D1362256

THE MINISTER'S OWN

MENTAL HEALTH

CONTRIBUTORS

GEORGE C. ANDERSON

DONALD BLAIN

SAMUEL W. BLIZZARD

ANTON T. BOISEN

GOTTHARD BOOTH

CARL W. CHRISTENSEN

WALLACE DENTON

RUSSELL L. DICKS

JAMES E. DITTES

EARL W. FURGESON

SEWARD HILTNER

REUEL L. HOWE

DEAN JOHNSON

JOHN P. KILDAHL

CHARLES F. KEMP

FREDERICK R. KLING

JOHN G. KOEHLER

ROBERT C. LESLIE

JULES HYMAN MASSERMAN

ALBERT L. MEIBURG

JOHN A. P. MILLET

WAYNE E. OATES

RALPH T. PALMER

JAMES G. RANCK

WILLIAM RICKEL

HARRY B. SCHOLEFIELD

LEONARD SMALL

SAMUEL SOUTHARD

EDWARD E. THORNTON

PAUL TILLICH

HAZEN G. WERNER

DANIEL D. WILLIAMS

CARROLL A. WISE

RICHARD K. YOUNG

THE MINISTER'S OWN

MENTAL HEALTH

Edited by
WAYNE E. OATES

Developed from the articles
by ministers, psychologists,
psychiatrists and theologians
in two special issues of 'Pastoral Psychology' magazine,
with many new contributions

Published by Channel Press, Inc., Great Neck, New York

Copyright © 1955, 1956, 1958, 1959, 1960, 1961 by PASTORAL
PSYCHOLOGY PRESS

The selections in this book that have not previously
appeared in *Pastoral Psychology* magazine are used by
permission of the authors or holders of copyright and
publication rights, listed among the Acknowledgments
beginning on the following page, and may not be
reproduced without their permission.

Library of Congress Catalog Card Number: 61-5264

PRINTED IN THE UNITED STATES OF AMERICA

ACKNOWLEDGMENTS

THIS VOLUME stems from the publication in May, 1958 of a special issue of *Pastoral Psychology,* titled "The Mental Health of the Minister." Dr. Simon Doniger, editor of that magazine, did the basic work in bringing the issue into print, and I had the happy privilege of serving, at his characteristically gracious request, as guest editor of that issue. To him goes a great measure of my indebtedness for the kind of persistence it takes to nurture such a project as this.

I am indebted also to my friend and fellow Baptist minister, Wesley Shrader, now pastor of the First Baptist Church, Chapel Hill, North Carolina, for the stimulating and provocative correspondence in connection with his article in *Life* Magazine of August 20, 1956. His article nettled me out of my professorial lethargy and prompted me to begin a detailed investigation of what research, if any, had been done on this subject about which Mr. Shrader wrote with such enthusiastic certainty and "peppery" satire. For such stimulation I would be remiss indeed if I did not express my great indebtedness to him. Most of all, however, the real work on this book has been done by the research men whose articles comprise its content. Each of them will be introduced to the reader in an editorial note at the beginning of his contribution. Warm appreciation from the publishers and the editors outreaches our means of expressing it to each of these authors.

The following contributions have not previously appeared in the pages of *Pastoral Psychology,* and to the authors, publishers and holders of copyright or publication rights, we extend our deep gratitude. The order of these copyright acknowledgments follows the order of the articles' appearance in this book.

"Emotional Health of the Clergy," by the Reverend George Christian Anderson, S.T.B., Director, National Academy of Religion and Mental Health. By permission of the author.

"A Discussion of Gotthard Booth's Paper and Article," by Robert C. Leslie, Pacific School of Religion. A paper from the proceedings of the June, 1959, Conference on Motivation for the Ministry, Southern Baptist Theological Seminary. By permission of the author and the Lilly Foundation.

"Motivation and Mental Health," by Samuel Southard, Southern Baptist Theological Seminary. A paper from the proceedings of the June, 1959, Conference on Motivation for the Ministry, Southern Baptist Theological Seminary. By permission of the author and the Lilly Foundation.

"The Parish Minister's Self-Image of His Master Role" and "The Protestant Parish Minister's Integrating Roles," by Samuel W. Blizzard. Publication rights to this material are held by the Russell Sage Foundation, 505 Park Avenue, New York City, New York.

"Role Attitudes of the Minister's Wife," by Wallace Denton. This material is scheduled to appear in a forthcoming special issue of *Pastoral Psychology* devoted to the subject of the minister's wife, and is used by special permission of Dr. Denton, who is to be guest editor of that issue.

"Emotional Disorders of Persons in Church-Related Vocations," by Edward E. Thornton, The Institute of Religion, Texas Medical Center. By permission of the author.

"Facts and Fantasy in the Minister's Mental Health," by James E. Dittes, Yale University Divinity School. By permission of the author.

"The Occurrence of Mental Illness in the Ministry," by Carl W. Christensen, M.D., reprinted from the *Journal of Pastoral Care,* Winter, 1959, Issue. By permission of author and publisher.

"Work and Personality Adjustment," by Leonard Small, consulting psychologist, New York City. By permission of the author.

"The Significance of an Educative Analysis for the Parish Ministry," by Harry B. Scholefield, First Unitarian Church, San Francisco, California. By permission of the author.

"A Report on An Institute for Advanced Pastoral Studies," by Reuel L. Howe, Institute for Advanced Pastoral Studies, Bloomfield Hills, Michigan. By permission of the author.

"The Hazards of High Callings," by John P. Kildahl, clinical psychologist, New York City. By permission of the author.

"Religious Conservatism-Liberalism and Mental Health," by James G. Ranck, consulting psychologist, New York City, and Adjunct Professor of Psychology and Religion, Drew University Theological School. By permission of the author.

"Fostering the Mental Health of Ministers," by Daniel Blain, a chapter reprinted from the book, *The Church and Mental Health,* edited by Paul B. Maves. Copyright 1952, 1953 by Charles Scribner's Sons. By permission of the publisher.

TABLE OF CONTENTS

Introduction   1

PART ONE: THE HEALTHY MINISTER   3

The Healthy Minister, *by Wayne E. Oates*   5

Fostering the Mental Health of Ministers,
by Daniel Blain   18

Emotional Health of the Clergy,
by George Christian Anderson   33

PART TWO: THE VOCATIONAL INTENTIONS AND
INNER STRESS OF THE MINISTER   41

Vocation in the Christian Ministry,
by Daniel D. Williams   43

Value Structures and the Minister's Purpose,
by Frederick R. Kling   51

Religious Conservatism-Liberalism and Mental Health,
by James Gilmour Ranck   65

Unconscious Motivation in the Choice of the Ministry
as Vocation, *by Gotthard Booth*   76

ix

A Discussion of Gotthard Booth's Article and Paper,
by Robert C. Leslie 86

Motivation and Mental Health, by Samuel Southard 97

PART THREE: THE MINISTER'S SELF-KNOWLEDGE
AND FUNCTIONAL EFFECTIVENESS 109

The Parish Minister's Self-Image of His Master Role,
by Samuel W. Blizzard 111

Preaching and Personality, by Earl H. Furgeson 123

Self-Understanding in Pastoral Counseling,
by Dean Johnson 132

The Protestant Parish Minister's Integrating Roles,
by Samuel W. Blizzard 143

PART FOUR: THE MINISTER AND HIS FAMILY 157

The Minister as a Family Man, by John G. Koehler 159

Role Attitudes of the Minister's Wife,
by Wallace Denton 167

Emotional Disorders of Persons in Church-Related
Vocations, by Edward E. Thornton 179

Divorced Ministers, by Seward Hiltner 188

PART FIVE: THE INCIDENCE AND KINDS OF
ILLNESS AMONG MINISTERS 199

The Hazards of High Callings, by John P. Kildahl 201

Facts and Fantasy in the Minister's Mental Health,
by James E. Dittes 209

Are Ministers Breaking Down? by Hazen G. Werner,
Reuel L. Howe, and Carl W. Christensen 223

An Overview of Research on the Mental Illness of
the Minister, by Samuel Southard 229

The Hospitalized Minister: A Preliminary Study,
by Albert L. Meiburg and Richard K. Young 237

The Occurrence of Mental Illness in the Ministry:
Introduction, by Carl W. Christensen 245

PART SIX: THE SELECTION OF MINISTERS AND THE
PREVENTION OF MENTAL ILLNESS   259

Occupational Information for Church Vocation,
by *Charles F. Kemp*   261

Work and Personality Adjustment, by *Leonard Small*   270

Psychiatric and Psychological Tests for Missionary
Personnel, by *Jules Hyman Masserman and
Ralph T. Palmer*   278

PART SEVEN: THE RE-EDUCATION AND THERAPY
OF THE MINISTER   299

Is Psychotherapy a Religious Process? by *William Rickel,
Paul Tillich, Carroll A. Wise, John A. P. Millet, Russell
L. Dicks, and Anton T. Boisen*   301

The Significance of an Educative Analysis for the Parish
Ministry, by *Harry B. Scholefield*   318

A Report on an Institute for Advanced Pastoral Studies,
by *Reuel L. Howe*   330

THE MINISTER'S OWN

MENTAL HEALTH

POPULAR magazines have sensationally focused the attention of the public on the health and welfare of the minister. *Life* Magazine (August 20, 1956), *Harper's* Magazine (July, 1957), *United Church Observer* (February 1, 1957), *The Baptist Program* (November, 1959) featured just a few of the many articles that have appeared. Only recently the autobiographical story of a recovered mental patient who is a minister has been published. Through such writings, lay people have been provoked to reconsider their relationships to and expectations of their ministers. On the other hand, however, such reports have raised serious questions as to what the exact state of affairs really is concerning the minister's mental health; and they've pointed up the need for something more than the casual observations of interested people.

Therefore, professional journals, especially *Pastoral Psychology*, have called upon research men and teachers in the interrelated fields of religion and mental health to give more careful and detailed attention to the problem. This research has brought to light a number of valuable studies already in existence, and set into motion additional and new studies of the mental health and related problems of the minister.

Probably one of the most important results of the popular "broadsides" aimed at this problem has been the vivid way in which *research,* as such, has become more important to and appreciated by ministers. Ministers have found themselves judged by broad, casually-put-together, and sensationally-dramatized generalizations. Consequently, the ministry has become a great deal more aware of the value of statistical evidence, careful analysis of data, and thorough investigations as a basis for utterances and judgments.

Now the purposes of this volume become apparent. First, we aim to present in their original form the research papers which have been written on the mental health of ministers. Second, we hope to interpret cautiously and relate meaningfully these documents to each other. Third, our purpose is to bring together in one volume the modest body of literature in order to stimulate and encourage additional research, and to bring to light hitherto undiscovered studies.

As editor of this volume, my task will be that of organizing (hopefully), the data into a meaningful whole and contributing editorial comments from time to time through the manuscript. All of this is done with an eager desire for collaboration with readers who have information on the subject about which I am unaware. I have been amazed at the variety of persons who have patiently performed good work in this area of concern. There are more, I am sure, than we have been able to know.

This is a professional research volume written for pastors and teachers. It makes no pretense at popularizing the material for a lay audience. Nor does it pretend to be a self-help book for emotionally disturbed ministers. Doctors, psychologists, theologians, pastors, and chaplains have written the papers. And all have approached these subjects from the context of specific training, experience, and discipline in specialized study and work.

PART ONE

THE HEALTHY MINISTER

EVER since the establishment of the posterity of Aaron as the priesthood of Israel, men have—sometimes articulately and sometimes tacitly—expected that the minister of the Bread of Life be "without blemish." The Levitical law says:

And the Lord spake unto Moses, saying, Speak unto Aaron, saying, Whosoever *he be* of thy seed in their generations that hath *any* blemish, let him not approach to offer the bread of his God. For whatsoever man *he be* that hath a blemish, he shall not approach: a blind man, or a lame, or he that hath a flat nose, or any thing superfluous, Or a man that is brokenfooted, or brokenhanded, Or crookbacked, or a dwarf, or that hath a blemish in his eye, or be scurvy, or scabbed, or hath his stones broken; No man that hath a blemish of the seed of Aaron the priest shall come nigh to offer the offerings of the Lord made by fire: he hath a blemish; he shall not come nigh to offer the bread of his God. He shall eat the bread of his God, *both* of the most holy, and of the holy. Only he shall not go in unto the veil, nor come nigh unto the altar, because he hath a blemish; that he profane not my sanctuaries: for I the Lord do sanctify them. And Moses told *it* unto Aaron, and to his sons, and unto all the children of Israel. (Leviticus 21:16-24).

3

This same legalism pervades the minds of people today. Yet the wisdom of Barnabas and Paul at Lystra, when they refused to be treated as "gods who had come down in the form of men," reaches more deeply than the Levitical requirement of being without blemish. They said: "We also are men of like passions with you, and preach unto you that you should turn from these vanities unto the living God . . ." (Acts 14:11-15). The ministry is like a treasure, as Paul puts it: "We have this treasure in earthen vessels in order that the excellence of the power may be of God and not of us" (II Cor. 4:7).

The contemporary minister feels the pull between these expectations of blemishlessness and his own confession of humanity, earthenness, and weakness. The perfecting of the strength of God through our infirmities seems to be the divine intention. This section is devoted to the healthy minister, a grappling with the creative tensions which arise out of these contrary, paradoxical demands felt keenly by the working minister in the church of today.

The Healthy Minister

By Wayne E. Oates
Professor of Psychology of Religion,
Southern Baptist Theological Seminary

The healthy minister is one who participates both as a man who has his commission from God as a shepherd of his flock, and as a man who has laid hold of the treasures of empirical science to help him implement this commission.

Health is a valid, proximate goal of the life of the working minister. However, it is not the ultimate goal of his existence. When health is made the primary value of life by a minister, he may easily become like the man who quit work and spent full time worrying about his health. This in itself may be a state of disease. The idolatry of health has taken many forms in history. One of the most recent appears in the tendency to take the criteria of therapeutic ideologies as *the* sole standard of the effectiveness of the Christian minister. Having said this, one must hasten to say that the health goal set forth by modern therapists is *one* of the values inherent in the Christian faith. It is certainly not, however, the primary value nor by any means the only value intrinsic to the Christian faith and thus to the life of the minister. The minister, therefore, is healthiest who keeps his concern

5

for health subordinate to, and in focus with, the chief end for his existence, namely, "to glorify God and to enjoy him forever."

The Christian faith affirms that the Providence of God is not restricted to time, but extends from everlasting to everlasting. The forces of nature are to be subdued by man for the service of God, the lengthening of life, and the enjoyment of both by man. But ultimately the intentions of God for man transcend health, life, and even death. The minister's certainty of this purpose is a fountain of renewal for his health. As Gotthard Booth, the psychoanalyst, has said, the psychiatrist has "theoretical and empirical reasons" for believing that the person who has found something in the world "for which he wants to live and die" is healthier than the person who has not.[1] Within the context of the discovery of such a clear sense of purpose, the minister begins to see that illnesses are of at least two kinds: the illness which is "adopted as a way of life," and the illness which is at one and the same time a failure of an inadequate way of life and the discovery of a better one. In this latter case, a man's life is shifted from the foundation of the temporary to the foundation of the Eternal, from sand to rock. This may happen *after* for any of a variety of reasons he may have decided to be a minister.

Examples of this are conspicuous in both our time and in Christian history. Harry Emerson Fosdick, in his recent biography, relates the writing of his book, *The Meaning of Prayer,* to a nervous breakdown through which he had to find his way. The clinical pastoral training movement itself was born out of the suffering of Anton Boisen, who tells the dramatic story of his illness in his book, *The Exploration of the Inner World.* Russell Dicks, suffering from the ravages of a tubercular elbow and a collapse of his hitherto secure beliefs, came through the illness to write, with Richard Cabot, the book, *The Art of Ministering to the Sick.* Lest we think that this happens only in the lives of men who later become interested in the ministry of counseling and the care of the sick, let it also be said that H. Wheeler Robinson, the eminent Biblical theologian, recounts a severe

[1] *The Church and Mental Health,* ed. Paul Maves (Scribner's, 1955), p. 55.

illness of the spirit in which he discovered a new way of life. Also, Frederick W. Robertson, in the throes of illness, discovered a larger purpose for his life. These more or less recent examples could be placed alongside those of Bunyan, Fox, and others. This is not to glorify illness as a way of revelation, but it does serve to re-focus some of the easy moralisms which attach themselves to discussions of the health of the minister.

1. Achieving Clarity of Purpose

Likewise, the foregoing discussion points up the relevance of the minister's clarity of purpose and sense of obedience to, approval from, and fellowship with God in his inner appropriation of that purpose. How, then, can this be achieved?

In the first place, clarity of purpose is achieved by courageously facing and dealing with the impediments of past and present commitments that obscure the minister's vision of God and understanding of his purpose. One older minister who had come through some trying fires of suffering was commenting to me on the preaching of another older minister. The other minister for twenty years had real difficulty in preaching a sermon without referring to conflicts he had had with his now deceased father. His friend said a wise thing about this. He said that he felt that the preacher should go to some one who could help him and "pump that old trouble with his daddy out of his system" so he could preach without "sloshing it on his listeners." In II Timothy 2:4 we read that "no soldier on service gets entangled in civil pursuits. . . ." This man's involvement with his father certainly was an entanglement which needed attention.

Another such entanglement is the minister's involvement with a given social class, whether it be the class into which he was born, the one into which his education has thrust him, or the one into which his congregation would make him fit. The minister may become limited, bound, isolated, and diverted by confusing the folkway-mores of any one social class with the purpose for which he is a minister. More than this, he may completely reject the proven ways of functioning of the professionally educated class of people. Thus he will become overworked, confused, and frustrated to the point of sickness from sheer neglect of the disciplines of the ministry in behalf of a sense of calling from God and a need for a "chummy" friendship with everybody to whom he has to minister. We will pay more attention to this later in this article, but the main point here is to note how a minister stays entangled in the attitudes, ways of doing things, and even the values of the social class into which he is born. Let us consider, as one example, the minister who goes from an unsophisticated, lower-middle-class, agricultural society.

When he is expected by his parishioners to handle his time, energy, money, and relationships in a disciplined manner more characteristic of such other professional persons as teachers, doctors, lawyers, and the like, he reneges and thereby becomes overwhelmed by a number of demands that cannot be handled through informal, personal friendships. In such an instance, he either remains in a church small enough to be handled this way, or he has some sort of illness as the pastor of a large church which by its very nature protects him from too much responsibility.

Yet at this very point the minister has an acute conflict in his ideals. He reads his Bible and studies the lives of great pastors, both of which were produced under the conditions and ideals of an agricultural or rural society. Yet his professional training in the seminary keeps reminding him that he will have a heavy administrative task as the "pastoral director" of a diverse organization. With one image of himself as a "hair-shirted" prophet he is confronted with another image of himself as "a man in a gray-flannel suit." Little wonder it is that his romantic ideal suffers some real decay and failure of idealism. He is confronted with four alternatives. He can reject all the disciplines of his calling as a profession, and yet he becomes anxious for the financial, leadership, and prestige values that go with doing so. In this event he is likely to become sour on the world, complaining, and vindictive. Second, he can take one of the working roles of the minister, such as administration, preaching, teaching, pastoral care, etc., and become a special pleader for it, neglecting and even despising the other disciplines. This ill-prepares him for almost any type of ministry, although some men foolishly think that going into teaching or the chaplaincy or denominational work will accomplish this, when in fact all the working roles of the minister are required to greater or lesser degree in either teaching or in the chaplaincy. Third, the minister may "turn professional" and yield to the secular counterparts of his various roles in business administration, social work, public relations, psychotherapy, etc., and reject the more distinctly pastoral definition of his purpose in life.

The fourth and more difficult way of achieving clarity of purpose in the minister's life is to recognize that his work is both calling and profession, pastoral and professional (in the sense of learning certain basic information and skills). He participates both as a man who has his commission from God as a shepherd of his flock, and as a man who had laid hold of the treasures of empirical science to help him implement this commission. The healthy minister is the one who is willing to take this ambiguity upon himself, bearing in his own self the reconciliation of the two. The healthy minister, in a word, is the one who can bring things both old and new from his treasure, see the relation between them, and through prayer and discipline cause them to glorify God in the love of his neighbor.

2. Using the Resources and Learning the Disciplines of the Ministry

This, however, requires that a minister submit himself to the disciplines of his work if he is to maintain his health. Such submission pre-requires that a minister basically *want* to be a minister, that his reasons for doing this work are his and not someone else's—internal, and not external; voluntary, and not compulsory. He does his work "readily" and not out of constraint. The vividness of the role of the minister as a representative of God, as a bearer of the Good News of God in Christ, as a representative of the "gathered community" of the friends of God in Christ varies from community to community. I quite agree with Daniel Blain in his observation that the minister's security, adequacy, and health is somewhat dependent upon the clarity of his task in the minds of those for and with whom he seeks to serve. However, I note two signs of neuroticism at this point in ministers, which even appear in some of the writing on this subject. First, the people of any culture expect a minister to know more about this than they do, whereas many ministers tacitly expect their people to work this out *for* them. Second, the minister, in behalf of a "buddy buddy" kind of "regular fellow" chumminess with people, tends to reject the distinctly religious and spiritual content of his role. Thereby he cuts himself off from the resources of his role. He is left to face the demands of the ministry with no more resources than he would have had if he had never been ordained or trained for his task.

This last observation accents the necessity for a minister to interpret his role to his people—to explain what a minister is for, what he does, what he can do for people, and what he cannot do. This calls for teaching. The minister, particularly in a culture where his role is not clearly defined, has the painstaking task of interpreting his work to his people. This begins when he first confers with the congregation. It continues in his conferences with his leaders, should be prominent from time to time in his preaching, and it must be repeated at the outset of his relationship to counselees. He demonstrates the meaning of his work in the symbolism of what he does and does not do in his daily routine. For instance, when a patient is going home from the hospital, the best thing the pastor can be doing is to confer with him about the problems of his convalescence. He *could* use the same hour to make a special trip to carry the patient's flowers, radio, and suitcases home. But the former task is more uniquely that of the pastor, and the latter can be done by anyone.

The pastor is overworked, not by the *many* things he does, but because he does not plan his time for the things which he uniquely can do. If he does not see distinctly religious meaning in these tasks, it may be because he lacks powers of interpretation, or it may be that he fears rejection by referring some needs to someone more adapted for meeting them. Deeper than this, he may lack the capacity to let go of any responsibility, to permit someone else to do it. Some ministers have had breaks in health because of "overwork." Closer study, however, sometimes revealed that their churches had been trying to get them to build a staff of co-workers to share the responsibilities—and that they would not. One such minister, just before his death from a heart attack, said that he would never have anyone in his church "usurping the place" of the pastor! A "horse-back" opinion is that some men break because of their inability to share, delegate, and correlate responsibility with other people, not because of overwork. The prima donna complex will get a flashy minister into the orbit of success, but it will not keep him up there. What will?

First, the healthy minister necessarily learns to pass opportunities for the "limelight" around to others. Younger ministers, members of his church, student pastors who are entering the ministry from his congregation, and many others look upon a recommendation from the outstanding minister as a ministry in and of itself. The minister stands or falls, furthermore, as he moves from the "tycoon" conception of success to the "chief of staff" conception of effective teamwork in his organization. But this calls for an inner discipline within the pastor himself. Until he solves this, no number of additional workers will be able to relieve his load. For they will see themselves as his "flunkies," and not as responsible people with a clearly defined future. He, in turn, spends more time recruiting assistants because of the fast turnover.

Second, the healthy minister necessarily learns to use more than one pastoral resource for meeting people's needs. He reflects on whether a letter will not be more helpful than a visit, a telephone call more penetrating to the need than a home visit, an office conference more securely meaningful than a chance meeting spent with divided and distracted attention. He may choose to spend five half-hour conferences with one person rather than one whole afternoon at the expense of his sermon preparation for that night. He may reach out and draw upon the resources of teachers, doctors, lawyers, business people, and many others to do things for which they and not he are more especially trained. They in turn may help him reach people with his distinctly religious ministry whom he would never otherwise have met. These are a few of the skills taught in pastoral care, a discipline as old as the church itself. Training in pastoral care enables the pastor to do what he must do in a carefully planned and pastorally resourceful way that brings the "love of God and neighbor" to those who need it without causing the Christian shepherd to "wear both himself and those who seek him" out. (Exodus 18:18)

3. Maintaining Directness and Expressing Hostility

Such clarity of purpose and wisdom of discipline, however, requires that the pastor be sure of his own experthood in the word and work of the Christian faith. He cannot carelessly let other people decide for him exactly how and on what bases he will do for them what they need done. In the name of non-directiveness, which occasionally is another name for indecisiveness, we overlook the fact that we are working in an uncontrolled environment far different from the interview-room of the professional counselor. We are asked and told to do many things by anxious, trouble-laden people. We live our lives in hopeless confusion and get sick ourselves if we attempt to do everything everyone asks us to do in the way *he* decides it must be done. Yet at the same time we are faced with the necessity of staying in the good graces of even persons who would seek to manipulate and use us at times.

Therein lies the rub! We, in America particularly, are supported by the people whom we serve, not by the state. As a result we cannot as pastors be as direct, frank, and open as even professors in schools can be. Yet when we as pastors do not maintain this directness, a burden of hostility and feelings of injustice falls back upon us. This becomes an unresolved set of guilt reactions because we in our idealized image of ourselves are called to be loving and kind. Yet we really wonder whether the loving and kind thing is always the sweet and cheerful thing. The research of Fitzhugh Dodson, Harold Massey, and others points to this as *the* major problem of ministers in maintaining good mental health. They tell us that the minister is more intrapunitive than other control groups with whom their studies compared them. How can a minister come to grips with this problem for his own and other persons' well-being? Let me suggest several methods.

First, the minister should discipline his congregation to support him through the church and not to give him private gifts "for services rendered" or to allay hidden guilt feelings, or to bind him in obligation to them as individuals. For example, a minister allowed his congregation to "give" him a new car. This was repeated three times in twelve years. By the time the third car was given, the son of the minister was a teen-ager. He drove the third car one evening and had an accident, tearing the fender off. When the proposal arose that a fourth car be given the minister, the men refused to do so because "that young hellion would take it out and tear it up." The minister had to stew in the silence of his feelings. Whereas, if in the first place he had insisted that the car be the property of the church as a staff car and that his salary be such that he could afford his own car, he would have avoided the latter situation. If anyone had said anything about his son's wreck he could have had the satisfaction of saying that it was *his car* and *his son!*

Second, the minister can, through counseling and psychotherapy for himself, gain insight into his guilt feelings about being direct in the presence of authority persons, about the rightness and wrongness of hostile feelings, and about the importance of transparent relationships to his people. He can develop a sense of humor in the presence of his darker feelings and a confidence in his power to channel his aggressions toward justified and worthy targets. He can learn to be a good marksman and cease to waste his ammunition on small and unworthy targets. We can learn to stand and having stood all to stand in the "whole armor of God."

Third, the minister can handle his hostilities by working with a group of other ministers and professional people in either informal or formal group relationships where professional problems can be discussed in conference. This is one of the real advantages of the effectively constructed staff meeting in a larger church situation. I know that one of the most meaningful aspects of the staff work of my own departmental fellowship as a professor is the way in which my colleagues and I can explore together without fear of exposure or personal hurt the feelings of inadequacy, hostility, or affection we may feel in any given service situation.

Fourth, the minister learns best to practice directness and to express his true feelings, be they sharp, mellow, or rancorous, in his own face-to-face encounter with God in prayer. The Psalms have been a lasting aid to me here, because I cannot always say how I feel. They help articulate my inmost strivings. For this I am grateful that the more imprecatory Psalms were not left out by some uninspired and hyper-pious scribe who was miraculously prevented from getting hold of the Holy Writ. Otherwise, some of the chafings of the spirit, the blazings of anger, and the direct challenges of my spirit would never find words before God. Our Lord loves and accepts a man with no guile, and he helps us in the inner privacy of our spirits to come to that feeling of forgiving acceptance before the sun goes down and in turn to forgive realistically those who attempt to use us. This is one of the minister's sure sources of healthful renewal.

4. Ventilating Relationships

In the fourth place, the healthy minister maintains what I have chosen to call "ventilating" relationships. This implies that the unhealthy minister is a "stuffy" person. He talks only to religious people, attends only religious conferences, hears only religious language, until he is breathing the same old air over and over. But the healthy minister walks in the open air of the example of our Lord Jesus Christ. He is a friend of publicans and sinners. He is not an ingrown personality. He seeks "those on the outside of the church" not only for their good but his own. Thus he stays in touch with life and human need. This has several implications, but I can identify only two or three of the most important for the minister's health.

The minister can best ventilate his life by participating in friendship, comradeship, and inter-stimulating insights with teachers, lawyers, doctors, social workers, and law-enforcement workers. For instance, ministers of Louisville walk and ride the beat with police officers several evenings each month. Also, from time to time some of us have profited greatly by teaching in the university in courses other than religion. Participation on committees and boards of community agencies helps the minister to see and know his community from a more ventilated perspective than stained glass windows ever afford. A minister trained in counseling would be fortunate indeed to take an occasional or regular assignment as a counselor with someone who does not see him as a minister.

Furthermore, the minister can use his vacations to great profit. One of the purposes of a vacation is to get out of one's accustomed social role. A few weeks spent on a university campus taking a course in English literature, or in a center of government such as Washington, D. C., reading in the libraries, and visiting law-making bodies, museums, and hearing policy-making addresses, or in New York finding out what American dramatists are saying, or in a deep Southern city getting one's own impression of the way of life—all these and many other strategies will get the minister up out of his stuffiness.

5. The Use of Time

The mention of vacations raises the whole problem of the healthy minister's use of time. The minister is, more than other people, tempted to use his time to meet certain needs of certain individuals and groups and to neglect the needs of the persons for whom he is primarily responsible, namely his congregation. He may leave a whole series of sick people to fend for themselves emotionally while he takes on an extra duty "for the denomination." The sick people manage to get along well enough without him so do not think of calling for him when they really need him the next time. This often leaves the minister with a burden of guilt. While the minister does not restrict himself to doing "what he is getting paid for," he nevertheless *is* getting *paid for doing certain things—and he cannot expect to "stay well" emotionally unless he knows clearly what he is getting paid for doing and does at least that.*

Many hyper-idealistic plans for the use of time have been drawn up to find their ways into my and your wastebasket or to gather dust on our shelves. The most reasonable way of using time is the most flexible one. All that a minister has to give away is time. He should do this with more skill than that with which businessmen give away, invest, and earn dividends on money. A flexible, shrewd use of time is necessary to the minister's own health as well as to his effectiveness. Several suggestions have been useful to other ministers as well as to myself.

First, a day should be planned in such a way that "inasmuch as in the minister lieth," he gets full use of "the best two out of three" portions of the waking day. If the minister is to be busy morning, afternoon, and evening of every day, he cannot stay well indefinitely. Therefore, if he is to admit that he is as other men, he must have a part of each waking day free. It cannot always be the same. If he finds the morning and afternoon full, he should angle to have the evening free. If the afternoon and evening are full, he should shoot for having the morning fairly free. If he has the morning and evening full, he should work toward having the afternoon at least partially clear.

Furthermore, the mythical "day off" is really a mirage! Many times the minister will work for three or four weeks without a day off. If he could work on the same basis as do firemen, policemen, etc., and *accrue* his days off for an occasional short jaunt away from the city, he will do himself and his family a service. These days could be used for family outings, or, on a clearly understood basis with his congregation, they would be used as our Lord used them, for prayer, meditation, study, and reflection. Sometimes an illness accomplishes just this in the life of a minister: it gives him some time and protection in which he can let his spirit catch up with him through quietness, meditation, and prayer.

Finally, good communication with one's family is necessary for the minister's health. He should plan his week, "pausing for station identification" with his wife at the beginning of the week. Insofar as a week can be seen ahead, a weekly conference with the family should be held. Also, a daily clearance and reminder

of these plans saves about a fourth of the frayed nerves, hurt feelings, and feelings of being neglected in the family. Also, the events of a month and year can be visualized with enough forethought that "anticipation becomes the greater part of delight" for the whole family. I am convinced, out of several years of partial failure and partial success, that living life on a twenty-four-hour basis is a necessity for good health, but that foresight should be aided by reflection as to the total meaning of each year of life. A year should be allowed to have a certain number of things in it that are planned in terms of our total life purposes. Then it should be "closed out" for any further appointments. This in itself should be the excuse for saying "no" to people. And, when the sum total of our lives and poor health are added up, we will be able to say that it was our friends' insistence and our feeling that we are indispensable that finally "did us in," not overwork! It was at the point of decision, indecision, and the need for our friends' approval that we became sick, not at the point of doing and getting things done.

For all of this, the healthy minister needs at least a part of an hour every day when he is by himself. If he can be quiet then, it is good. If he can be still, it is better; if he can pray without feeling that it is expected of him, it is even better. For then does the ordering of life and the focusing of purpose become clear. Out of this comes the renewal of life. Even so, as the minister "numbers his days and gets himself a heart of wisdom," he realizes that he is a man of like passions with other men who, like himself, live a certain number of years and are not exempt from the discipline of death. Through his faith in the Lord Jesus Christ, he has died to sin and been born into the resurrected existence to walk in the newness of life. Whereas death does not come to him as a total surprise, he nevertheless has not tried to kid himself into believing that just because he is a Christian and a minister at that, it does not apply to him. By reason of the realism of his faith, he "joins the human race" and does not ask for exemption from his share of pain and death. He knows that these are but the gates of a new life into which he is about to be born.

Fostering the Mental Health of Ministers

By Daniel Blain, m. d.
Medical Director, American Psychiatric Association

*One of America's outstanding psychiatrists, himself the son of a
minister, outlines the basic dangers to the minister's mental
health, as well as the basic principles upon which he can build a
mentally healthy life for himself, his family, and his parish.*

An experienced hospital chaplain has said that it is difficult to
minister to illness out of illness. This is so because the person
who is ill is too preoccupied with his own suffering to be sensitive
to the needs of others. Indeed, he is likely to *use* others to relieve
his own distress, even at the expense of aggravating their problems.
However, unless one has had some experience with illness in
one's own life, it may be difficult to sympathize with or to minister to illness in another. No pride is more overweening than
that of the man who boasts he has never been ill a day in his
life . . . who implies that it is unnecessary for anyone else to be
ill. Perhaps this paradox is best resolved in the minister who has
wrestled successfully with some of the ills that beset us all in our
common humanity and is ready to turn to help others through
similar difficulties. At any rate, it is important that the minister
have a reasonable degree of freedom from illness so that he can

18

minister to others. A primary part of the professional preparation for the ministry is to resolve inner conflicts and achieve freedom from compulsions arising in the unconscious. Regeneration would seem to be the prime requisite for true ordination. Another part of professional life is to maintain mental health in the face of stresses so that one can continue to minister to others in stress.

It is quite possible that the reader, if he is a minister, will not warmly welcome a topic which turns the spotlight upon himself. If this is so, he may comfort himself with the knowledge that the psychiatrist also, when playing his professional role, tends to shrink from the suggestion that he should think of his own mental processes. Indeed, one may note many similarities between ministers and practitioners of psychiatric medicine. They have a common motivation for the practice of their professions rooted in a humane sympathy for the suffering, and a desire to relieve human distress. They need the same perceptive skills and capacity for empathy. Both attempt to help troubled persons. They possess a similar belief in the dignity of man. Both seek to remove the stumbling blocks to personal integration and the building of more satisfying social and spiritual relationships. And, like the psychiatrist, the minister may welcome an intelligent interest in his inner life that may promise to bring him increased satisfaction, and so will accept the discomfort of self-analysis.

In my experience, most ministers have a high degree of mental health. That is, they "are able to live happily and productively with other human beings within the limits imposed by bodily equipment."[1] This is not to say that the best adjusted and most successful ministers do not, like other human beings, have their trials and tribulations, their sorrows, their anxieties, and even occasional periods of discouragement or moods of failure. But they, like most other persons, meet their obstacles courageously and emerge hopefully from each crisis, wiser with respect to themselves, more understanding of others, and closer to their Creator.

But leadership is often a lonely function and one that is beset

[1] George H. Preston, *The Substance of Mental Health* (New York: Rinehart, 1943).

with special psychological and health hazards. Each profession tends to have its own pitfalls and occupational neuroses. An awareness of some of the pitfalls to be encountered in the ministry may help one to steer clear of them, and a better understanding of their nature may help one to climb out of them if he should be drawn in.

1. Health Hazards in the Ministry

To begin with, the sacrifice which is demanded in the ministry may be a real source of maladjustment. A minister usually receives less of this world's goods than others of equal training, education, and responsibility. Filled as he is with a desire for service, the minister may at first find it easy to disregard the absence of most signs of comfortable living, the low salary (sometimes difficult to collect), the apparent belief on the part of many that it is all right for his clothes to be threadbare, to get along with his worn-out car (often dangerous to drive), and to be the recipient of special gifts such as food, clothes, odd bits of furniture, and the like. He may be appreciative of the spirit of the gift but sometimes may wish that he had the financial income which others have, and could meet his obligations as others do. In moments of weariness, he may occasionally suspect a condescending attitude on the part of the giver that may strip the gift of its generous implications, and reduce it to its materialistic proportions. On a deeper level, in a materialistic culture which gauges value and confers status in terms of income, the minister often interprets his low income as lack of appreciation of his services and the denial of prestige in the community. This situation may produce resentment and moments of rebellion. Such resentment may find its outlet in preaching that nags, scolds, or is judgmental and displays many rationalizations about the blessings of giving and the virtues of poverty, or the selfishness of parishioners.

This may be successfully met by the minister himself, but what of his family? Some families may not be so dedicated, so imbued with the spirit of service, so desirous of filling a humble position. Wife and children may, at times, complain or, perhaps worse, bear the situation with an outward resignation and acceptance that may hide anxiety or resentment. Or they may put pressure on him to strive for a position of higher status or to spend his time finding ways to raise his salary which may divert his attention from ministering to the members of his parish.

Furthermore, the necessity to receive, in a worldly sense, more than one gives, may have a pauperizing effect, leading one to go through life expecting gifts, looking for help with more than usual avidity, and even demanding special concessions and favors. This may lead to a kind of professional hypochondria or public martyrdom which ends up by having the congregation supporting a minister who plays a dependent, improvident role, rather than a minister who is free to play an independent, supporting, and leading role. At times, the demoralizing effect may not show itself for many years, when one begins to face the future with less certainty and perhaps with some specific burdens of ill health and discouragement. Then it is that an accumulation of such pauperizing effects may contribute to a willingness to succumb to defeat rather than to continue to keep up the good fight.

While such sacrifice may be a potential source of stress, it may also be productive of more good results than bad. The possession of worldly goods and high social status may not be an unmixed blessing but may bring its own special stresses. The children of the minister may have to "work their way" through school and usually do. Lack of money in the minister's family is most often accompanied by greater than usual incentives for the best of education, and often for a great deal of it. Many ministers' children enter the professions and often become outstandingly successful in creative arts and sciences. It may well be that it is an advantage to have had to live in a somewhat austere environment, to have to "work one's way," and it is doubtless a strengthening factor when success is attained in such an environment.

Another hazard is that ministers may succumb to the pressure to restrict personal pleasure and to deny themselves a normal emotional expression. Worldly pleasures are often thought to be unbecoming to a minister and his family. (The wherewithal is usually withheld.) In our tradition, austerity and even asceticism often have been linked to godliness. It may be said that self-denial has its virtues and that a surfeit of rich food or amusement or anything pleasurable brings its own devaluation, and it is true that too much time in amusement leaves little time for honest work and productive activity. However, most people would prefer to be their own judges, and not have a straitjacket forced on them by reason of their position in society. That this is relative goes without saying. Generally, ministers have enough flexibility to fit easily into the customs of their neighbors, and it is the standard of pleasure and amusement in the community, as well as personal standards of morality, that should restrict the limits of expediency for the minister's family.

Different groups expect different things. The minister will be judged by the most circumspect and not by the average. Those in the congregation who are most austere, most denying of the flesh, are often the ones who set the pace for the minister's family. For various reasons, it may be proper for the minister to live on this austerity plan but, again, such may be more of a burden than appears on the surface.

What is true of the expression of joyful emotion is true also of the negative emotions. Emotional outlets are less common in the life of a minister when, I suspect, they may be more needed. Fear, anger, desire are often thought to be inappropriate in one who stands as a leader. It is too often believed that one who calms the fears of his flock must not show his own anxiety, or that one who deplores hatred between a man and his neighbor must not be irritable at home when he is tired—or grouchy at an unannounced caller who takes an unwarranted amount of time. By the same token, it is often believed that righteous indignation for social evils must never be allowed to become personal.

Not only the minister but also his wife and children are expected to be good examples, and they have to bear the strain of such a position from beginning to end of life.

Conscious suppression of such emotions is therefore commonly called for, and this constant need for self-control gets tiresome when too frequent. The penalty for active expression of emotionally charged attitudes sometimes may make passivity a virtue and lead to neglect of social reforms, a neglect not difficult to rationalize. Unconscious repression of emotion may have more deeply hidden roots than are suspected. Fires of hidden emotion may burn more fiercely than surface indications suggest. The organism protects itself by use of defense mechanisms. But these defenses may be unsuccessful, and the resulting strain may appear in various symptoms.

The suppression of emotion, when it slips over into repression, may be responsible for depression of spirit and a flattened personality devoid of color or attractiveness. It may break out in compulsive hostility toward special groups or the promulgation of restrictive patterns for others.

The minister may need courage to face the fact that it is impossible to please everyone in the community, and that the attempt to do so would strip him of his own character. A minister needs what Adler called "the courage of one's own imperfections."

Third, the position of a minister entails, on occasion, a lack of freedom and personal privacy that marks any man in an important post. His life is to a large extent an open book, and his children's a gold-fish bowl. Or it may be said that he lives his life upon a pedestal where he is not only in full view but is expected to behave differently from most of his parishioners. He is believed to be a professional "good man," and his family members are expected to exemplify all the virtues the Christian life is supposed to confer. It is forgotten that he and his family as well as all other Christians are in the process of becoming, and that they like all other persons make mistakes, fall short of their accepted ideals, and have periods of regression.

This may lead the minister to attempt to cover up his deficiencies and to bring pressure upon his family to conform outwardly to a standard which they have not inwardly assimilated. This leads to a denial and a suppression of the true self which may be the beginning of a neurotic trend. The popular concept of the profligate character of the minister's son is evidence of the distortion so common when people occupy the spotlight of prominent position. Frequently, behavior which is considered normal for the average parishioner is regarded as especially sinful when seen in the minister's family. Not only does each member of the family have this cross to bear, but each in turn may be concerned as to how well the others are bearing up, and this is often more of a strain than appears on the surface.

On the other hand, the people may not be nearly as conscious of the behavior of the minister and his family as he is of his own. If he has the courage to be himself, his parishioners may find it quite a relief, especially as a self-conscious example may be an expression of pride and condescension.

The fourth health hazard in the ministry is found in the clergyman's relations to his ecclesiastical superiors, for while he is expected to be a leader in his own congregation and community, he is often a member of an organizational hierarchy of church discipline. The role of leader gives way to the role of humble follower. One's superiors are themselves human beings who are subject to the corruptions of power, who are fallible in their judgments, and who do not always exhibit the highest qualities of leadership. Often a minister is subject to frequent transfer from church to church with great inconvenience to himself and his family. If the minister has unresolved problems in relation to authority, his relationship with his superior may be marked by difficulty. A series of unfortunate experiences at the hands of an insensitive superior and an inability to express his feelings to his superior may produce a chronic paranoid suspicion toward the hierarchy, which in turn accentuates his difficulties in relation to the system.

Fifth, dealing with constant emotional appeals for help is wearing, and the need to be sympathetic yet objective is trying. There is always the danger that the minister will succumb to the pressures put upon him to play the roles demanded by persons to support their neuroses rather than to define his role therapeutically. Illness, poverty, personal problems, disappointments, bereavements, conflicts are an increasing part of a minister's daily life. In dealing with persons, he must feel their need without losing his own identity. He must be one with his people, yet not assume their positions himself. There is always the hazard that empathy will lead to identification and that he will respond to transferences with counter-transferences of his own unless he has resolved most of his conflicts and has been trained to handle himself wisely in these situations. An example is that of the lonely woman who falls in love with the minister, not for himself, but because of what he represents to her as an ideal loving father. Without insight into his own need, the clergyman may respond by falling in love with her. Or, again, some may respond to the clergyman with hostility because he represents to them a hated father. If the clergyman takes it personally and responds with anger, he only accentuates the situation.

Along with this, the minister's judgment is deferred to and his parishioners may expect him to have an authoritative opinion on every subject so that he may come to regard his own judgment as infallible and may assume a competence in fields where he has no competence. It is easy (because it is flattering) to fall into the role of advice-giver, and to assume the power of deity in acting as the interpreter of deity. It is hard to define one's limitations objectively and to admit ignorance when pressured to be an omniscient parent by dependent and insecure people. Humility is sometimes difficult in one who must be strong enough for others to lean on. This humility must be real and not merely worn as a garment on suitable occasions. The role into which the community casts the minister conspires to make this difficult. Furthermore, in this day of changing culture and conflicting cultures ministers may become confused about their role and find the confusion very frustrating.

The sixth hazard increases in proportion to the minister's competence and grows out of the constant importunities for him to assume leadership and to help. He will be sensitive to need, and desirous of meeting need. He will be besieged by those in need to give of himself and of his skill. It will be hard for him to limit himself to that which he can do without experiencing diminishing returns in terms of his effectiveness and his personal and professional growth. Unless methods of recuperation are developed and used, the wearing-down process will exceed the building-up process. Energy will diminish and patience will ebb. Small things will harass; the minister will become exhausted physically and spiritually. Unless he guards his time to insure growth and opportunity for study, his potential usefulness will be impaired. Unless he has time to plan strategies and priorities in relation to his work, he may lose sight of objectives and fall into a rut of ceaseless and often useless activity.

This is not peculiar to leadership in the spiritual field. It occurs in all positions of responsibility. It is in this aspect of the job that balance of work and rest, production and recreation, intake and outgo, must be sought.

Another hazard that is rather peculiar to the ministry is the danger of separating thoughts from feelings. An analytical study of prayer, for example, may focus attention on various elements that constitute prayer, to the exclusion of praying. Moreover, it is hard to be objectively analytical of abstract concepts without losing the existential value of the concept itself. To intellectualize brings the danger of losing the power which flows from the dynamic quality of the idea itself as a plan for action. To have faith is to believe, and to believe is to feel and to act. Faith is not subscribing to verbal propositions, but living a life. Intellectualizing is often a defense against participation. Patients sometimes talk endlessly of their activities and thus protect themselves from facing their conflicts. Ministers and sometimes parishoner may feel that to talk about a thing is to have done it. The tendency to slant statements for publicity purposes often ends with the advertiser believing his own publicity—in short, institutionalized wishful thinking.

The final hazard to be discussed here is the feeling which the minister may develop that because of his profession he ought to be spared the common ills of life. But it is important to remember that the minister, as well as others in authority, is not omnipotent, and shares with all others the possibility and normal expectancy of illness. He is a potential statistic among those who develop rheumatism or heart disease, cancer or tuberculosis, or one of the major mental diseases. He should not be surprised if he becomes tense and nervous at times. In fact, the peculiar stresses of his position may bring greater vulnerability to anxiety and functional disability. Such conditions as stomach ulcers or hypertension or coronary disease are thought to go with the so-called high-pressure positions of life. Professional people are distinctly vulnerable to some of these. A strong sense of dedication assists in determination to overcome obstacles. But a wholly commendable and unselfish desire to do one's work in the most exemplary fashion does not eliminate the risk of breakdown. One may still succumb to exhaustion, infection and nervous strain, and illnesses that are potential in one's constitutional make-up. Every minister must have a mental reserve against a possible break in the period of service, even though he marshals all his assets for health and makes use of the not inconsiderable resources that his position makes available to him.

In view of the professional stresses and hazards which endanger the health of the minister, what can he and those who work with him do to strengthen him against them and to foster his health in order that he might minister more effectively to others?

2. Safeguarding the Minister's Health

First, he will have an elastic concept of health, and cultivate a capacity to accept limitations and to work within those limitations. Health, after all, is always a relative matter and many persons do good work in spite of even severe disabilities while the strongest and most efficient are not entirely free from defects. Persons who are crippled, who are blind or deaf, or who are confined to wheel chairs often do excellent work provided the work is in a field where their disabilities do not weigh heavily, and provided special facilities are available for them. One could cite the illustration of a clergyman who has no arms and who eats, writes, and uses a telephone with his feet and toes. Or the clergyman who is blind and carries on the responsibilities of a normal parish with the aid of a seeing-eye dog.

Persons have even made important contributions in spite of such mental defects as epilepsy and anxiety states or extreme mood swings. Even those with an average or somewhat low I. Q. may do good work under some circumstances.

Second, he will attempt continually to clarify his objectives in order to maintain a strong sense of direction and purpose. He needs to know where he is going and to feel that he is making some progress toward a goal to gain satisfaction from his work. It may be ventured that much frustration in the present-day ministry is due to loss of objective—and to confusion about the role the minister ought to play in the community—growing out of the cultural changes going on in the modern community. It has been observed that in the more conservative sections of the country, where urbanization and industrialization have not developed to any great extent, ministers are more sure of their role and gain greater satisfaction from their work which in turn is related to the definiteness of the response to their efforts.

If we draw a figure from navigation, it can be noted that the North Star does not change, but our compasses are susceptible to variation depending upon the elements that are close by, and that we have to correct the errors due to drift or deflection if we are not to be lost.

Correlative to this, if he is to maintain a sense of well-being through noting movement and progress toward a goal, continual evaluation and measurement of progress must be made. It is at this point that those who work with intangibles have their greatest difficulty, particularly when results are often not apparent until a long time has elapsed. Knowing where we are and merely staying afloat is not enough, if we may continue our nautical allusion. Evaluation means keeping records and developing instruments of measurement. Impressions, guesses, and estimates are not enough to give assurance of progress. The psychiatrist has learned that accurate and complete records of his interviews are an indispensable part of his therapeutic effort. Records keep him oriented, reveal clues for strategy in treatment, measure progress or failure, and give perspective on his relationship to the patient. Tested evaluative instruments help him to know what he is up against and correct his biases.

Third, he will learn to accept emotionality or excitement and its expression as an inseparable part of perceiving and acting, and will cultivate the capacity to love, to fear, to dislike, and to desire. Love is used here as the tender emotion, the feeling of compassion, adoration, desire for nearness, willingness to share.

In moral terms it is altogether good and never causes trouble except in its absence. Fear is useful in the presence of real danger, unless it becomes excessive—when it may become a serious hindrance to action—or unless it continues as anxiety after danger has passed. Dislike and even anger are appropriate in the face of that which is frustrating or threatening, since they stimulate useful avoidance reactions or generate extra energy to cope with the situation. In excess, as hate or rage, anger becomes a useless and dangerous emotion not subject to rational judgment. Desire stimulates us to work to secure food, clothing, protection, to reproduce and to win social acceptance. Only when it becomes emotionalism, unattached to useful productivity and pleasure, an end in itself, does it become both obstructive and destructive of the proper functioning of the individual.

Love, fear, dislike, and desire need to be given some form of acceptable expression when appropriate and in terms of sound priorities; need to be suppressed when inappropriate in accordance with a hierarchy of values; and even need to be repressed in certain areas; and often need to be sublimated. Always these effects must be balanced or in compensation with each other. Suppression is the conscious and willful denial of an impulse that one wishes to avoid, and it is an important part of the socializing and civilizing process. Repression is by definition an unconscious process and not subject to will power. It is, in part, a useful protective mechanism which relieves the mind and spirit of an overload of care and responsibility or psychic stress beyond human endurance. It is also a kind of selective inattention which relegates to the storehouse of the mind some material best reserved for future use. Unfortunately, this inattention often becomes habitual and we forget what we have put into the storehouse unless unusual events allow awareness to emerge. Sublimation is the diverting of a strong drive from an unacceptable or impossible goal into one that is socially acceptable and partly satisfying.

Fourth, the minister will seek to establish an adequate program of recreation, refreshment, and replenishment which will serve to restore his energies and nourish his mind and spirit. One of the basic elements in such a program is to secure sufficient rest and relaxation through sleep, taking naps, or simply loafing. High creativity seems to depend upon these fallow periods, and new insights and inspiration often come during or just after such quiet times. Periods of prayer and meditation may serve the same purpose if they are relaxed rather than tense, if they are periods of waiting rather than worrying. Another aspect of such a program is to rest the much-used parts of the organismic structure by activating other parts. So a change of activity or occupation may in itself be restful. Fortunately, the ministry usually entails a wide variety of activities so that it often has a kind of built-in recreation. Hobbies may serve a recreational purpose if pursued spontaneously and voluntarily rather than compulsively and competitively in hope of gain, prizes, or prestige. Still another aspect of recreation is to engage in activities in which we can "let ourselves go," speaking from the "motor" point of view. Such activities serve to release tensions built up by the necessity of inhibiting dangerous or distracting impulses which arise in the course of our work, out of fear, anger, or anxiety. Walking, bowling, gardening, and carpentry are examples of such activities. Finally, a recreational program will serve to round out the personality, express talents, and satisfy needs in a way not achieved during the practice of one's vocation. Such a program is often difficult for professional men to achieve because of a genuine compassion for those who need help, the constant importunities for help he receives, the compulsions to work which are all too frequently reinforced, approved, and even exploited by our culture. Moreover, many persons are ashamed to play because in Protestant culture play has often been equated with sin, and sanctions have been applied to keep persons at work. There may be times when one must choose to spend himself lavishly, but this is a conscious compulsion for glory.

Finally, the minister will avail himself of the therapies of human fellowship in which he may satisfy his need for dependence and interdependence, and find affection, emotional security in personal relationships, and a sense of personal significance.

Too often the minister who is a confidant and confessor to many persons finds himself in the position of having no confidant or confessor to whom he can turn other than God. An understanding wife or an intimate friend may help. A ministerial fellowship may be extremely therapeutic if the competitive, moralizing, and punitive elements are minimized and if one may be himself and be accepted as he is in the fellowship. Unfortunately, too few official professional fellowships are free of those negative elements. It may be that a select and small group of ministers, or even an inter-professional fellowship of like-minded persons, will serve better to provide one with a secure base of operation. If the minister's emotional needs are met through his non-professional relationships, he may not succumb so easily to temptations to exploit his parishioners.

At times the minister may find it necessary or helpful to turn to a trained psychiatrist for personal help. This is not an easy thing to bring oneself to do, any more than it is easy to undergo radical surgery. Frequently it involves a long, painful, and expensive process of treatment; and since in our society there is still some stigma involved in admitting mental illness, psychotherapy may be even more difficult to face than surgery.

However, the greatest boons of life are often painful and expensive—including parenthood and professional training. Many men are stronger, better, and more effective for having experienced illness, including mental illness, and particularly in view of what they might have become without it. Even as the psychiatrist may realize his dependence on God and turn to the Church to support him in life's common ventures, so the clergyman may be forced to admit his need for succor from the ministries of the healing profession.

In conclusion, it may be stated again that while health is a relative concept which defines the ratio of satisfaction and function to inherent capacity, one can minister to illness only out of a fair degree of health. Therefore, the minister will avail himself of all the therapies which are open to him and will attempt to live and work in the light of the realities described by mental health principles. He will be on guard against the mental health hazards surrounding his profession, and he will accept its risks fortified by the insights we have into the nature of these hazards.

Emotional Health of the Clergy

By The Rev. George Christian Anderson, S.T.B.
Director
National Academy of Religion and Mental Health

The minister should seek for maturity in life; his emotional problems spring from immaturity. The minister must overcome his dependence upon stereotypes of the ministry. These get in the way of his full understanding of his own task, and contribute to his health problems.

Clergymen as a group probably have as good a physical health record as any other group in the community. Indeed, insurance records indicate that the life expectancy of ministers is somewhat higher than that of people in other professions. But what of the emotional health of clergymen?

What do we mean by emotional health? Psychiatrists tell us that emotional health is another term for maturity. There are many definitions of maturity, but it is generally agreed that it means emotional growth resulting from a person's continual inner awareness of himself. Such growth is not easy, since the content of our unconscious accounts for a significant part of our total personality; and only as we are able to come to terms with what is hidden within us can we really achieve maturity.

This fact is not generally understood. Many people are convinced that they can control themselves by a sheer effort of intellect. But the best intellect is unable to quench certain powerful emotional drives. Psychiatry has learned to observe and classify various kinds of human behavior which obviously are the result of unconscious emotional drives and conflicts. Many behavior patterns are symptomatic of trouble within. Whenever a person's behavior is immature there is a good likelihood that he has a deep-seated emotional problem.

1. Marks of Maturity

Some of the characteristics of maturity obviously are an inner sense of security; the ability to experience self-esteem and a feeling of one's own worthwhileness without a severe sense of guilt; the capacity to form love relationships; the ability to control resentment and to laugh and have fun; a realistic attitude toward society and life; the capacity to withstand reversals and to adjust to and cooperate with all experiences of life. The mature person has adequate bodily desires and the ability to respond to them without excessive use or an undue sense of guilt; the competence to appraise himself realistically, without overcondemnation, and to accept himself completely, even though some of his thoughts and desires may not be socially acceptable (this implies the capacity to control the expression of such thoughts and desires).

Maturity involves a sense of morals; a conscience that is not overly rigid; satisfactory life purposes and goals; the ability to learn from experience; the capacity to satisfy the important requirements of one's own group; and, finally, the ability to be independent of group opinion. In a general way, these attitudes and types of behavior define what is meant by maturity or good mental health.

Maturity is growth from emotional patterns of childhood into adult patterns. When childish patterns persist in the adult, emotional good health has not yet been attained. Emotional growth is often hampered by anxiety-producing conflicts in early childhood. These conflicts may be hidden in one's unconscious; nevertheless they can influence adult behavior. Indeed, whenever infantile characteristics persist in an adult to the point of real unconscious conflict, there is a possibility of predisposition to neurosis.

Childhood patterns can be seen in adults who are prejudiced, egotistical, highly competitive, emotionally frustrated, unduly sensible of inferiority, inflexible, hostile and excessively guilt-ridden. The need for security, attention and love may be arrested at the childhood level, and often these repressed needs betray themselves in neurotic behavior.

2. *Exploiting the Clerical Profession*

To illustrate: Some clergymen consciously or unconsciously exploit their profession to satisfy childhood needs for attention. Children who are insecure or who lack affection endeavor to obtain these things by attracting attention to themselves. We are familiar with the child who makes a nuisance of himself by "showing off." But as the child grows, he is usually able to satisfy his needs for affection and security in a way consistent with his stage of development. However, some persons never outgrow infantile needs for attention and, not having the emotional maturity to satisfy these needs in an appropriate way, continue to behave like children.

Thus clergymen who continually use their chancels or pulpits as a stage upon which they can attract attention to themselves display childish emotional patterns. There are mature and immature ways of using the drama of worship. Obviously, the minister who exploits it to satisfy his need for attention is acting childishly on an occasion which calls for maturity and so reveals his own inner immaturity.

Incidentally, the chancel or pulpit is not the only place that may be perverted to satisfy neurotic needs. The professions that bring public attention and esteem—medicine and education, for instance, as well as the ministry—may assist in maintaining childish personality patterns. The man who is totally dependent on "status prestige" to bolster his ego reveals immaturity. Spoiled as a child by his mother, then by his sisters, then by an admiring congregation, a clergyman may become dependent on constant

admiration for security. Such ministers often attain high positions in their denominations. They never fully understand why
they feel a need to be authoritarian. In later years, they may
develop more serious character disorders.

3. "Know Thyself"

A mature person is aware of his inner drives without excessive
feelings of guilt. Clergymen are often unaware of their unconscious guilt, but by pouring out hostility and threats in their
sermons they reveal their disorder. It would be interesting to
measure the amount of hatred that emerges from the mouths
of preachers Sunday after Sunday. Such hatred is often symptomatic of the preacher's unconscious guilt, hostility or anxiety—
in other words, of his emotional illness.

The very fact that a man has chosen the ministry for a vocation may indicate some kind of inner disorder. Carroll A. Wise
has commented at length on the problem of what has been called
the "neurotic need for helping other people." Of course it must
not be inferred that the desire to help others is always a sign
of emotional ill health. But if the desire stems from unresolved
unconscious needs, there is a good chance that only limited insights concerning the problems and needs of others are possible.

4. Masochistic Martyrdom

A little caution is necessary in evaluating the degree to which
a clergyman makes a "martyr" of himself. While suffering often
brings us nearer to God, it is important to understand the real
nature of the suffering one is experiencing. Psychologists have
observed that an unconscious seeking after suffering, a deliberate
"martyrdom," may reflect an emotional disorder termed masochism. Whether masochism is conscious or unconscious, it becomes a self-inflicted handicap which has no relationship to a
genuine love for God. Those who make unusual sacrifices may
be experiencing infantile needs for punishment. To suffer because of obedience to righteousness is a mature action; but to
seek suffering merely for the sake of suffering may have emotional
implications.

Another indication of emotional illness may be seen in the minister's attitudes toward the customs and traditions of his particular church. One who is excessively rigid and unable to acknowledge the possibility that an opposing viewpoint has validity may be revealing fear and insecurity. He may consciously or unconsciously feel himself threatened and consequently becomes overly rigid. There is an interesting correlation between such persons and extreme neurotics. Maturity implies flexibility and the capacity to modify one's point of view.

Probably the most significant mark of a predisposition to neurosis among clergymen is the inability of some to free themselves from the traditionally imposed patterns of a minister's life and thought. Some clergymen apparently feel that they are required to throw themselves into some kind of mold and completely lose their individuality. No doubt there are those who are quite content to follow the traditional concept of what a preacher should be. Those who must be protected by the "system," who are unable to deviate from what is expected, who feel themselves very much apart from the world of other men, and particularly those who feel superior in this separation, are revealing anxiety and insecurity. Sometimes there are unconscious elements of guilt. The childhood pattern of wanting to be protected by the family and especially by the mother or father can be seen in the adult's desire to cling to a group under the protection of the "mother" church. Undoubtedly, for some, ecclesiastical organizations provide enormous feelings of security—for this world and the next! But clergymen who require this kind of security may have serious pathological disturbances and certainly cannot be said to have good emotional health.

5. Pinning One's Faults on Others

Another symptom of emotional illness is the projection of one's own character disturbances or deviations upon another. Enough evidence exists to demonstrate that we hate in others that particular personality trait which we find most threatening to ourselves. More than likely, the trait is in our unconscious mind, for often we are unaware of having those objectionable and even horrifying traits we see in our fellow men. Clergymen who condemn certain behavior in others should be reminded of the possibility of similar behavior on their own part. This is what Jesus implied when he said, "Judge not, that ye be not judged." Inability to forgive is a sign of immaturity.

Still another manifestation of emotional ill health is the unwillingness to accept oneself regardless of the character of one's behavior. To accept is not necessarily to condone, but a realistic awareness of oneself is essential to good health. Excessive guilt or anxiety may be characteristics predisposing to neurosis.

Occasionally one observes jealousy in a clergyman, or resentment over another preacher's success. Some preachers have powerful competitive drives. Such dynamic aggressiveness is often a symptom of inner disturbance. One sometimes speculates why certain clergymen work at such a terrific pace. Frequently such behavior is linked to a desire to atone for conscious or unconscious misdeeds. Guilt and repressed anxiety are also found in such persons. Occasionally marital disharmony or frustration lies behind the parson's overbusyness. He feels a compulsion to be a leader and to prove that at least to his parish and his community he is an acceptable and needed person.

6. How to Foster Emotional Health

What can be done to help clergymen maintain or recover good emotional health? Unfortunately, the need for help is often greatest after ordination. Yet important steps can be taken before a man enters seminary to check certain attitudes which might intensify a latent disposition to neurosis. Good counseling services and even psychiatric help should be provided for all seminarians. More frequent use of projective tests such as the Rorschach or the Thematic Apperception test could be advantageous.

Such services should be available in every area where clergymen—particularly young clergymen—work. Bishops or denominational heads should employ a trained counselor whose chief duty is to help clergymen deal with their emotional problems. A psychiatrically trained counselor can render significant service

in this field. Many clergymen who have acquired some understanding of depth psychology are beginning to feel that they
would profit by personal psychoanalysis. Insights into one's own
unconscious problems and resources is almost a prerequisite for
dealing with the troubles of other people.

The emotional difficulties of clergymen and their families
constitute one of the most perplexing and time-consuming
problems that face bishops and others in authority, and their
wisdom is not always sufficient. Trained clerical counselors are
needed.

If the clergy are to help others toward emotional health, they
themselves must have good emotional health. "Physician, heal
thyself" is as good advice today as when Jesus gave it 2,000 years
ago. Emotionally ill clergymen tend to perpetuate the pathology
of the congregation. Fortunately, the majority of ministers are
mature and intelligent. But there are enough of the other kind
to constitute one of the important problems of our day. The way
organized religion meets these needs may determine the growth
or decline of the church.

PART TWO

THE VOCATIONAL INTENTIONS AND
INNER STRESS OF THE MINISTER

The emotional disturbances of mankind are both clinically and existentially rooted. Specific syndromes of symptoms must be dealt with medically. But recent investigations by such authorities as Booth, Frankl, May, Mowrer, and Wolff indicate that these symptoms are deeply related to the sense of meaninglessness of destiny. In ministers as well as others symptoms may be "ditching" symptoms, in the sense that they boil over out of otherwise unbearable responsibilities. They may be "doing in" symptoms, in the sense that they convince other people of the same feelings of unworthiness which clutch the minister himself. In every instance, the symptoms of a minister bear some real relation to his motives for being a minister.

Therefore, no discussion of the emotional health of the minister gets very far before the problem of his motivation is mentioned. The externally motivated or "other-directed" minister is likely to be "tossed to and fro, and carried about by every wind," thereby reflecting his immaturity. The compulsive minister is driven by blind impulses, not having "the eyes of his inner understanding opened." The good shepherd of his flock, to the contrary, is enjoined by the author of I Peter as follows:

> Feed the flock of God which is among you, taking the oversight thereof, not by constraint, but willingly, not for filthy lucre, but of a ready mind, neither as being lords over God's heritage, but being examples to the flock.

This part of the research is devoted to discussions of the sense of vocation in the minister, the value structure of the minister as it is related to his purpose, the unconscious motivation of the minister, and a summary of the Lilly Foundation-supported research conference on motivation for the ministry.

The inseparable relation between freedom of motivation and healthy function in the minister will become apparent in these research articles. The tensions of contrary demands upon him are felt keenly. The ancient wisdom of the Pastoral Epistles becomes painfully contemporary as one reads this research.

Vocation in the Christian Ministry

By DANIEL D. WILLIAMS

Professor of Systematic Theology

Union Theological Seminary, New York, New York

Ministers experience profound inner tensions between their sense of call and the day-to-day demands laid upon them. They are torn between a sense of holiness of their task and their own personal feelings of unworthiness. They wistfully yearn for an adequate theology of vocation.

Every conception of the Christian ministry has its foundation in Christ's ministry in the world and in the church. T. W. Manson makes this clear in *The Church's Ministry* as he points out the sense in which there is only one ministry in the Church: Christ's ministry. All special ordination and calling within the Christian faith can only be an extension of or response to that one ministry.

While this basis of all Christian ministry is clear, the nature of the special ministries of the church has been subject through Christian history to a continuing theological search. It has created deep divisions, and at the present time has led to another period of widespread self-examination on the part of churches and ministers. In this article I should like to deal with certain of the problems about the ministry which lie on the boundary between the theology of the church and vocation and the experience of ministers in the church today.

At the outset we have to recognize that many things are being said today about the difficulties of ministers under the pressure of responsibilities. Temptations to self-pity and self-seeking abound in the ministry as in every other place in life. We cannot deny that many of our problems as ministers are our own creation. Here, however, I take all such moral reflections for granted. It still must be pointed out that there remain some profound tensions in the life and faith of the Christian minister today which cannot be explained away by reference to moral failure. They arise both from the Christian faith itself and from the attempt of the church to realize its mission in this kind of world. To cover up these tensions is to invite increasing confusion and to weaken the power of the ministry in the guidance of the church. I shall speak of three problems and make two brief suggestions as to ways of meeting them.

I

Few ministers do not find at some time a sense of discrepancy between the call of God to love and serve men, and what the minister finds himself doing from day to day. I want to point out that this comes partly from the profound inner tension in the Christian conception of the "calling."

In our time we are in difficulty about the meaning of "vocation" because both pietism and Calvinist puritanism identified the calling too easily with the single action of direct service to God in daily work. St. Paul's words, "let every man remain in the calling wherein he was called," became the foundation of the Protestant doctrine that all are called, not only the "religious." It released the energies of Christianity in the modern world, especially in its Calvinist version, as men regarded every legitimate activity in life as sacred in the sight of God. What was lost from sight in this dynamic movement was the realization that the calling of God—that is, the summons to be conformed to the mind of Christ and to be *his* servants—is a call to reform and reshape every circumstance of life. It is both an acceptance of the given order and a judgment upon it.

When this point is grasped, it becomes clear that a sense of discrepancy between the calling of God and our immediate way of life, whatever it may be, is inevitable. It is a sign that we are approaching the depth of the New Testament understanding of the calling.

The Christian minister finds the question of the meaning of his calling opened up in many ways today. He may be acutely conscious of the influence of historical accidents, of cultural pressures, and of the special aspects of his personal biography which have brought him to his decision for the Christian ministry, to his particular communion, and to his position in it. It was fairly easy for some of our theological forebears to identify all this process directly with the will of God, and to read his providence as a kind of assurance that whatever is, in the church at least, is right. But we are certainly at a time when the forms of culture and church are being ploughed up and transformed, and we are far less ready to see the explicit decision of God in the circumstances of our life. There are theological issues here concerning the meaning of Providence, and the way in which we can know God's will; but whatever our theology of Providence, our realistic sense of history prevents us from a simple identification of our professional calling with the will of God. We have to look deeper than ecclesiastical order for our understanding of the calling which comes to us as persons and leads us to the ministry.

Again, the minister today cannot help but be conscious of a discrepancy between the summons to the sacrificial life and the position of relative comfort and privilege which in many cases he enjoys. The church reflects the economic, social, and national structure of our life. Whatever problems are created by American wealth among the poorer nations of the world, or by racial divisions, or by the pressures to conformity and security in the present technological age, are not escaped by the church and its ministers. To have an ecclesiastical position is to be a part of the system. Any sensitive conscience recognizes that. Just because ministers are often one step removed from the bitterness of economic and political conflicts, they may have a heightened sense of injustice and of the judgment of God upon all "vocations."

It is probable that the development of new ministries (and the opening up of a variety of ways of fulfilling one's ministry today) has added to the problem of realizing the meaning of vocation. To be sure, the increasing recognition that there are specialized ways in which interests, training, and skill can be used within the parish ministry and beyond it, has given a new reality to the personal vocations of many. But at the same time the decision concerning the ministry has become more complex. Every observer of seminary students, for example, is aware that even when the decision about "ministry" has been made, the seminary years are apt to be full of self-searching and sometimes agonizing decision among several alternative forms of ministry in teaching, chaplaincy, hospital, or mission field. We must have a theology of "calling" which enables us to face the kinds of dilemmas and choices which ministers make in the church today. Vocation is not an escape from decision.

II

A second major source of difficulty about vocation today arises from the life of the church, and is so well known that we need not dwell upon it. This is the discrepancy between what ministers believe they ought to be doing to serve the Lord as preachers and pastors, and the expectations of churches that whatever else the minister does, he shall be the executive of a complex time-consuming organization. Dr. Blizzard's studies and others have shown how deep the sense of discrepancy at this point is in the American ministry today. It is often pointed out that the minister is not the sole judge of what constitutes his greatest service to the church. No one can deny that what churches do on the whole are things that must be done if those churches are to live and grow in our culture. But this only sharpens the problem of where the criteria are to be found for the church and its ministry. If the minister simply allows the immediate pressures of the parish or hospital or theological seminary to define his own calling, then he may have surrendered the very heart of his vocation to what is external and accidental. If he tries to reshape and redirect his own life and the institution around him, he will encounter some of the resistance which makes him doubt his own calling. Or he may discover that he is called to be a reformer with all the painful risk and self-doubt that this involves.

III

A third cause of self-searching about the ministerial vocation comes from the nature of the ministry as a public and visible embodiment of the "sacred calling" to represent the body of Christ and to preach the Word of God. There is a personal restlessness which many ministers experience concerning this identification of the office with the "holy." There is the personal sense of unworthiness. There is the loneliness of the inevitable distance which is created between the minister and people. The pastor and his family live in a special relationship to church and community. It is not these aspects of the matter, however, that I wish to emphasize. It is rather to the fact that the Christian faith itself points away from the distinction between minister and layman. As Dr. H. Richard Niebuhr has stressed in his book, *The Purpose of the Church and Its Ministry,* the Christian minister is one who shares in the ministry of Christ. The existence in the church of an order of priests and pastors may obscure the reality of the shared ministry of all. It is not that the minister is necessarily restricted in his freedom to think, to be, and to do what his conscience and faith direct. Grant for the moment that he has all such freedom. But he may still find himself desiring to be able to say things not because they conform with sacred doctrine, but because they are true; to speak of service to God and man not because he is ordained to preach this, but because every man is called in Christ for this purpose. In a world divided between the sacred and the secular realms, a way of life publicly and explicitly identified with "the holy" may produce a sense of violation of reality and of separation from the fullness of God's service. Holderlin's words sting with the truth:

> Who follows sacred calling like a trade,
> His face is false and cold and dead, as are his gods.

There are paradoxes in this relation of the minister to others. It is true that his ordination gives him in many ways the opportunity to meet each person where he is. When the mission of the church to bring healing and forgiveness along with judgment is understood, this fact may enable the minister to realize his own humanity and his relationship to others. But he cannot escape the problems created by the power of "religion" to separate life from life. Our Lord was not ordained. His message seemed, to the most religious of his hearers, to be filled with challenge which they could not understand.

IV

These problems all point to the need for a theology of vocation. Toward that theology two suggestions can be briefly stated here. First, let us recognize that emphasis upon the special circumstances and special call of each individual is foreign to the New Testament understanding. There is only one calling in the Gospel. In the Pauline interpretation of it, this is the summons of God through His Word incarnate in Jesus Christ to give life in service to God and to the neighbor. That is the election and choice of which the Fourth Gospel speaks in the words, "Ye have not chosen me, I have chosen you" (John 15). "To walk worthily of the calling wherein ye are called" is for Paul to respond to the whole summons of Christ, not to give any final place to one's particular station in life. To be sure, there are diversities of talents and gifts. Not all are called to do exactly the same thing. The calling of God comes in the concrete situations of life, not as something removed from them. But when Paul says in I Corinthians 7, "let every man remain in the calling wherein he is called," surely in the light of his whole outlook it is clear he is not focusing attention on particular circumstances of life as constituting the calling. Paul did not remain in the work in which he was engaged when the Lord spoke to him. Many of the disciples certainly did not remain in their "daily work" when Jesus summoned them to follow him. Paul in I Corinthians is surely giving good practical advice to the Christians to begin where they are. In that situation to stay in their present daily work was the part of wisdom. But to make more of this, and to treat the various professions and situations of life as in themselves identical with "vocation," is surely to misrepresent the Gospel.

The one calling, to love and serve God and our neighbor, underlies all vocation including that of the ordained ministry of the church. To know that every man is called in Christ to the use of his powers and his freedom in meeting the tasks of life as they are set before him, is to find a solid basis of reality. Of course there will be a discrepancy between that calling and many of the circumstances and ambiguities of life. That is part of the reality of the situation and points to the significance of grace and forgiveness as aspects of all "calling."

A minister of Jesus Christ cannot find his own vocation apart from his helping the people to whom he ministers to find theirs. He should remember that those who sit before him in the congregation or the counseling room very often cannot begin with their daily work, or their profession, or their situation in life as the key to the meaning of their "calling." They can be helped to begin with the one calling which comes to all men, and which gives the stature and dignity of service in every struggle with the problems of life. Then it may be that some realistic sense of a personal vocation can begin to grow.

The other point which needs to be kept clear is the requirement of decision in all response to calling. So long as we think of our vocation as something provided for us by the form of the church and the expectation of society, so long as it is a mould to which our life conforms, we shall certainly either become sentimentalists or futile rebels. To be called is to be challenged with the realization of our personal freedom where we are. It is to begin to live for God and the great community of His people. We take up our own life in response to Him. No matter how much our personal fate may be determined by inward and outward pressures over which we have little control, there is at the core of selfhood the power to live freely and responsibly in trust and commitment, and to begin to allow the spirit of love to reshape our own world and that around us.

The divine call is always a summons to creativity and a new life in the midst of the old. We will see a deep gulf between what we are intended to be and what we are; but we are called only to serve in the spirit of love and to believe in the reality of the Kingdom of God, not to create a perfect world or church according to a pattern. To enter the special ministry of the church is a decision taken with the same reliance upon grace, the same commitment of self, and the same acceptance of the uncertainties of life as any other serious Christian decision. The minister who undertakes his work in that spirit shares in the universal comradeship of all who live by faith.

Value Structures and the Minister's Purpose

By Frederick R. Kling
Director, The Ministry Study Educational Testing Service

The Educational Testing Service is conducting an empirical study of the goals, identity, and effectiveness of the minister. The director of this study gives a detailed discussion of the values of the minister as they are related to his purpose.

The Christian ministry has been the subject of careful study and extensive literature to a degree with which, historically, few other vocations can compare. We may in part explain this greater attention to the minister's job by the greater literacy of ministers who up through the time of Lyman Abbott's *The Christian Ministry* (1905) and John Henry Jowett's *The Preacher: His Life and Work* (1912) were predominant among the more educated and more vocal members of the community. But we would be amiss if we overlooked the continuous attempt of ministers to understand their own vocation better and to improve their own capacity to serve both God and man. The degree of literary attention the ministry has received reflects both the complexity of the job and the will to see it done well.

Recent years have brought new approaches to the task of understanding a vocation. It is interesting to observe a secular em-

51

ployer who is serving on a pulpit committee attempt to formu-
late a job description to assist the committee in its search for
the "right" minister. He knows the procedure helps in his business, but he is frustrated in applying it to the Church. While
many denominations are working in this direction, we have as
yet no thoroughly developed methods of fitting ministers and
churches so that the combination will function most effectively
in the Church's business—the definition of this "business" being
one of the problems. Again, the sociologist or the educator may
take a fresh look at the ministry and try to apply the insights of
his discipline to help in the understanding of the ministry or in
the training of ministers. Despite the extensive literature on the
ministry, it is noteworthy that such approaches have had to
break new ground—as for example, S. W. Blizzard's application
of the sociological concept of role to the minister and his work.

Not least among the new disciplines taking a fresh look at the
ministry is psychology, and in particular that part of psychology
having to do with vocational guidance and counseling. Seminaries, denominational departments of vocation, and local in-care
groups are continually striving to improve their programs of
recruitment, selection, and guidance of ministerial candidates.
Increasing experimental and practical use is being made of a
wide variety of psychological tests and instruments. But how are
such tests chosen or devised? How are they checked for accuracy
in measuring the traits and characteristics they are intended to
measure? The task of evaluating these instruments for their pertinence to the ministry, as distinguished from other vocations, is
one of the assignments of the Ministry Study at Educational
Testing Service, and it is this task that necessitates additional
study, from the psychologist's point of view, of the ministry as a
vocation.

The procedure the Ministry Study is using for evaluating a
test is to follow up the students who took the test a number of
years ago, when they entered seminary, and find out where they
are now and, if they are in the parish ministry, what kind of a
job they are doing. To compare their present performance to
their old test scores (and thus to evaluate the test) necessitates

having some sort of measure of the nature and quality of their work. To fill this need, the staff of the Ministry Study, with the guidance of its Advisory Committee drawn from representative denominations, developed a test-like instrument entitled "The Work of the Parish Minister." In the course of the analysis of the data gathered through this instrument it becomes possible to further refine our knowledge of the basic dimensions of the minister's job as revealed by empirical descriptions of actual ministers obtained from the ministers themselves and from their laymen—in short, to take a fresh look at the ministry.

The minister's work is difficult to "capture" in an empirical instrument. To be sure, he performs certain functions, such as preaching, visiting, counseling, administering the affairs of his church, and so forth, in which he might be rated by himself or by others. We have done this in "The Work of the Parish Minister," and we have gone yet a step further and obtained as well descriptions of the *manner* in which he performs these functions —that is, the aspects of his personality that can be so important in determining whether or not his preaching communicates, his visiting is effective, or his counseling mediates healing. The analysis of these sections of the instrument is now in process and must await a future report. This article is confined to sections of the instrument that attempted to go yet deeper. *Why* does the minister perform these functions? What is he trying to accomplish? How does he see his purpose and how do his lay people see his purpose in terms of the effect he is trying to produce in human lives? This is the "business" of the Church in the truest sense, the part of the job description that eluded our employer above.

These questions, reaching as they do into the less tangible areas of the minister's role, might be expected to prove the most resistant to the behavioral scientist's tools and techniques. A number of approaches were considered, partially developed, and then rejected. Items for an objective instrument conceivably might be written that would distinguish between the minister who needs to have people dependent on himself and the minister who values their own integrity, or that would differentiate among ministers who want people to experience life and the Christian faith in the optimistic mood of American progress and self-indulgence, the Puritanical mood of moral obligation, or the Kierkegaardian mood of a tragic human predicament. We even *tried* to write such items. We gave it up. Another attempt which we would like to have carried further but felt it wiser to abandon was to obtain a picture of a minister's message and impact in terms of the thirteen "Ways to Live" extensively investigated for different cultures by Charles Morris (*Varieties of Human Value*). Our fear here—later confirmed by what we *did* do—was that the philosophical language and subtle distinctions in the "ways" would be too abstruse for some of the lay people to handle adequately. Whatever would a Kansas farmer, aged 60, graduate of eighth grade, a leader in his congregation, understand by "the dynamic integration of enjoyment, action, and contemplation" even if it were the very thing his pastor sought for his people?

While our final solution left much to be desired, we felt that it came closest to our intention of translating such abstract definitions of the minister's purpose as "the increase among men of the love of God and neighbor" (from Richard Neibuhr's *The Purpose of the Church and Its Ministry*) and "relating the Word of God to the needs of men" (from somewhere, from seminary days) into everyday language in such a way that we could obtain a picture of a minister's purpose, i.e. what he represents to his congregation in terms of what life is all about and what value people should seek. The twenty goals of the "General Goals of Life Inventory"[1] were modified slightly to allow for a greater emphasis on religious goals for inclusion in "The Work of the Parish Minister" in the following form:

1. Self-sacrifice for the sake of a better world
2. Peace of mind, contentment, stillness of spirit
3. Serving the community of which one is a part
4. Devotion to God, doing God's will
5. Being genuinely concerned about other people
6. Enjoying life to the full

---

[1] Published by Cooperative Test Division, Educational Testing Service.

7. Achieving personal immortality in heaven
8. Finding one's place in life and accepting it
9. Developing a sense of personal communication with God
10. Doing one's duty
11. Promoting the most happiness for the greatest number of people
12. Making a place for oneself in the world; getting ahead
13. Power; control over people and things
14. Disciplining oneself to a wholesome and clean life
15. Providing love and security for one's family
16. Being able to "take it"; brave and uncomplaining acceptance of what circumstances bring
17. Self-development; becoming a real, genuine person
18. Preserving the best in human culture
19. Understanding oneself; having a mature outlook
20. Participating fully in the life and work of the Church

The ministers in our samples (some about six years out of seminary and some between 30 and 50 years of age, from eight representative denominations) were asked to select two lay people, a man and a woman most informed about their ministry. Each minister and his two lay people independently ranked these twenty goals according to two criteria: (1) the value structure underlying the "American way of life" and (2) that particular minister's "total message." The instructions spelled out these criteria a little more fully:

(1) We hear a great deal about "the American way of life." Despite the great differences that exist between different groups in our country, there is the notion of a typical way of living or common value system that is shared by the majority of Americans. The purpose of this section is to determine what you personally feel this American way of life actually is. A list of twenty "goals of life" is given below. Please indicate the order in which you feel that these goals describe the value system underlying the lives of Americans as a whole . . .

(2) The purpose of this section is to determine what you feel that your minister stands for in the eyes of his congregation. The same twenty "goals of life" used before are repeated below

. . . describe the over-all way of life your minister upholds before his congregation (through his preaching, his teaching, his
counseling, his personal example—his total impact). . . .

The table which appears below gives the mean response of
226 ministers, 226 men, and 226 women (about half our total
sample) in ranking the twenty goals according to the two criteria. Two goals were assigned to each rank, from zero as the
least descriptive of the criterion to nine as most descriptive of
the criterion. The standard deviation of responses about any
one of the means in the table averaged about 2.0. Because of
the ranking procedure, the average mean is 4.50 for each column
in the table.

We had many reasons for asking these two questions, but only
a portion of our inquiry based on them can be reported here.

MEAN RATINGS FOR TWENTY GOALS OF LIFE

ITEM (see pages 54-55)	I. Ratings of the "American Way of Life"			II. Ratings of the Ministers' Total Message		
	Ministers	Men	Women	Ministers	Men	Women
1.	2.92	3.23	2.93	5.36	5.09	4.79
2.	5.21	5.29	4.75	4.08	4.73	4.78
3.	5.63	5.60	5.61	4.73	4.76	4.50
4.	2.75	4.70	4.52	8.61	8.58	8.67
5.	4.10	4.79	5.01	7.36	6.40	6.88
6.	7.02	5.16	5.21	2.48	1.71	1.96
7.	2.16	3.36	3.06	3.88	4.94	4.48
8.	5.23	4.86	4.61	4.00	3.49	3.40
9.	2.61	4.21	4.20	7.84	7.67	7.67
10.	5.61	5.15	5.18	4.35	4.46	4.19
11.	4.60	4.03	3.73	3.78	3.88	3.75
12.	7.34	6.06	6.01	.50	1.16	.97
13.	4.59	2.94	3.19	.32	.64	.32
14.	3.62	4.38	4.57	5.41	5.96	5.82
15.	7.19	7.40	7.36	5.29	5.04	4.98
16.	4.11	3.31	3.34	2.98	3.01	3.52
17.	5.05	4.68	4.83	4.82	4.25	4.48
18.	2.99	2.69	3.22	2.31	2.73	2.90
19.	4.24	4.08	4.43	4.76	3.83	4.24
20.	2.77	4.09	4.25	7.19	7.69	7.75

Our primary purpose was to obtain "portraits" of individual ministers against which to evaluate psychological test scores. Compared to the other sections of "The Work of the Parish Minister" which deal with the more *functional* aspects of his job, the portraits of *purpose* which we found tend to be more alike and thus less distinguishable from one another and less useful for our investigation. This analysis, and other comparisons such as differences among denominations or among rural, urban, and suburban churches, are beyond the scope of this article. Our attention will be confined to a sort of average minister among our respondents, and to the differences in the way he sees himself and his lay people see him as contrasted to the way the same people see the value structure underlying the American environment.

The mean response of the men and women for each of the entire group of forty items (both questions) have been compared in Figure 1 on page 58. If the means had been exactly the same, the points in the figure would have fallen on the diagonal line in this graph. It is possible to investigate statistically whether the departures from this diagonal lines are too great to be accounted for by chance fluctuations. As it turns out, there are not enough big differences (only two out of forty at the 1% level of significance) between the mean responses of the men and the mean responses of the women to throw any serious doubt on the hypothesis of chance fluctuations. In other words, we are justified in assuming that for both questions the men and the women are talking about substantially the same thing and, even more surprisingly, seeing it eye to eye!

The second figure shows a quite different result. It contrasts the mean response of the ministers and the mean response of the lay people (men and women combined) in describing the minister's total message. For the twenty items in this second question, the ministers' mean responses were significantly different at the 1% level from the men's responses in ten cases and from the women's in seven. It will be noted that these 20 points lie close to the diagonal line, but that a number of them stand somewhat off from it and represent inversions in the way the ministers rank themselves and the lay people rank them. (See page 60.)

Both the ministers and the lay people agree that four of the goals of life are clearly the most descriptive of the ministers' position:

4. Devotion to God, doing God's will
9. Developing a sense of personal communion with God

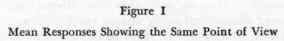

Figure I

Mean Responses Showing the Same Point of View

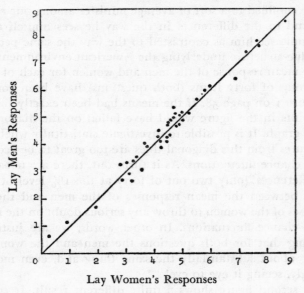

Lay Women's Responses

20. Participating fully in the life and work of the Church
5. Being genuinely concerned about other people

Interestingly, however, the lay people tended to rank "participating fully in the life and work of the Church" significantly higher than the ministers, and the ministers tended to put "being genuinely concerned about other people" higher than the lay people thought they did. A second group of statements,

14. Disciplining oneself to a wholesome and clean life

15. Providing love and security for one's family
 1. Self-sacrifice for the sake of a better world
while far below this first group of four, occupy a clear second
place in these descriptions of what the ministers stand for.
There are again significant differences, the lay people stating
that the ministers emphasize "disciplining oneself to a wholesome and clean life," while the ministers feel that they in fact
emphasize "self-sacrifice for the sake of a better world" and
"providing love and security for one's family" about equally as
high.

At the bottom of the scale of what ministers represent, we find
two items clearly in last place:

12. Making a place for oneself in the world; getting ahead
13. Power; control over people and things
A cluster of goals somewhat less objectionable to the ministers
again demonstrates a significant inversion. The lay people feel
that the ministers take a very dim view of (6) "enjoying life to
the full" as contrasted to (16) "brave and uncomplaining
acceptance of what circumstances bring" and (18) "preserving
the best in human cultures." While it is quite possible that the
ministers have placed a different interpretation on the meaning
of enjoying life, as for example with the reservation that true
enjoyment comes only in doing God's will, this result is in keeping with the other stoical, dutiful emphases that the lay people
see in the minister's total message.

More dramatic differences are found in comparing the ministers' concept and the lay people's concept of the American way
of life. These are depicted in Figure 3 on page 61. Here the
ministers' means differ significantly from the men's in ten cases
and from the women's in twelve. A curious relationship exists
between the *differences* of Figure 3 and the *rank order* of Figure
2. Lay people have a much higher appreciation than the ministers
do of the way Americans actually are living in terms of the goals
of life that are important to the ministers, namely:

 4. Devotion to God, doing God's will
 9. Developing a sense of personal communion with God
20. Participating fully in the life and work of the Church

5. Being genuinely concerned about other people

14. Disciplining oneself to a wholesome and clean life.

The ministers, on the other hand, seem to feel that what Americans are looking for in life are the things that they, as ministers, tend to rate low. Their idea of the extent to which Americans value (6) "enjoying life to the full" and (12) "making a place

Figure II

The Minister's Total Message

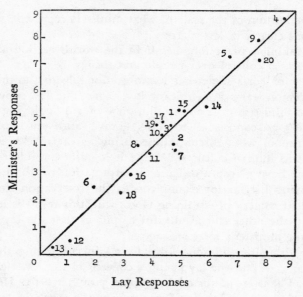

Lay Responses

for oneself in the world; getting ahead," and to a lesser extent, (13) "power; control over people and things," (11) "promoting the most happiness for the greatest number of people" and (16) "being able to 'take it'; brave and uncomplaining acceptance of what circumstances bring" is much higher than the lay people's evaluation of the same goals.

Special attention ought to be drawn to item (7) in both Figure 2 and Figure 3, as it accounts for greater differences than any other item. "Achieving personal immortality in heaven" occupies the very bottom position on the ministers' evaluation of the American way of life, and it is also quite low in the value structure they try to encourage for their congregations. The lay people, on the other hand, place it much higher in both value structures. In both figures the differences involved are differences

Figure III

The American Way of Life

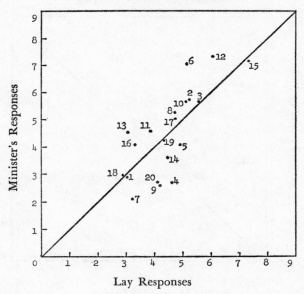

Minister's Responses

Lay Responses

of *perception* of the *same* value structure. If we may assume that the ministers are the more accurate judges of their own message and the lay people the more unbiased judges of the American way of life, it would appear that this especially sensitive item is one in which they most misunderstand each other. The layman is not hard to find who is sincerely and even painfully perplexed by his minister's lack of evangelistic zeal, nor the minister who is disillusioned by his lay people's more ready acceptance of a formula for achieving personal immortality than of a commitment to a deeper understanding of the Christian life.

The ministers' rankings and the lay people's rankings have been pooled in Figure 4, which compares the composite view of the minister's total message with the composite view of the American way of life. In this figure, no discernable cluster around

Figure IV

The Value Structures Compared

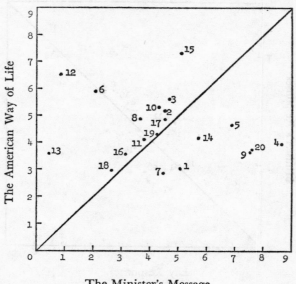

The Minister's Message

the diagonal line exists at all, but instead, a negative relationship is evident between the two sets of composite rankings. The tension is vividly portrayed between the way that this group of respondents looks at the American way of life and the way they look at the ministers' presentation of the proper values of life. As might be expected, the cluster of religious goals (4, 9, 20, 5) and the cluster of self-indulgent goals (13, 12, 6) weight down the ends of this distribution. Thus the minister's role is quite definitely seen by these respondents as being in conflict with the value structure of the environment in which he performs his role. His job is to bring about changes in the way people live and the goals of life they pursue.

It is interesting to note the *degree* of conflict as each group of respondents sees it. The pooled rankings in Figure 4 result in a negative correlation between the two criteria of −.19. If we compute the correlation for each group separately, the men's means correlate +.08 under the two situations, the women's +.05, and the ministers' −.48. Thus the minister sees a much greater discrepancy between the two value structures than the lay people do. From his point of view, a much greater "about face" is called for, a much greater task for the Church envisioned.

The conclusions drawn from an analysis of the type described in this article will sometimes be what the researcher anticipated in advance and will sometimes take a more surprising turn. We expected to find a conflict between the two value structures, but we did not expect to find the same picture from the men and women and a different picture from the ministers. We expected to find the approximate ratings that we did, but again some of these were surprising, such as the very low rating given to "preserving the best in human culture" in both value structures. A good experimental design must allow for either the expected or the surprising to emerge. The "objectivity" of a measurement device is one of its fundamental qualities. It provides a test of the researcher's hunches and theories without allowing him to color the basic data with the very ideas he expects to find.

On the other hand, a measurement device sacrifices much of the flexibility and insightfulness of the human observer, thinker, and reporter. It can go no deeper than the items in the instrument, which are often short and somewhat ambiguous. For the task of comparing psychological test scores and present performance in the ministry, there is no avoiding this handicap. For the task of understanding the ministry as a vocation, however, it has been possible as well to visit ministers in their parishes and to interview them about their purpose as ministers. While this aspect of the Ministry Study, too, must await further reporting, it can be definitely said as a concluding note that these interviews support and amplify the findings of the present report. Ministers from very unlike denominations do look upon their purpose primarily in terms of people and of the value structures underlying their lives. They regard their work as imparting to these people the insights that will enable them to see through and to avoid the inviting but shallow emphasis of life described above as the self-indulgent cluster of goals and to seek instead within the framework of the Church and of Christian commitment a more meaningful, worthwhile, and satisfying conception of life. They verbalize it with varying facility, and find it much easier to give examples of "what they're trying to accomplish," examples that seem invariably to involve people whose lives have been made happy and valuable by a new structure of values.

Religious Conservatism-Liberalism and Mental Health

By James Gilmour Ranck, Ph.D.,
Clinical Psychologist,
New York City, New York

Experienced ministers get a sneaking hunch at times that rigidity of orthodoxy—be it of the fundamentalist or the liberal variety— has some connection with the emotional health of the minister. Is this so? James G. Ranck, a discerning and disciplined clinical psychologist, has done extensive doctoral research on this.

Although the rapprochement of psychology and theology is something quite new on the American intellectual scene, there is a current and growing interest, in centers of theological training, in the psychological understanding of religious ideology, behavior and motivation. One indication of this interest is an increased emphasis on the training of theological students in the relationships between religion and personality, in counseling theory and practice, and in pastoral psychology. Another such indication is the use of psychological tests and the psychiatric interview in the admission of students to theological schools, and as aids in counseling them during their period of training. Similar procedures have been and are being adopted by boards of missions, annual conferences, and other church administrative bodies, for the placement of persons in various types of religious vocation.

Within the context of this acknowledged utility of psychological insights in the selection, training and counseling of religious professionals, a study was recently conducted of the relationships between personality and theological attitudes and beliefs. The sample was composed of 800 male Protestant theological students, representing the entire theological continuum from extreme conservatism to extreme liberalism. Drawn from twenty-eight theological schools throughout the United States, the subjects' places of home residence included every major geographical area of the country.

I

For the purposes of this study, religious conservatism was defined as essentially theistic, God-centered, supranaturalist, absolutist in dogma, and conceiving of religious experience as consisting primarily of a dependent relationship with an "Other," identified as a person, institution, ritual, or dogma, and usually some combination of the four. Religious liberalism was defined as essentially humanistic, man-centered, naturalist, antidogmatic, and conceiving of dependency upon institutions, rituals and an anthropomorphic Supreme Being as unnecessary and even undesirable in religious experience. The whole compass of religious attitude and belief was conceived of as being on a continuum between these two poles of thinking and believing.

Ten standard psychological personality scales, two scales for measuring religious ideology and attitudes, and a specially prepared opinion questionnaire were used to obtain the data. These data were expected to shed some light on the following questions: Is there a significant relationship between the kind of person one is, and the kind of religious attitudes and beliefs one holds? If so, in what areas of the personality are these relationships found to exist?

It was hypothesized that significant relationships exist between one's position on a continuum of religious ideology and (a) authoritarian attitudes and beliefs and (b) submissiveness. It was hypothesized, further, that significant relationships do not exist between psychopathology, as conventionally measured, and position on a conservative-liberal religious continuum. The testing of these hypotheses yielded the following statistically significant results.

Authoritarianism:

1. The more conservative that persons are in their religious ideology, the more they tend to exhibit prejudice against, and to reject, such outgroups as Negroes, Jews, and persons of other nations, and to idealize the corresponding ingroups. Conversely, the more liberal the religious ideology, the greater the rejection of both outgroup prejudices and ingroup idealization.

2. The more conservative persons are in their religious ideology, the more they exhibit such personality characteristics as authoritarian aggression and submission, conventionalism, identification with power figures, projectivity, punitiveness, and stereotypy. The more liberal the religious ideology, the less are such personality characteristics exhibited.

3. The more conservative persons are in their religious ideology, the more they emphasize discipline in child training, the dominant-assertive male, and the rigidly conventional female. Conversely, the more liberal the religious ideology, the greater the emphasis on self-expression, and the less the contrast of sex roles.

Although the correlations between conservative religious ideology and authoritarianism were substantial, the apparent distance from a one-to-one relationship suggested considerable variability among conservatives in this regard. In part, this variability might be explained by previous studies which suggested that tolerance is associated with stability of religious convictions, self-accepted rather than coerced conformity, and depth rather than superficiality of commitment, relatively independent of whether the nature of the religious ideology is conservative or liberal.

In the general light of these findings, the characterization of religious conservatism as either psychologically immature, or mature, appeared tenable. The immature conservative may be described as an exaggeratedly dependent individual, with externalized needs for security and ingroup status. To the degree to which his religious ideology is a part of, or a displacement from, early authoritarian parental attitudes, the tendency toward prejudice, aggression and hostility toward outgroups might be construed legitimately as the consequence either of displacement from, or identification with, the feared Deity as parent symbol. On the other hand, the mature conservative may be described as an individual whose religious attitudes and ideology may or may not be derived from parental sources, but in any case are genuinely autonomous, and who exhibits attitudes of dependence upon and deference to a suprahuman object who is primarily loved rather than feared. Presumably, such an individual would be equalitarian rather than authoritarian in his interpersonal relationships.

Data from the present study suggested that the tendency of religious liberalism to be associated with democratic rather than authoritarian ideology was either a consequence of relative freedom from coercion in the early environment, or a generalized process of reaction from authoritarian parental attitudes and ideology. Again, however, the data far from suggested a one-to-one relationship between religious liberalism and generalized democratic attitudes and beliefs. In the one previous study of known liberal theological students reported in the literature, half of the subjects could not be identified as accepting or rejecting externalized authority, and exhibited tendencies to withdrawal from interest in and contact with other persons, into a world of intellectualization and abstraction.

The substantial relationship of extreme religious conservatism and authoritarianism did suggest that *authoritarian attitudes and practices, as distinguished from rational expressions of authority, may indeed be a serious form of pathology.* Freud may have been quite right, within the limits of his viewpoint and terminology, in describing religious conservatism as a substitute for private neurotic tendencies. Though not identifiable as such by the currently accepted psychological measurements, *all expressions of authoritarianism may be equally or even more destructive to the individual and his interpersonal relationships than most of the presently acknowledged syndromes of pathology.*

Submissiveness:

The data suggested that the more conservative religious persons are in their religious ideology, the more submissive they tend to be in face-to-face situations. Conversely, the more liberal the religious ideology, the greater the tendency to be dominant in interpersonal relationships.

Although the statistically significant correlation between submissiveness and conservative religious ideology was high enough to warrant the above conclusion, it was regarded as being too small to be of any predictive value. One explanation for the relatively low correlation may be that the dependency needs of religious conservatives are satisfied primarily through submissive attitudes to suprahuman and more abstract forms of authority, e.g., God, the church, religious dogma, ritual and symbol, rather than in the everyday face-to-face situations with other persons. Further, religious conservatives, who, as in this study, are also theological students preparing to assume positions of spiritual and moral authority in society, may identify more strongly with religious leaders as power figures than do religious liberals, and conceive of their professional role as a dominant one. Perceiving themselves as mediators between God and man, they may be concomitantly submissive to the former, and more dominant with the latter.

A second explanation may be that professionals in religion, regardless of theological position, tend to be dominant in one situation and submissive in another in face-to-face relationships, depending upon what may be perceived to be the differing demands of (a) Christian ethics, e.g., the "turning the other cheek" principle, or (b) the role of authority and leadership expected of the clergy.

A third explanation may be that belief in and deference toward a suprahuman being does not necessarily decrease self-confidence, but rather, in many instances, tends to increase it. *If so, serious doubt would be cast on the theoretical assumption of Freud and others that submission to a suprahuman personal authority necessarily tends to encourage crippling dependent and submissive interpersonal behavior.* To the extent, however, that submission to suprahuman authority is essentially a displacement from or extension of attitudes toward parents, it might be expected that such attitudes would generalize to other human authority figures.

Psychopathology:

1. A small but statistically significant correlation suggested that religious liberals exhibit greater tendencies to overproductivity and impulsivity than do religious conservatives. A tenable explanation may be that religious liberals tend to be persons who have exchanged the relative security and certainty of conventionalized religion for greater freedom, experimentation, and trial and error searching, in religious matters. Such a situation plausibly would be accompanied by increased anxiety, expressed in hypomanic behavior. Particularly in the early adult years characteristic of the subjects used in this study, religious liberals may be persons whose religious ideology is as yet not fully reasoned and integrated with the personality.

2. The data suggested significantly that religious liberals tend to have more feminine interests than do religious conservatives. The stereotype of the authoritarian individual includes the characteristics of activism and aggressivity commonly associated with the male role, while greater passivity and aesthetic sensitivity, as well as less dichotomous definition of sex roles, have been associated with the more democratic individual. Since liberals in religion, as well as in other matters, appear to be persons opposed to the various forms of authoritarianism, a reasonable explanation of the data is thus afforded. Feminine interests, as measured in this study, cannot be assumed to be associated with homosexual tendencies without confirmatory evidence.

3. The following psychopathological syndromes were found to have no significant relationship with tendencies to conservative or liberal religious ideology: (a) Defensiveness against psychological weakness, deliberate distortion of communication for the purpose of making a more "normal" appearance, or deliberate efforts to make a poor impression. (b) Hypochondriacal, depressive, and hysterical symptomatology. (c) Oversensitivity, suspiciousness,

and delusions of persecution. (d) Obsessive-compulsive behavior, mild depression, excessive worry, lack of confidence, and inability to concentrate.

It should be emphasized that the reported relationship between religious liberalism and overproductivity, impulsivity, and feminine interests, is too small to be of predictive value. Data reported in previous studies of the relationship between psychopathology and position on a continuum of religious ideology were equivocal, and their general inconclusiveness tended to be confirmed by the preponderance of insignificant data obtained in this study.

Cultural conflict, which has been found to be a crucial variable in the incidence of psychopathology among religious persons, appears, among extreme conservatives, in the form of severe moral taboo and consequent guilt, and the greater emotional trauma occasioned by emphasis upon crisis-conversion. It may be that these conservative forms of conflict tend to be counterbalanced by the fact that religious liberals are usually dissenters from the status quo of religious and parental convention, and as such are subject to increased feelings of guilt, insecurity, and anxiety. It appears that the psychologically negative aspects of religious conservatism and liberalism tend to offset each other, and that the same may be true of their corresponding psychological gains.

II

The data thus far discussed were obtained entirely from the use of the twelve scales measuring psychological and religious attitudes and beliefs. An overall examination of these data suggested the possibility that conservatism in theology may tend to be a continuing expression of conformity to parental attitudes and ideology, and liberalism in theology an expression of a measure of freedom from such conformity. Consequently, additional data obtained from the subjective opinion questionnaire were examined for further evidence concerning these relationships. This part of the study was confined to those cases which fell within the upper (extreme religious conservatism) and lower (extreme religious liberalism) quartiles of the total sample. These data yielded the following statistically significant results:

1. Religious liberals more markedly change from their early patterns of religious attitudes and belief than do religious conservatives.

2. Religious conservatives differed significantly from religious liberals in major influences upon their religious attitudes and beliefs. Both conservatives and liberals regarded clergymen as being the most important influence upon their religious ideology. For theological students, this finding reasonably might be attributed primarily to identification processes, related to anticipated self-fulfillment of the role. For conservatives, the parents appeared to have exerted the most influence after that of the clergyman; for liberals, college and graduate school teachers replaced the parents as the second and third most important influences. For both conservatives and liberals, the mother exerted greater influence than the father. In summary, the results suggested that the religious ideology of conservatives tended to be acquired early in life within the family, and was retained. That of liberals appeared to be acquired during later years, and to represent a change from earlier, family-influenced religious ideology, and from a more emotional to a more reasoned view of religion.

3. In matters of *secular* familial attitudes and beliefs, e.g., attitudes toward child rearing and conventional morality, liberals differed from their parents significantly more than did conservatives. Both conservatives and liberals differed more with their fathers than with their mothers. However, liberals tended to differ more with their mothers than did conservatives. The greatest differences were at the extremes of measurement, where conservatives regarded their familial attitudes and beliefs as "almost identical" more than liberals, and liberals regarded theirs as "drastically different" more than conservatives.

4. In matters of *religious* attitude and belief, liberals differed from their parents significantly more than did conservatives. Conservatives differed more with their fathers; liberals differed more with their mothers. The greatest differences were at the extremes of measurement, where conservatives regarded their

religious ideology as "almost identical" more than liberals, and liberals regarded theirs as "drastically different" more than conservatives. Comparison of these religious ideology responses with the responses for secular familial attitude and belief, suggested a very close relationship between familial and religious ideology. It appeared that the religious and family history of conservatives tended to follow the same pattern of similarity to that of the parents, while that of liberals tended to follow the same pattern of difference.

5. Stated in terms of religious conservatism and liberalism, liberals differed from their parents markedly more than did conservatives. Liberals regarded themselves overwhelmingly as more liberal than their parents. Comparatively few regarded themselves as more conservative. Conservatives tended to be as conservative or more conservative than their parents. Conservatives regarded themselves as more in agreement with their mothers than with their fathers; liberals as more in agreement with their fathers than with their mothers.

6. Parents of conservatives approved significantly more than did those of liberals of the subjects' choice of the religious vocation. Mothers of both conservatives and liberals expressed stronger approval than did fathers. More fathers than mothers were regarded as neutral in their attitudes, and more fathers of liberals were regarded as neutral than were those of conservatives. Greater neutrality among fathers may have been due not so much to preference for some other choice of profession, as to lack of interest in and concern for religious matters. This was true most plausibly of the fathers of liberals.

Summarizing the results obtained from the opinion questionnaire data, they suggested that religious liberals tend to change their religious ideology as they become adult, and that the shift among them in major influences upon their religious ideology is from the parents to college and graduate school teachers. Liberals appeared to differ from their parents substantially more than conservatives in matters of religious ideology, and markedly similar results were obtained in matters of secular familial ideology. Conservatives tended to be as conservative or more so than their parents, and relatively few came from liberal homes. The religious ideology of conservatives and liberals was more similar to that of the mother than of the father. However, liberals differed with the mother substantially more than did conservatives, suggesting that religious conservatism is more mother-oriented. It may be inferred from the data that the greater differences between liberals and their parents were due either to their being allowed more freedom to choose their own familial and religious attitudes and beliefs, or to reaction to authoritarian parental attitudes.

III

In summary, the data obtained in this study appeared to support the hypothesis that significant differences do exist in certain areas of personality structure along a conservative-liberal continuum of religious attitude and belief. For the variables examined, these differences appeared to be substantial only in relationships between authoritarian attitudes and ideology and tendencies toward conservatism in religious attitude and belief. Statistically significant but small correlations suggested tendencies for submissiveness to be associated with religious conservatism, and for overproductivity, impulsivity, and feminine interests to be associated with religious liberalism. In the main, psychopathology, as it is currently identified, did not appear to be related significantly to position on a continuum of religious ideology.

The substantial correlations between authoritarian attitudes and ideology, and religious conservatism, may be due in part to the greater susceptibility of both to attitude and opinion forming influences in the broader cultural milieu, when contrasted with submissiveness and psychopathology. Further, the religious conservative may tend to be less exposed to the more sophisticated social attitudes which appear to influence persons toward liberalism, and may retain more readily the prevailing general conservatism of his basic secular environment.

Conservative secular family ideology emerged as the authoritarian factor most closely related to conservative religious ideology. It appeared that the more authoritarian attitudes of religious conservatives, and the more democratic attitudes of religious liberals, were primarily the consequence of family attitudes experienced early in life. This conclusion seemed tenable, whether the attitudes lay in the direction of similarity and presumed conformity with the parents, as was the case with religious conservatives, or of difference and presumed reaction, or freedom to differ, as was the case with religious liberals.

The overall conclusion suggested by the results was that position on a continuum of religious attitude and belief was not, in the main, significantly associated with pathological signs, unless authoritarianism be admitted as a form of pathology. Rather, it appeared to be primarily a cultural phenomenon, related, as a product either of conformity, permissiveness, or reaction, to the early family environment. The crucial question remains to be answered: why some individuals, conservative or liberal, are able to achieve a mature religious autonomy, while others are not. In seeking the answer, detailed consideration must be given to the underlying structure and dynamics of the individual personality.

Unconscious Motivation in the Choice of the Ministry as Vocation

By Gotthard Booth, M.D.
Psychiatrist and Associate of the Seminar
on Religion and Health, Columbia University.

The intrusion of the deepest unconscious level into the vocational development must be taken as valid expression of the underlying transcendental character of man. It depends on the solidity of the inner structure of the person and on the right understanding of the environment whether the labor of the irrational crisis will end in a spiritual still-birth or will lead to a religious rebirth.

In the course of the current century the concept of unconscious motivation has become increasingly popular and acceptable to the educated layman. In general this is considered mainly from the point of view of individual health and effectiveness, but in the case of the minister the importance of unconscious attitudes is most significant for the people around him. The parishioners are subjected not only to the overt influence of their spiritual leader, but also to the operation of his unconscious bias. The latter may cause serious problems because for all practical purposes, a minister may appear healthy, intelligent, industrious, and what he says may agree with the best values of his professed faith. If, in spite of all these qualifications, a significant number of individuals in the congregation, or the congregation as a whole, are not faring well, the tendency is to rationalize disappointments.

The minister in particular will be inclined to blame the influence of his predecessor, or the characters of the parishioners, or the social setting, or the inadequacy of the parish resources. The cause, however, may be in his own personality. For instance, his unconscious motivation may be the drive for individual leadership, uninfluenced by others because he grew up with a defensive attitude regarding the demands and emotional influences of his family or of his social milieu. Parishioners are liable to feel the underlying spirit of rejection even though they may be at a loss to explain adequately why they feel uncomfortable with the man.

To some extent people may use cues which the minister provides unconsciously by the mechanisms which Freud described in his *Psychopathology of Everyday Life:* slips of the tongue, of the pen, forgetting, accidents, etc. He pointed out that people often do not even notice their own mistakes, or that they dispose of them by means of some rationalization such as pressure of work, fatigue, etc.; but outsiders notice and often they interpret their observations correctly even without benefit of psychoanalytical training. Motivations stemming from the childhood experiences of the minister and causing neurotic complications are real, but represent only the most superficial level of the unconscious mind which may affect the success of the ministry.

The research of Szondi[1] has provided proof that people react to each other also on a deeper level of the unconscious: the inherited psychological constitution. The latter communicates itself by way of physiognomical expression to which people respond intuitively according to their own constitutions. On this

[1] Szondi, L., *Experimental Diagnostics of Drives,* New York, 1952; Szondi, L., *Trieb Analyse,* Bern & Stuttgart, 1952; Szondi, L., *Ich Analyse,* Bern & Stuttgart, 1956; Deri, Susan, *Introduction to the Szondi Test,* New York, 1949.

basis Szondi developed a test series of forty-eight pictures, composed of six sequences of the same eight types of psychiatric case. The latter are all victims of eight different extremes of psychological needs which to some extent are common to every human being: affection, aggression, capacity for control of affectionate or of aggressive impulses, acquisitiveness, enjoyment of relationships, tendency of the ego to set itself apart from the world and tendency of the ego to fuse with the world. According to one's individual psychological constellation one responds with sympathy, antipathy, or indifference to the eight types of representative faces. Such reactions take place irrespective of what the conscious impression of the faces may be. It could be demonstrated that interpersonal relationships in work, marriage, and friendship are governed to a considerable extent by the interaction of specific constitutional dispositions which are unconsciously drawn toward one another.

A still deeper level of the unconscious is involved in the choice of the ministry: the religious archetypes to which Jung[2] has devoted the major part of his research. He demonstrated that humanity may express its religious side in forms which on the surface seem to be completely different and even contradictory. Analysis of the symbolical meaning of these forms, however, reveals a striking similarity of the unconscious process in which man transcends his earth-bound instinctuality and reaches out for spiritual freedom. This deepest level of the unconscious processes in the minister rarely becomes accessible to direct observation except under the conditions of Jungian analysis. In some cases, however, the transcendental realm of the soul breaks through into the conscious ego and produces an overwhelming conversion experience such as Saint Paul's on the road to Damascus. Similar events seem to be characteristic of the lives of many great religious leaders, but not of the average minister. Few people seem to have a strong enough ego which is capable of staying rational under the direct impact of the numinous.

---

[2] *Symbols of Transformation,* C. G. Jung, New York, 1956; *The Psychology of Jung,* New Haven, 1943.

Boisen[3] has given a vivid account of his own psychotic episode which moved him to become the religious leader in the current efforts for the integration of religious and psychiatric knowledge. He collected other historical and clinical examples of spiritual reorganization following a period in which the original values and thought processes of the personality had been shattered. In many cases, however, the individual proves incapable of integrating the experience and ends in chronic psychotic islation. In such cases the individual may identify himself with superpersonal powers and become a caricature of the mystic's experience of God. As Jung pointed out repeatedly, particularly in *Psychology and Religion*,[4] "sacred images expressive of important unconscious factors, together with the ritual, since time immemorial, [have] been a safe way of dealing with the unaccountable forces of the unconscious mind."

A healthy instinct causes most people to avoid the direct experience of the transcendental world, even after as popular a writer as Aldous Huxley[5] encouraged the use of mescalin as an easily available method for visiting the world of the mystics. This author claimed that "to most people mescalin is almost completely innocuous," but he omitted to emphasize the important fact that the only people who use mescalin habitually do so as part of a religious ritual, pagan in the case of the Mexican Indians, christianized by the members of the Native American Church in the United States. Their transcendental experience is tied safely to concrete symbols. Those who took mescalin for experimental purposes and gained important insights from it were often, as Huxley reminds us, "men of first rate ability," well enough grounded in human reality that they were capable of withstanding the impact of supernatural experiences. Some individuals, however, can be seriously damaged by such "artificial psychosis," as this writer discovered when he and a number of his colleagues served as guinea pigs in a mescalin experiment more than thirty years ago. One participant

[3] *The Exploration of the Inner World,* Anton Boisen, Chicago, 1936.
[4] C. G. Jung, *Psychology and Religion,* New Haven, 1943.
[5] Aldous Huxley, *The Doors of Perception,* New York, 1954.

became a chronic schizophrenic, another suffered greatly. Most of those who gained very positive insights still did not feel any temptation to repeat the experiment.

Spontaneous, as well as artificially induced, psychotic episodes with religious content are often experienced as equivalent to a direct call from God. From the psychiatric point of view many times such visions or auditory hallucinations must be considered as a serious trial of vocation rather than as proof of it. "Many are called, but few are chosen." On the other hand, the intrusion of the deepest unconscious level into the vocational development must be taken as valid expression of the underlying transcendental character of man. It depends on the solidity of the inner structure of the person and on the right understanding of the environment whether the labor of the irrational crisis will end in a spiritual still-birth or will lead to a religious rebirth. Although this type of motivation for the ministry is rare, it calls for consideration on account of the danger that this type of candidate be considered in a one-sided manner, either too positively on account of the religious content, or too negatively on account of the psychiatric form of his experience.

A similar dilemma presents itself to the psychiatric examiner when he studies the motivations which stem from the personal circumstances under which the candidate grew up. Often one finds certain typical childhood situations which suggest that the candidate seeks the ministry as a compensation for various childhood frustrations—for instance, isolation because he has been an only child or the only boy in a series of girls, or because he has been physically handicapped. In many cases the boy grew up under the influence of a mother who dominated the father intellectually or socially; in other cases the boy came from a poor socio-economic background but fitted into a more cultured social group through his intellectual ability or his aesthetic sensitivity. Others had a loveless or broken home and the church alone gave them the feeling of being "in one's father's house." Religious vocation may then appear as superficial rationalization for such egotistical needs as socio-economic or emotional security, escape from aggressive competition, or from normal sexuality. Sometimes the candidate may seek not so much the service of God and man, but rather, motivated by fantasies of wielding magic powers, the position of a primitive medicine man, although his theology may be orthodox.

Having been the examiner,[6] and in many cases the therapist of well over 500 ministers and candidates for the ministry over the last twenty years, this writer has come to the conclusion that these "all too human," selfish motivations should not be overestimated. In some cases unworthy motivation causes guilt feelings which unconsciously force the candidate to eliminate himself from the ministry, e. g., some with excellent college grades fail academically in seminary, some misbehave compulsively in sexual matters or in the form of excessive drinking. Often, however, non-religious determinants prove to be incidental to a man's valid feeling that he has a vocation for the ministry. The infantile motivations should certainly be considered carefully, but only as part of the total personality, because in other people they lead to different vocational choices such as medicine, the armed services, the stage, faith healing, or the like. What Freud observed about the relationship between infantile trauma and neurosis holds equally true for the relationship between childhood milieu and vocation: the decisive element for a constructive or destructive development is the quality of the inherited constitution. The latter is determined by the relative strength and direction of the psychological needs, which can be tested by the Szondi method mentioned in the beginning of this article.

The average minister presents in the Szondi test the following profile: his affectionate needs are balanced between personal and sublimated objectives. In the task of maintaining this often difficult balance he is aided by the tendency to devote his aggressive tendencies to impersonal goals and to subordinate it to the control of conscience and to inhibit the display of personal emotions. He is inclined to hold on to the personal relationships he has formed and to enjoy them. His ego is characterized by the re-

[6] Booth, Gotthard, "The Psychological Examination of Candidates for the Ministry," *Academy of Religion and Mental Health* (New York, 1958).

pression of tendencies to isolate himself and a conscious or unconscious need to become part of a transcendent relationship with the world. This description should not be understood as a rigid formula to separate the sheep from the goats. Particularly in the individual case, one has rarely the opportunity to establish a basic profile because one has rarely an opportunity to administer on successive days the full series of 6-10 tests which would reveal the stable and unstable features in the given personality. Furthermore, outstanding achievements may come from individuals who deviate from the social norm. The prophetic type of minister is likely to differ from those who work within the framework of a tradition.

The preceding remarks indicate that this writer does not consider psychological testing of the unconscious motivations of ministers a method which by itself alone provides clear-cut answers to the question of vocation. This estimate agrees with the conclusions of H. Richard Niebuhr, D. D. Williams, and J. M. Gustafson (*The Advancement of Theological Education,* New York, 1957), who report on their study of testing procedures in twenty-eight representative seminaries, namely, that their use of the tests is of an experimental nature and relevant to the counseling rather than to the admission of students. This experiment, however, is strongly recommended under the condition that the selection and use of the tests is adapted to the particular purpose. Having seen a considerable number of psychiatric and psychological reports which failed to serve their purpose, this examiner wishes to make the following points:

1. The psychological examination should not be used primarily as a means of *screening out psychiatric cases.* Very rarely does one find pathology which is so serious that it would definitely exclude a man from the attention of the clergy and layman who saw him before he came up for psychological examination. This does not mean that the psychiatrist may not find disturbances in the private lives of candidates who made an impression of being "socially well adjusted." The problem of the psychiatric examiner is to evaluate the significance of such findings for the future health and ministry of the given person,

particularly if he deals with a young man who is still inexperienced and untried in many spheres of existence.

2. Psychological tests should not be of the questionnaire type, such as the Strong Vocational Interest test, the Allport-Vernon Study of Values, the Bernreuter and the Minnesota Multiphasic personality inventories. They do not reach the unconscious motivations, and they therefore invite responses determined by wishful thinking. The only tests which reflect the unconscious layers of the personality, regardless of the verbalizations used, are the so-called *"projective techniques"*:

a) The Szondi test, described above, is based *on the affect elicited* by portraits which do not reveal their psychiatric classification to the conscious mind of the observer.

b) The Rorschach test[7] is based on the interpretation which the testee gives to *non-representational inkblots*.

c) The drawing tests of Koch[8] and of Machover[9] are based on the way a person *draws a tree and a person*.

The three testing approaches complement each other because they are focused on three different manifestations of the unconscious: the emotional tension of eight different psychological needs, the way ten different life situations are experienced in the Rorschach cards, and the way an individual places himself actively into his environment represented by his drawings.

3. The tests should be interpreted against the background of *two self-images* which the candidate gives of himself in writing:

a) His spontaneous autobiography.

b) His self-evaluation with respect to the specific functions which are important for the ministry: thinking, authority, sex, aggression, community, anxiety, religion, ministration, an insight into his strengths and limitations, his special abilities and leadership.

4. The examiner should *discuss with the candidate* those aspects of the self-image which deviate from the conclusions sug-

---

[7] Rorschach, Hermann, *Psychodiagnostics* (New York, 1942).

[8] Koch, Karl, *The Tree Test* (New York, 1953).

[9] Machover, Karon, *Personality Projection in the Drawing of the Human Figure* (Springfield, 1949).

gested by the tests. Important motivations of which the candidate seems to be unconscious can be suggested to the candidate in a constructive, non-traumatic way by facing him with his own pertinent imagery as it is apparent in the Rorschach and in the drawings. The reaction to such *self-confrontation* clarifies the interpretations of the examiner, particularly regarding the possibilities of spontaneous growth, or of psychotherapeutic help. This procedure appears to be far superior to abstract formulations of a problem in judgmental psychological terms such as hostility, dependency, exhibitionism, and latent homosexuality. Such terms are easily resented and repressed, but the self-produced imagery is apt to be remembered, even if the candidate tries to rationalize it away during the interview.

5. *Psychological reports* to the ecclesiastical authorities should be specific and concrete in the same way in which the candidate is given a picture of his particular personality, in terms of a future in the ministry. Obviously the examiner must use judgment whether he will tell the authorities more or less than what he told the candidate. Since psychological evaluations are always difficult and their usefulness dependent on the personalities involved, it is desirable that the examiner know the recipient of his report, particularly his capacity for pastoral use of the information given. More important, however, is the capacity of the psychological examiner to communicate the salient facts about the past life of the candidate without use of technical jargon so that the churchman can evaluate them in terms of his own frame of reference.

As Carroll Wise points out in his article "The Call to the Ministry" (*Pastoral Psychology,* Vol. 9, No. 89, December, 1958), "the call to the ministry is not a matter of fact; it is a theological interpretation of a complex constellation of processes and experiences in the life of a person." This writer has participated for the past two years in a group discussion of ministers, psychologists, and psychiatrists in which each participant tried to give an account of the complex processes which led him or her to their respective vocational decisions. Often there seemed to be a chain of coincidences at work which could not be accounted for in terms of rational, causal developments. The psychologist recognizes in such events the power of deep unconscious motivations which brought people into certain decisive situations. Such so-called parapsychological phenomena appear as the manifestations of the deepest layers of the unconscious: the archetypes described by Jung[10] and in Szondi's analysis of fate.[11] Fateful, however, as these events appear, neither one of these two great psychotherapists has given them a fatalistic interpretation. Fate, as Szondi asserts most emphatically in his last works,[12] is only part of the human encounter.

In spontaneous situations and in psychotherapy, the decision is up to the transcendent spirit, the spirit which gives ultimate meaning to defeats as well as to victories in this world. In reporting to ecclesiastical authorities on the unconscious motivations of a theological candidate, the psychiatrist and psychologist can only try to present the individual psychological facts. They may comprise evil ranging from the demonic to the petty, and good ranging from divine inspiration to conventional morality. They may present themselves as psychotic or neurotic distortions of the human search for salvation. Such reports obviously cannot be written without expressing value judgments in the selection and weighing of the observations, but the psychiatrist or psychologist should above all always keep aware of the possibilities of conversion. It is not within the province of the scientist to make the final judgment, whether the candidate has merely been called or whether he has been chosen.

[10] Jung, C. G., *Synchronicity, an Acausal Connecting Principle in: The Interpretation of Nature and the Psyche* (Bollingen Series, vol. 51. New York, 1955).

[11] Szondi, L., *Schicksals Analyse* (Basel, 1948).

[12] Szondi, L., *Ich Analyse* (Bern & Stuttgart, 1956); *Heilwege der Tiefenpsychologie* (Bern & Stuttgart, 1956).

A Discussion of Gotthard Booth's Article and Paper[1]

By Robert C. Leslie
Associate Professor of Pastoral Psychology and Counseling,
and Director of the Pastoral Counseling Service,
Pacific School of Religion,
Berkeley, California

This paper is taken from the proceedings of The Conference on
Motivation for the Ministry *(held in Louisville, Kentucky, at the
Southern Baptist Theological Seminary, June, 1959 under the
auspices of the Lilly Foundation). It takes up and discusses many
of the points of the preceding discussion.*

The importance of unconscious factors in motivation for the
ministry is now quite generally accepted. The impact of psychoanalytic thinking on our day has been so real that in educated
circles, at least, common sense explanations of motivation are
recognized as inadequate until the underlying dynamics have
been considered. Dr. Gotthard Booth's article "Unconscious
Motivation in the Choice of the Ministry as Vocation" under-
scores the emphasis that popular writers have made in recent
days in trying to analyze vocational problems that the minister
faces.[2] An earlier study by Karl Menninger pointing out a

[1] *Pastoral Psychology,* IX (December, 1958), 18-24.
[2] See especially Wesley Shrader, "Why Ministers Are Breaking Down,"

similarity between ministers and doctors in their vocational motivation, stressed four factors, largely unconscious:

1) The wish to relieve the anxieties of childhood by allegiance to a belief in the infallibility either of a God or of a philosophy or of a technique (science).
2) The search for a solution of the problem of conflict with authority.
3) The need to assuage the unconscious guilt arising from long repressed hostility toward various members of the childhood family by the psychological process of undoing.
4) A glorified curiosity about the human body, particularly the mother's body, and the great mystery of creation.[3]

Menninger's list reinforces Dr. Booth's thinking about the influence of the early experiences of home and family.

The well-known, careful study of James M. Gustafson of the variety of types of students found in theological schools across the country further supports Dr. Booth's emphasis. Gustafson categorizes theological students into 10 groups which, for purpose of easy reference, I have labeled as follows:

1) Coerced
2) Disturbed
3) Manipulating
4) Resistant
5) Sheltered
6) Zealous
7) Skeptical
8) Humanitarian
9) Searching
10) Maturing[4]

Life, XLI (August 20, 1956), 95-104; William H. Hudnut, "Are Ministers Cracking Up?" *Christian Century,* LXXIII (November 7, 1956), 1288-89; James B. Moore, "Why Young Ministers Are Leaving the Church," *Harper's,* CCXV (July, 1957), 65-69; and *Pastoral Psychology,* IX (May, 1958), entire issue.

[3] *Love Against Hate* (Harcourt, Brace, 1942), p. 208.

[4] See Appendix 1. For another, more positive categorizing see Frederick R. Kling, *The Motivations of Ministerial Candidates.* (Educational Testing Service, Princeton, New Jersey, February, 1959), especially pp. 22-25.

In the first five categories the distinguishing characteristics are largely unconscious. In a brief study which I have made of two entering seminary classes, 50% of the students fell in these first five groupings.[5] Gustafson's study goes on, however, to indicate that the great majority of those who have been accepted in seminary can be helped to become effective ministers. Thus, even though the motivation that leads a man into seminary may leave much to be desired, the emphasis is to be placed not so much on what a man brings to theological school (overt pathology of course being excluded) as on what he takes out with him. As Dr. Booth makes clear, the use of the projective-type test is not primarily for screening out unsuitable candidates but is rather for helping men to be alerted to some of their less conscious needs that are seeking expression.

It would be useful if we had information about men who have been turned away from the ministry on the basis of psychological examination based on projective tests. Presumably any candidate appearing before the psychological examiner has been recommended for the ministry by some responsible persons or committees. One brief study by the Episcopal Diocese of Massachusetts reports that out of 65 applicants processed in the three years prior to June 1, 1952, 16 or 25% were rejected.[6] It is not made clear to what degree these rejections were due to factors uncovered by the psychological testing which included a Rorschach, but presumably this was a major factor.

In this same report of the Episcopal Diocese of Massachusetts a recommendation is made regarding the Szondi Test which Dr. Booth uses:

---

[5] See Appendix 2 for the complete tabulation. See also Robert C. Leslie, "The Background and Intention of the Theological Student," Paper presented at the Association of Seminary Professors in the Practical Fields, (Boston, June, 1958).

[6] Gordon W. Allport and Rollin J. Fairbanks, *An Evaluation of Present Methods for Selecting Postulants in the Episcopal Diocese of Massachusetts*, (The Diocese of Massachusetts, 1 Joy Street, Boston 8, Massachusetts, September, 1953), 3.

We recommend that the psychologist discontinue the use of the Szondi Test (because of its poor reliability and validity as shown in recent research). While he may wish to continue using it for his own research purpose, it should not be made to sustain diagnostic judgments.[7]

The preference of this particular research committee is for the Rorschach which as they say, "is probably the most universally used test, and is also the heart of the diagnostic battery employed in Massachusetts."[8] It is obvious that any test becomes more useful to any individual tester the longer he uses it, and Dr. Booth's intimate acquaintance with the Szondi makes it particularly useful for him, especially as it is supplemented by the Rorschach and other projective devices and complemented by the self image as consciously perceived.

My own experience in the seminary leads me to feel that a psychologist who has worked intimately with the questionnaire-type tests and who has developed a special feel for norms for theological students can find far more about the student through tests such as the MMPI or the California Psychological Test (a modification of the MMPI) than Dr. Booth is prepared to grant. I have worked intimately with two different psychologists, both well experienced in testing and well oriented to the ministry, who have written evaluations of students on the basis of findings from the Strong Vocational Interest Test, the MMPI or the California Psychological Test, some tests of academic aptitude, and a detailed Life Experience Summary (including a self-image index), and I am constantly gratified at how close these reports come to catching the man as he really is, as we come to know him in the intimacy of a small school over the three-year period. It seems to me that the more intensive series of projective tests is not needed for the average theological student provided adequate persons are available to interpret the group type tests mentioned above. However, the desirability of a battery of projective tests for questionable cases might well be considered.

I note with interest that Dr. Booth emphasizes the importance

[7] *Ibid.*, p. 23.
[8] *Ibid.*, p. 23.

of interpreting projective test results in the light of the applicant's self-perception. Gordon Allport has made a strong case
against the use of projective tests by themselves, pointing out
that conscious goals and purposes may be more significant than
the unconscious needs also present. This point is of special
significance in dealing with the place of religion in a person's
life. Allport makes his point in his usual cogent manner:

> In a person in whom the religious factor serves an obviously ego-
> centric purpose—talismanic, bigoted, self-justificatory—we can infer
> that it is a neurotic, or at least immature, formation in the per-
> sonality. Its infantile and escapist character is not recognized by the
> subject. On the other hand, in a person who has gradually evolved
> in a guiding philosophy of life where the religious sentiment exerts
> a generally normative force upon behavior and confers intelligibility
> to life as a whole, we infer not only that this particular ego
> formation is a dominant motive but that it must be accepted at its
> face value. It is a master motive and an ego ideal whose shape and
> substance are essentially what appear in consciousness.[9]

Allport's point is of special significance when we consider the
older man who decides to enter the ministry after successful
achievement in other areas. Conscious decision, arrived at after
genuine soul-searching over an extended period of years, seems
to be characteristic of the older man who chooses the ministry.
It seems quite clear that conscious motivation may play a larger
role in the life of such a person than the more subtle unconscious
factors. A brief and beginning study of the older student in
which I am now engaged seems to bear this out, as I will attempt
to demonstrate.

In two entering classes of students in a small (150 students),
interdenominational seminary, 14 men and 4 women out of a
total of 75 had been employed in some full-time vocation other
than the ministry. In every instance, as far as we could determine
from reference papers, the work had been successful and had
been terminated on the initiative of the student. The ages ranged
between 25 and 43. Specific data on the 18 students is given in
the following chart.

9 Gordon W. Allport, "The Trend in Motivational Theory," in Clark E.
Moustakas (editor), *The Self: Explorations in Personal Growth* (Harper,
1956), p. 37.

EIGHTEEN OLDER STUDENTS WHO CHANGED VOCATION

Former Occupation	Sex	Age	Number of Children
Teacher (elementary)	F	25	0 (single)
Boys' Club Worker	M	27	0 (single)
Dry cleaning business; owner	M	28	2
Accountant	M	29	1
Chemistry lab technician	M	29	3
Teacher (secondary)	M	32	0 (single)
Insurance claims adjuster	M	32	3
Research writer	F	33	1 (divorced)
Accountant and officer manager	M	33	3
Farmer, owner and operator	M	33	4
Food brokerage concern, manager	M	34	3
Teacher (adult education)	M	35	2
Research supervisor, aircraft industry	M	36	4
Publishing company, manager	M	36	2
Teacher (elementary)	F	36	0 (single)
Teacher (elementary)	F	40	0 (single)
Bookkeeper	M	42	0
Machinist, aircraft industry	M	43	1

In categorizing this group on Gutafson's 10-point scale, my evaluation of the individuals, arrived at on the basis of a) our introductory testing battery with the psychologist's evaluation, b) admission papers, c) an autobiography written as a part of class work, and d) personal conferences and contacts, is as follows:

Number	Category	Men	Women	Total
(1)	Coerced			0
(2)	Disturbed			0
(3)	Manipulating			0
(4)	Resistant			0
(5)	Sheltered			0
(6)	Zealous	4		4
(7)	Skeptical	1		1
(8)	Humanitarian	6	2	8
(9)	Searching	2	1	3
(10)	Maturing	1	1	2
				18

It is to be noted that the older students fall largely in the last five categories, the ones that stress largely conscious motivation. The common theme running through their life experience was the gradual dissatisfaction with the way in which they were spending their time, the gradual increase in lay leadership in the church, the growing conviction that their abilities and interests could be put to work best in full-time religious leadership. In several instances a real struggle was involved as serious financial sacrifice was faced along with disruption of established family life. One man who sold out a successful business to enter seminary writes:

> [With a second child and a successful business] we seemed to have everything anyone could want. However, we were restless, until we began taking our children to the _____ Church school . . . The Church and its ministry seem to be the only realistic fulfillment of my life's work.

Another student who now works a 40-hour week while going to seminary writes of how he found himself spending more time in a lay capacity, and wanting to give more than "off hours" to the Church.

> Through the ministry and fellowship of the Church I have found fulfillment as a person, and our family life has been strengthened immeasurably . . . I have concluded that a person's life with God is of most vital importance—that a mature, personal relationship with God is his most crucial need.

This note of personal fulfillment occurs again and again in the testimony of these older men. One of those categorized as zealous (No. 6) describes his pilgrimage from a secular occupation of money, position, and importance to the ministry. His description of his relationship to God carries with it something of the numinous that Dr. Booth speaks of.

> I found myself again rebelling; this time against conformity to a structured pattern of living which seemed to me to lack any real purpose or meaning. I began to question the meaning of existence and to feel more and more that I was just going through motions leading to goals with which I could not truly identify. It was during this period that I began associating closely with the church

for the first time in many years and in 1950 I first broached the subject of going into the ministry. My wife scoffed at the idea . . . At my lowest ebb I turned to God for help admitting that my own strength was not enough and asking to be shown the way— His way not mine. Since then I have constantly prayed that His will for me be done and the way my life and outlook has changed I would not have believed possible if I had not experienced it myself.

I have experienced the redemptive power of God's love and the joy and satisfaction of turning my life over to Him and I am now seeking training for the ministry so that I may be in a position to help others find the joy and fulfillment of truly turning to God . . . Many, many people are using their abilities to promote further material abundance and prosperity in the belief that they are thereby helping to solve the basic problems of the world. I wish to devote whatever talents I may have to preaching what I believe to be the only answer and hope for humanity, the love of God and the message of His Son Jesus Christ our Lord.

The largely conscious nature of the decision for the ministry is expressed by another student whose plans were many years in maturing.

For 15 years I have wanted to express my interests and aptitudes for spiritual and ethical concern by preparing for a full-time Christian vocation . . . I am strongly convinced that religion can offer a vital and in some respects, a unique contribution toward resolving the dilemma in which modern man is ensnared.

Another student, categorized as humanitarian (No. 8) tells of a similar long-term struggle. He refers to contacts while in secular work with two theological students, then writes:

What effect these fellows had on me I don't know. Whatever it might have been I shoved it down into my subconscious, because religious interest, vocationally speaking, lay dormant for over 15 years.

Something of his inner struggle is indicated as he reviews what happened 15 years later at a point when a new job was opening but when he was being urged to study for the ministry by two friends who were ministers:

I was really up a tree. Should I go backward or forward? Was the ministry really a call from God to serve the Kingdom or was it just a desire to escape?

After a month of lots of thought and some clumsy prayer, my wife and I reached what appeared to be independent decisions that the future should be with God. We were probably the most naive pair of budding ministers ever to make the decision. Even after it was made there were moments of concern over how it could be brought off. However, after we started moving in this direction momentum picked up and since then much has been accomplished. It was a call and it was the right decision but not without some faltering on my part.

It is to be expected that the search for the right vocation does not stop with acceptance into seminary. Of the 18 included in this study, two have left or are leaving seminary to return to the work from which they came (boys' club and secondary teaching —both service vocations). One student speaks for category No. 9, "searching" as she writes in her autobiography:

Perhaps I may best be called a seeker; I have been searching for faith . . . The autobiography left me feeling small and fragmented, and apologetic for even presuming to bring my tangled self to the doorstep of this seminary. Yet there is a whole and upright self whose voice needs to be heard, who is here because of high ideals and not low motives; who believes that God can cup His will about a life and move it in strange and wonderful ways; and whose dearest hope is that God has so commanded hers.

These words sound the final note which seems important to me, that commitment around high ideals plays a role as significant as that played by unconscious motivation, that a determined adventure, especially in older students, cannot be passed over lightly in favor of lesser motives. When we are able to bring to the minister of steadfast commitment a deeper understanding of his personal needs, whether through clinical pastoral training or therapeutic interviews, our task has been made complete.

APPENDIX 1[10]

"What Kinds of Persons Seek Theological Education?"

(1) Coerced
There is the student who is in seminary because his parents, pastor, and home congregation have decided for him that he will make a good minister.

(2) Disturbed
A man may be suffering from deep wounds in himself and seek through theological education to heal his own disturbed mind and spirit.

(3) Manipulating
A student who functions well in interpersonal relations and anticipates the prestige and success that will be forthcoming from a ministerial career will find his way to seminary.

(4) Resistant
A person who has prematurely tasted the fruits of success in a church career as a boy evangelist, dynamic youth leader, or student movement executive must complete what are to him often only *pro forma* requirements for ministerial status.

(5) Sheltered
The man who decided for the ministry at an early age, frequently out of a sense of alienation in the world, and who enjoyed the protection of the preministerial group in college will find his way to seminary.

(6) Zealous
A zealous spirit characterizes the student who has found a gospel and knows its saving power. He wishes to share his good news with the world.

(7) Skeptical
Religion and theology present themselves as objective intellectual problems to a searching mind, and the theological school seems to be the place to pursue a study of these problems.

(8) Humanitarian
An experience of a tragically disorganized society, or of disordered minds, often leads a student to study for the ministry. He sees the Church as an institution out of which flow healing processes for the social and personal evils of our time.

---

[10] James M. Gustafson, "Theological Students: Varieties of Types and Experiences," in H. Richard Niebuhr, Daniel Day Williams and James M. Gustafson, *The Advancement of Theological Education* (Harper, 1957), 146-7. (The headings are editorial additions.)

(9) Searching

Frequently found in the present generation is the man seeking for a faith adequate to bring order into the intellectual and moral confusions that have characterized his previous personal and academic experience.

(10) Maturing

Finally, there is the rare student of mature faith who lives in the knowledge that it is God who saves and justifies. He is seeking to become an adequate servant of his Lord.

APPENDIX 2

Students Classified According to Gustafson's Categories

Number	Category	Students in two entering classes	Older students who changed vocation
(1)	Coerced	7	0
(2)	Disturbed	7	0
(3)	Manipulating	3	0
(4)	Resistant	3	0
(5)	Sheltered	18	0
(6)	Zealous	4	4
(7)	Skeptical	4	1
(8)	Humanitarian	11	8
(9)	Searching	13	3
(10)	Maturing	5	2
		75	18

Motivation and Mental Health

BY SAMUEL SOUTHARD
Associate Professor of Psychology of Religion,
Southern Baptist Theological Seminary,
Louisville, Kentucky

*In June, 1959, a three-day conference on "Motivation for the
Ministry" was held at Southern Baptist Theological Seminary.
Samuel Southard, chairman of the conference, has summarized
in this article some of the data of this conference as it bears upon
the mental health of the minister.*

"Why do men enter the ministry?" This was the question before
theologians, psychiatrists, psychologists and sociologists at the
Conference on Motivation for the Ministry. Many themes were
woven into the discussion. One of the most significant was the
relationship of motivation to mental health.

1. The Dawning Awareness of God's Intention

Motivation and mental health are growing concepts. Ministers
must be judged in the light of a continuing motivational
process.[1] The roots of this process are found in the home, the
church and the culture of a candidate for the ministry.

[1] Transcript of Conference on Motivation for the Ministry (Louisville:
Southern Baptist Seminary, 1959), remarks of Fred Kling, p. 38, Southard,
p. 101.

Ministerial students often spoke of parents as an "indirect influence."[2] As yet there has been no clinical study of parents as a formative force for the ministry. Many questions will need to be answered. For example, a 1954 questionnaire to 1500 students of 20 denominations revealed that almost a third thought their home background was "moderately happy."[3] If a "happy" home develops mental health, what about these students? Does the ministry supply the psychological food that was denied them in childhood? Are they permanently thwarted by early deprivation or can they find fulfillment and new growth in a profession?

The pastor was a "particularly influential" factor toward the ministry for most of the students in a study conducted by Murray Leiffer.[4] How is identification with the pastor to be evaluated in terms of mental health? Hobart Mowrer approached the question in this way: Does the ministry present an ideal which will challenge commitment?[5] This must be answered through the pastor's way of life, for this is the sign of his spiritual vitality.[6] Although there has been little study of this important relationship, several comments are appropriate.

First, a strong pastor helps a young candidate in his struggle toward masculine self-identification. Seminary students are sometimes shaken by the thought that they could not stand the competitive world of "real men." Fitzhugh Dodson found that seminarians tended to feel guilty about this problem and to inhibit aggression.[7] The socialization of aggressive strivings is a major problem of young men. It would be especially acute for those who aspire to a profession which requires a balance of judgment and love, objectivity and compassion.

Second, a mature pastor provides the warmth and intimacy required by growing young men. This element in identification

[2] Conference on Motivation for the Ministry (Louisville: Southern Baptist Seminary, 1959), address of Murray Leiffer, p. 90.

[3] Samuel Southard, unpublished study, Southern Baptist Seminary, Louisville, Kentucky, 1954.

[4] Ibid., p. 89.

[5] Transcript, p. 55.

[6] Ibid., remarks of Carl Michalson, p. 67.

[7] Pastoral Psychology, May 1957, p. 46.

has been investigated by Eric Erickson in *Young Man Luther*.[8] It is the quality described by one seminary student in this statement: "I was not aware of how much the informal chats helped me as I dropped by his home on Saturday night. But it has had more effect than I realized."[9]

Third, a sensitive pastor can lead a young candidate to consider the relation of the Gospel to all areas of his life and thought. If the pastor's sole motivation is the salvation of isolated "souls," his counsel to candidates will be quite restrictive. A mountain preacher, J. C. Pipes, spoke of his own growth in this way:

> I discovered as I studied my Bible that the Gospel of Jesus meant more than saving souls from the standpoint that I conceived of a "soul." (In my background) the "soul" is a little thing inside of you and it's distinct and it's extracted and it goes to heaven and the rest goes to the devil if he wants it. I got a different view from studying the Bible—God was trying to save *people*. He wanted to save the whole man.[10]

The view of Mr. Pipes illustrates another major factor in the candidate's first thoughts of the ministry. This is the influence of culture or society. It varies widely. In the mountains of North Carolina, the motive back of the ministry "is the call of God and a definite experience with the Lord. [Mountain preachers that I know] are 'called to preach the gospel that people are either going to heaven or to hell.' "[11] On the plains of Texas, ministers of the Church of Christ "do not attribute their call to any special personal selection by God."[12]

An understanding of these stereotypes of the ministry is crucial for an evaluation of a candidate's mental health. An emphasis on "the call" would be proof of a ministry in one sub-culture and evidence of psychopathology in another. These cultural presuppositions were demonstrated for me at Camp Butner, North

---

[8] (New York: W. W. Norton, 1959.)

[9] Southard, Samuel, *Counseling for Church Vocations* (Nashville: Broadman Press, 1957), p. 24.

[10] Transcript, p. 11.

[11] *Ibid.*, p. 10.

[12] Conference address of Paul Southern, p. 30.

Carolina. The medical officer of a psychoneurotic ward asked me to interview a mild, docile patient from the mountains of North Carolina. The patient, a private, had been sent in by his captain because he would do anybody's work and never "bitched." A Jewish social worker, fresh from New York City, had interviewed the patient on admission. She had reported that he suffered from visions—"he saw Christ." He should be watched closely, for "he saw blood dripping from a cross." Furthermore, there were auditory hallucinations—"he talks to God and God answers him." The doctor was puzzled by this report, since it was not consonant with the patient's behavior. Since the officer knew I was reported to be religious, he asked me to talk with the man. I was serving as a medical corpsman.

I found the patient to be as mild and friendly as the doctor had reported. He was overjoyed to find that I was a Baptist. Although he was "pentecostal," he thought Baptists were "fine people." We immediately began to talk about his faith. As he "gave testimony," I asked how the Lord spoke to him. "Why, brother," he said, "not as you talk to me. But here, in my heart, I hear him. I tried to tell this to a young lady who came to see me, but she seemed frightened by my words." "Has not the Lord ever spoken to you as I speak?" "No! Lord forbid that I should think thus of a sinner such as I am. Ah, brother, I do love Him, though. He died for me." "And you see him on the Cross?" "Well, not as I see you . . ." A frown crossed him: "That lady who came to see me, she troubles me. She didn't understand. I have my humble testimony, but she kept asking questions." "She wanted to know if you really saw blood." "How could I, brother? Our precious Lord died 2000 years ago. But have I upset her?" "Well, I don't know—yet."

In my report to the staff, I recommended that visiting personnel avail themselves of the opportunity to survey through revival and other services to which the natives would welcome them these local pre-suppositions.

These cultural conflicts are evident in the ministry. Victor Glass found in a study of white and Negro ministers that the latter tend to emphasize charismatic gifts, visions and tongues.[13] These have been given up by many white preachers as evidences of a "call." Is the Negro's mental health to be called into question because he now accepts the criteria which white ministers extolled fifty years ago?

An identification of these stereotypes of the ministry would increase the exactness with which a clergyman's mental health might be assessed.[14]

2. Personal Needs and Denominational Demands

As motivation matures, the candidate and his church grow closer together. His cultural and personal expectations of the ministry must now be measured against the total perspective of his denomination. How does this influence his mental health?

One of the first issues to be considered in this area is the call of God and the call of the church. In his historical study of the Protestant concept of the ministry, Winthrop Hudson reported that in Reformation times the call of the church came first. It was not until the last century, under the impact of Lockian individualism, that the inner call gained priority.[15]

What is the significance of this shift? The answer is not yet certain, but the advantages of the earlier view for mental health are obvious. When candidates are chosen out of the congregation, they move forward with the approval and support of all. Their potential talents have already been detected by discerning leaders. Now they are to "stir up the gift that is in them."

Under Lockian individualism, a candidate may feel isolated from any Christian fellowship. Loneliness and competiveness replace fellowship and the sharing of burdens. In extreme examples, an inadequate candidate may protect himself by crying: "The *Lord* called me." The church, the seminary, the denomination are to defer before his assertion.

---

[13] An analysis of the Sociological and Psychological Factors Related to the Call to Christian Service of the Negro Baptist Minister, unpublished Th.D. Thesis, Southern Baptist Theological Seminary, 1952.
[14] Transcript, remarks of Tom Bennett, p. 81.
[15] *Ibid.*, remarks of Winthrop Hudson, p. 34.

During his seminary training, a candidate often faces a second issue. This is the confluence of "special" and "natural" leading. Fred Kling developed these terms to describe (1) those candidates who believed that God provides a special plan for each man, and (2) those who believe that God, like the author of an unfinished novel, would let man finish the plot with the potentials God had given him.[16] The students who held steadily to special leading would exalt the personal call of God and seek His counsel through prayer. Those who followed natural leading would try to find what talents they had for the ministerial profession and consult pastoral counselors.

The candidates who seemed to be in most psychological difficulty were those who held exclusively to one concept or the other throughout their education. The more adequate candidates appeared to be those who found a harmony in the relationship of the call of God to their personal abilities. The candidates' inner sense of motivation was strengthened by the demonstration of talents approved by the church.

Kling's conclusions were drawn from a careful analysis of the test scores of the Theological School Inventory administered in a representative group of seminaries.

Another approach was taken by Earl Loomis. It was based on his psychiatric training and interviews with theological students. He hypothesized that the ministry represents a special kind of healing commitment. The minister has a deep, inner need to help others. He is a helper who hurts until he can help others. The theme might be, "Woe is me if I preach not the Gospel." A candidate must have this need, he must recognize it, and he must fulfill it.[17]

The implication of this theory is that a man does not find serenity until he has found fulfillment in a mission. What does this say about his mental health? Viktor Frankl would say that this kind of motivation is essential for life.[18] Yet in other psy-

---

[16] Research Bulletin, February, 1959 (Princeton: Educational Testing Service).

[17] Transcript remarks of Earl Loomis, pp. 15-16.

[18] Viktor Frankl, The Doctor and the Soul (New York: A. A. Knopf, 1955).

chiatrists there might be some question. Has not this man committed too much in one direction? Does he have the balance of forces sought by the followers of Carl Jung? At this point a theological problem is manifest: is a man overbalanced by the power of Christ? Does not the call of God lead beyond the emotional placidity of those who are not "stirred up"?[19] As we move into the deeper questions of motivation we meet a fundamental problem in mental health: how may we distinguish between divine and human compulsion?[20]

Let us move from this area of mystery to another aspect of inner needs and community expectations. Tom Bennett proposed that a denomination satisfies the dependent needs of a minister. The clergyman is in a social system, his denomination. Laymen respond to him as the representative of that system.[21] Does the clergyman find satisfaction in the system to which he is committed?

If this question is to be answered satisfactorily, two things must occur. First, denominations must articulate their norms in clear and bold language. Candidates need to know the *type* of authority to which they are being asked to submit. One man may prefer a communion in which authority is mediated through the church, while another seeks to move under the "direct autonomy" of God.[22] As professor in a Church of God seminary, John Smith found that candidates who come from different churches tend to meet their needs in different ways through another denomination. Former Methodists have a tendency to say: "Well, thank the Lord that I am out from under all of this regimentation." Former members of congregational-type churches respond: "Well, I'm glad that we have got a little bit of system here." Institutional involvement elsewhere did not meet their particular needs.[23]

A second answer to the question is to be found in the candidate's willingness to accept the norms of his denomination.

---

[19] Transcript remarks of Samuel Southard, p. 74.
[20] *Ibid.*, remarks of Tom Bigham, p. 78.
[21] Transcript address of Tom Bennett, pp. 73-79.
[22] Transcript remarks of Graydon McClellan, p. 28.
[23] *Ibid.*, remarks of John Smith, p. 22.

His personal motivation must stand up under the judgment of forces beyond himself.[24] God in his inner life and the church in his public life must approve his profession.

The candidate's security is tested when there is a time lag between his commitment and the community's approval. Murray Leiffer pointed out the necessity for consonance between the transcendent authority of God, the mediated authority of the church, and the inner authority of self-confirmation.[25]

The ministry, therefore, is not the result of one "call." It is confirmed by a dialogue between God, his people, and the man who responds.[26] The psychological implication of this is that inner motivation requires interpersonal confirmation. The candidate does not make up his mind in isolation and minister alone. He must meet some expectations of God's people, he must find some support from the church in which he labors. Yet, we may ask, how many ministerial students and graduates look back with affection to their home church and to the denominational officials who supported them? How many prophets are there without honor in their own country?

When inner needs and denominational approval coalesce, the minister has a secure climate in which to grow. When there is imbalance, difficulties arise. Some of the psychiatric problems were described by C. F. Midelfort. In a study of 35 pastors, wives and relatives he found some Lutheran families who had over-emphasized authority at the expense of love and humanity. Families of Calvinistic background were noticeable for their devotion to duty, righteousness and obedience. They were resentful and discouraged. Methodist patients complained of overwork and domination by authorities in the denomination and the congregation.

In none of these men did Dr. Midelfort find the balance of love, mysticism and prophecy which would provide health and sanctification.[27]

---

[24] *Ibid.*, remarks of C. F. Midelfort, p. 27.
[25] *Ibid.*, remarks of Murray Leiffer, p. 25.
[26] Cf. *ibid.*, remarks of Earl Loomis, p. 19.
[27] Transcript of Conference on Motivation for the Ministry, address of

Whatever the cause may be, conflict between pastor and denomination should not be ignored. It may signal new growth in a communion, or it may be symptomatic of a pastor's psychological disconsonance with himself and his chosen group.

Self-surrender to the denomination is not the answer to any such conflict. Ministers who are tyrannized by expectations may soon degenerate into the "other"-directed men excoriated by David Riesman.[28]

Are ministers "other directed"? The frequency of secular success standards among ministers raises questions both about their motivation and their mental attitudes.[29] The strength of the ministry can only be retained when the inner direction of God's call is confirmed by a righteous and loving community, the church.

3. The Confirmation of Identity[30]

Confirmation of the call of God is a responsibility of the church. Here the dialogue between God-man-church centers upon denominational criteria for approval. In mental health terms, what level of emotional maturity is to be required of a candidate for the ministry? How much stress can a certain minister endure in a given pastorate? What will it mean for the bishop to transfer an aging member of his diocese to a field that provides less strain—and offers fewer secular rewards?

One type of confirmation is provided by a seminary. This is professional certification. It comes as a result of intellectual, spiritual and emotional growth during three years of intensive

---

C. F. Midlefort, pp. 7-10. In discussing this address, Carl Michalson asked: "What warrant is there for concluding that the doctrinal emphases specified by this paper as prophetic and mystical have produced the particular emotional reactions described in the cases? . . . Which is easier to explain: how apocalyptic beliefs produce nervous disorders or how people come to identify with apocalyptic groups in the first place?" *Ibid.,* p. 13.

[28] Riesman, David, *Individualism Reconsidered.*

[29] Cf. the data in Samuel Blizzard's study, *Pastoral Psychology,* December, 1958.

[30] A phrase introduced by Earl Loomis from the writing of Eric Erickson.

training. From the professors' viewpoint, motivation and mental health are to be seen as a process. The focus is to be on the candidate's ability to help others after graduation rather than upon the untried attitudes with which he entered the seminary.[31]

Another form of validation is offered by the denomination. There are many ways in which the church speaks to the candidate: Procedure of licensure, the ordination, the appearance before an official board, psychological and psychiatric evaluation. In each of these the church is investing faith and strength in the candidate. Men of maturity and experience are saying: "You want to belong to us? Good! We accept you. As you give yourself to us, so we give ourselves to you."

Such an investiture is an act of faith, for the hidden springs of motivation are never fully revealed. The unconscious motivation of ministers can often be judged only by the fruits of their labors.[32]

Perfection in the judgment of reviewers or in the personality of the candidate is impossible. Official boards must be warned to guard against the fallacy of mechanical standards. Ministers are not machines; they are men. They cannot be taken apart or judged by the perfectionistic standards of industry. The mystery of God's way with men is not readily discernible to even the most sensitive of His servants. Gotthard Booth spoke out of years of experience as an examiner of candidates for the ministry in this way:

> It seems to me that unless we all have courage to face risks we will not get anywhere. (Although we must see what the nature of the risk is) we don't think we can figure out any kind of statistical system about how big the risk is. We must have faith to decide. This is the best I can see, and I am willing to take this wise risk. Candidates and ordaining bodies and various people involved must be willing to face this . . . But everybody is so afraid of taking responsibility for something that cannot be figured out in exact scientific terms.[33]

---

[31] Transcript remarks of Robert Leslie, p. 18.
[32] Transcript remarks of Gotthard Booth, p. 73. See also his article reprinted in this volume.
[33] Transcript remarks of Gotthard Booth, p. 91.

Complete psychological integration cannot be expected of candidates or ministers. All the parts do not fit in any human. What we may reasonably ask for in the minister is a specific sensitivity to human relationships and some depth of spiritual insight.[34]

What is the exact model to which the minister is to be conformed? Is it to be the life of Christ recorded in the Gospels, or the Spirit of Christ, or both? During the Conference Carl Michalson was faced with the argument that humans make distortions in their understanding of doctrines. Michalson replied that there is a difference between psychological distortions of doctrine today and the actual sayings of Christ.[35] Winthrop Hudson presented the authority of God in Christ as our primary standard.[36] But the question was not completely answered. Are we to conclude that a "pure" image of the ministry would be derived from a study of the life of Christ? Or are there inevitable distortions of the basic faith that take place as the image of Christ is implanted into human personality? Can we require of a minister today the sinless perfection of the Master himself?

These questions are acute in psychiatric and psychological evaluations of ministers. The need for such inventories of personality were accepted by many participants in the Conference,[37] but many safeguards were proposed. Gotthard Booth emphasized the importance of personal knowledge of the person who was being evaluated. "There is no statistical way by which you can definitely rule certain people out without really looking at the person too."[38]

Both conscious and unconscious motives were accepted as a part of the minister's total growth and functioning. In a study of Robert Leslie, older students were found to have more clearly defined conscious goals than younger students.[39] Gotthard Booth

---

[34] *Ibid.*, remarks of Gotthard Booth, p. 16.
[35] *Ibid.*, remarks of Carl Michalson, p. 4.
[36] *Ibid.*, p. 23.
[37] Some men used Minnesota Multiphasic Inventory, others relied on Rorschach or Thematic Apperception Tests.
[38] *Ibid.*, p. 71.
[39] Transcript, address of Bob Leslie, p. 113.

stressed the necessity of "clear clergy motivation" during a paper on unconscious motives for the ministry.[40] Hobart Mowrer urged ministers to present a clear ideal of the ministry. Yet he also urged that we give a prominent place in our thought to the equation of the unconscious with the Holy Spirit.[41] The motivation and mental health of the minister must therefore be seen both in the light of defined objectives and the inner illumination of a Spirit that is like the wind.

When the Spirit of God is in man, the breath of mysterious depth and power causes us to stand in awe and humility. Yet we have courage to test the spirits, to see if they be of God. For the Spirit has revealed himself in flesh and blood as Jesus Christ, and has entrusted to the church the mediation and confirmation of God's call to the ministry.

---

[40] Transcript, p. 70.
[41] *Ibid.*, p. 55.

PART THREE

THE MINISTER'S SELF-KNOWLEDGE
AND FUNCTIONAL EFFECTIVENESS

THE minister's self-knowledge is a part of his encounter with God. The Psalmist said: "Search me, O God, and know my heart! Try me and know my thoughts! And see if there be any wicked way in me, and lead me in the way everlasting." (Psalm 139:23-24, RSV). Such searching, knowing, and trying reveal the minister to himself if he is not like the disciples who slept at prayer.

Self-knowledge does not essentially mean "having information about oneself," but being genuinely aware of one's identity, his self-hood, basically of "who he is" under God. This involves the minister's own perception of his mission in life. Inevitably, therefore, as Nelson Foote and Leonard Cottrell have clearly demonstrated, this clarity of identity involves his "interpersonal competence." (Nelson Foote and Leonard Cottrell, *Identity and Interpersonal Competence.* Chicago: The University of Chicago Press, 1955). These authors list six factors in interpersonal competence. Three of these, intelligence, empathy, judgment refer to the more objective self-hood of a person; and, three of them, health, autonomy, and creativity refer to his more subjective existence. Any consideration of the health of the minister involves, then, his objective self-knowledge and his subjective functional effectiveness.

The concern of this part of the volume is to deal with the identity and functional effectiveness of the minister in his "master" role and his working roles as minister.

The Parish Minister's Self-Image of His Master Role

By Samuel W. Blizzard
Professor of Christianity and Society,
Princeton Theological Seminary,
Princeton, New Jersey

The problem of the minister in the local church is to develop an image of himself that is congenial with his theological orientation, that adequately explains his function in the church, and that permits him to be related effectively to all personnel in the social system. (The author wishes to thank Donald R. Young, Leonard S. Cottrell, Jr., and Arthur L. Swift, Jr. for their invaluable help in conceptualizing the larger study of which this is a part.)

The parish minister is the professional leader of the local church, a social system oriented to a theological perspective. He is an actor (a word used in the sociological rather than the theatrical sense). The minister is a central actor in the social system because he not only symbolizes and articulates the ideology of the church but he also performs other essential interpersonal and intergroup functions. There are other actors in the system who perform a variety of roles and who may differ in the degree to which they accept its ideology. There are formal and

111

informal leaders, including staff personnel (assistant minister, organist or choir director, secretary, janitor, and perhaps others), church officers, and members whose opinions help shape policy. They are all actors in the system, whether professional or non-professional leaders, formal or informal leaders, members or non-members.

Each of the several actors in the local church performs a role that is essential to the creation and maintenance of the social system. The definition of their roles varies according to the expectations of persons functioning both within and outside the system. Theological outlook, denominational heritage, the history of the local church and its practice of religion, community traditions, and American culture are a few of the relevant factors that help create, maintain, and affect the role expectations within the system.

Actors in the local church, including the minister, are also participants in other social systems in the community. This broader participation in community activities and organizations affects the way in which their role in the church is performed. Furthermore, actors in other systems, who may have no immediate relationship to a specific local church, contribute indirectly to the concensus about the role definitions of actors in that church. This would include clergymen and members of other churches, community leaders and residents, and all persons, agencies and media that shape or convey public opinion. Success criteria in secular professions are applied to the clergy. Member and leader role definitions in voluntary community organizations are carried over into the church.

1. Sources of an Image of the Minister

The definition of the minister's role is crucial to the effective functioning of the church social system. There are many sources of the image that a local church has of the minister. Each actor in the system, regardless of the degree of personal involvement and commitment, has an image of the ministry. It is derived from the concept of the minister in the culture which is reinforced by the portrayal of the minister in history and literature, on the stage and screen, and on radio and television. Bishop Sheen, Billy Graham, Oral Roberts, Norman Vincent Peale, and other clergy are personalities who help maintain and shape the image of the clergyman through television and other mass media. The image is also reinforced by the generalized concept that the public has of the Catholic priest, the Jewish rabbi, or the varieties of Protestant ministers (Episcopal, Lutheran, Baptist, Presbyterian, Pentecostal, or Church of God).

The minister of a local church will be aware that his predecessors have left their imprint on the image that parishioners have of the clergy. They will show deference for some, sympathy or pity for others, and perhaps hostility or disdain toward one. In a parish served by the writer the members held up as a model a minister who had been their leader three decades before. There was much hostility expressed toward a more recent predecessor, who was respected by parishioners as a clergy role model because he was alleged to have been disrespectful of the sex, alcohol, and economic mores. In a multiple-clergy staff church some members may differ in their acceptance, or rejection, of the ministers individually. The young assistant who has just completed his theological training may find that his more mature clergy associate is a role model from the point of view of some parishioners who expect that he will be emulated. He may also find some members who approve of the assistant's ministerial ways because he does not perform the role in the same manner as his senior associate. Parishioners also derive their image to some extent from clergy serving other churches in the community, especially if it involves status identification. Their firsthand knowledge about clergy of other churches and denominations may be limited to observing them offer an invocation or benediction at a public community affair, but friends and neighbors who are members or adherents in other churches will share their firsthand experiences with, and observations or reflections about, their minister. Hence each clergyman in a community helps shape the image people have of the minister, but his own self-image is also shaped by the local church and community.

The problem of the minister in the local church is to develop an image of himself that is congenial with his theological orientation, that adequately explains his function in the church, and that permits him to be related effectively to all personnel in the social system. The general image that people have of the clergy in our culture and the socialization that they have toward the clergy through previous social interaction is a part of the parish context into which a minister must fit whether he is a novice in the profession or a person of long experience. The minister's self-image is a major factor in the situation.

A person who becomes a minister begins to form his image of the clergyman relatively early in life. His socialization into the profession was initiated when he first heard a person called "Reverend," or recognized a person as a minister. All of his experiences and interactions with the clergy prior to ordination helped him derive an image of the ministry and perhaps of himself professionally as a minister. His call to be a clergyman, his theological education and his ordination are additional stages in his professional socialization. Ordination is his formal initiation into the profession, and the ceremony will in part confirm his image of himself as minister. Post-ordination experiences contribute to the maturation of his self-image as minister. He will be testing out role models that have been an inspiration for him or that his teachers have described. In addition, he will have derived by trial and error new facets for his own role image. The problem of the minister is to bring all of these images, his own and that of others, into sharp and acceptable focus.

The lack of systematic knowledge about the image that ministers have of themselves and the image that laymen have of ministers has been a major handicap for the church and general public. It has hindered ministers in being fully effective, parishioners in knowing the full potential of the minister's professional services, theological educators in preparing ministers realistically for the parish, and denominational executives in using clergy manpower resources wisely. This article is intended as a contribution to our systematic knowledge of clergy self-images.

2. *The Master Role*

There are many facets to the minister's self-image. One is his concept of the ministry as an occupation distinguishable from the occupational role of other persons. This is his master role. Another facet is his self-concept in extra-professional and non-occupational roles. There are other types of clergy roles that may be analyzed from the perspective of the self-image. The integrative role orientation makes it possible for the clergyman as evangelist, educator, father-shepherd, community problem solver, etc., to focus his master role on specific goals, ends, or objectives.[1] The practitioner roles (preacher, teacher, priest, organizer, administrator, pastor) are means, professional skills, that he may use to attain the goals of his ministry.[2] This article is confined to the self-image of the master role, the minister *qua* minister.

The image of the minister consists of ideas, and opinions that describe and explain his position in the social system and the culture. The self-image is the minister's view of his own personality and what he believes about himself as a professional man and as a person with family, community, and societal relations and responsibilities. The minister reveals something of his self-image through his role behavior and by the way he describes himself. There are several dimensions of the minister's self-image of his master role.[3] Four dimensions have been selected for ex-

[1] For a fuller discussion of the integrative role orientation see: Samuel W. Blizzard, "The Protestant Minister's Integrating Roles," *Religious Education*, Vol. LIII, No. 4, July-August, 1958, pp. 374-380.

[2] The practitioner roles are analyzed in "The Minister's Dilemma," *The Christian Century*, April 25, 1956.

[3] The research data used for this analysis of the clergyman's master role were collected while the author was visiting professor of Social Science at Union Theological Seminary, New York, with a grant from the Russell Sage Foundation. The informants whose master role is reported are the 1,111 college and seminary trained clergymen who minister to local churches or parishes in the continental United States and who co-operated in an action research project conducted under the auspices of Union Theological Seminary and the Russell Sage Foundation. Four other seminaries participated in the project: The Protestant Episcopal

amination and analysis in this article: the ideological or theological and the functional definition of the minister in the church social system, and the criteria of ministerial effectiveness and success.[4]

Data for the ideological and functional dimensions were secured by asking each informant: "When you are explaining the work of a minister to people . . . , what is the major picture, image or conception that you seek to give them?" Data for effectiveness and success dimensions were secured by asking each ministerial informant to name "the personality traits or characteristics of ministers that seem to lead to effective parish work," and to describe "the ways that ministers conduct themselves that seem to assure their success . . ."[5] It was expected that in respond-

---

Seminary, Alexandria, Virginia; the Louisville Presbyterian Seminary, Louisville, Kentucky; The School of Religion (Disciples), Butler University, Indianapolis, Indiana; Garrett Biblical Institute (Methodist), Evanston, Illinois. Through the Department of Town and Country Church and the Department of Urban Church, National Council of Churches, twenty-two Protestant denominations cooperated. The social characteristics of the ministerial informants and the research methodology of the project are included in a forthcoming report tentatively entitled—*The Protestant Parish Minister*—A Behavioral Science Interpretation.

[4] The categories used in this analysis of the minister's master role were constructed inductively on the basis of replies received from the parish minister informants. Content analysis techniques were used to group answers having a common theme. The names used to designate dimensions and concepts were selected for identification purposes after, rather than before, the data were collected. Faculty colleagues at Union Theological Seminary gave informal guidance from a theological perspective. The author was assisted in developing the categories by the Rev. George A. Lee and the Rev. Beryl B. Maurer who supervised the coding of the master role orientation of each parish minister informant. The author gratefully acknowledges this assistance, and accepts full responsibility for the interpretation of the research reported in this article.

[5] The success question was asked in this manner because in the pre-test ministers resisted using the word success with reference to themselves. They responded more readily to the indirect and projective question focused on other ministers.

ing to these situational questions that minister informants would provide an image of the master role as they perceived it. It was an assumption of the questions that the minister is influenced in his professional behavior by the beliefs he holds about himself and by the image that the public holds of his master role.

3. The Theological and Functional Dimensions

For the ministry the ideological dimension of the master role is primary. The minister articulates the total ideology of the church. To the lay public he personifies religion. The theological beliefs that he has about himself are only a part of the total ideology that he accepts as normative. This lends added importance to those aspects of the ideology that constitute a doctrine of the ministry. The ideology about the ministry would serve to justify the clergyman's identification with the church as a social system and his integration into it as a professional leader.

The clergy whose self-image is analyzed in this research used two concepts to describe the ideological or theological dimension of their master role.[6] Since the question permitted the minister to select his own frame of reference, not all informants introduced the theological dimension in discussing their master role. The minister is a mediator, or worker in the relationship, between God and man. About 33 per cent mentioned this view, which is illustrated by the informant who holds that the minister is "an agent by which the heritage of the Christian faith is brought to these times, and through which the dynamic and eternal truths of the faith are put into contextual relationship to contemporary problems." About 22 per cent mentioned the servant of God view. In it the minister is "one called of God to give his life in Christian ministry," or "primarily a servant of Christ."

---

[6] These categories and those that follow are not mutually exclusive. A minister informant could be classified in each category. For example, a clergyman might include both concepts of the theological dimension in his response. Since multiple answers in each dimension were possible, percentages in each series of categories may add up to more than 100. The proportion of ministers reported in each category is preliminary and is subject to further checking before final percentages are published.

Some ministers see a functional dimension in their self-image of the master role. This dimension reflects the day-to-day functioning of the minister in his master role. It is operational rather than theoretical. One group of informants, about 32 per cent, represented the minister as a servant or used a service-oriented concept. One minister reported: "We are to be busy in our parish, in our community, ministering to the needy, the troubled, the sinful, the sorrowing, just as Jesus did." About 21 per cent hold the inspirational view of the functional dimension of the master role. The minister is "an example for his people"; he tries "to fight for what is right and to help [parishioners] overcome evil." A small number (4 per cent) expressed the pragmatic view which may be illustrated by the minister who reported: "All truth is God's truth and the free way of the congregational approach does not foist on the believer a lot of dogma which he cannot honestly accept." Or, the Church "has a stable worth for the individual and the community for the long pull."

Parish ministers vary in the degree to which they hold the ideological and functional dimensions of their master role. For purposes of statistical analysis the twenty-two denominations in which the informants are ministers were grouped as follows: Baptist-Disciples; Brethren; Lutheran; Methodist; Presbyterian; Protestant Episcopal; United Church of Christ.[7] As might be expected, the ideological dimension differs from denomination to denomination. The Lutheran, Presbyterian, and Protestant Episcopal clergy expressed the ideological dimension of the master role more strongly than the other denominational groups.[8] The functional dimensions were expressed most strongly by Methodist

[7] American Baptist, National Baptist, Church of the Brethren, Christian (Disciples of Christ), Congregational Christian, Evangelical and Reformed, Evangelical United Brethren, Church of God, American Lutheran, Augustana Lutheran, Evangelical Lutheran, Lutheran-Missouri Synod, United Evangelical Lutheran, United Lutheran, Methodist, Moravian, Cumberland Presbyterian, Presbyterian, U.S.A., Presbyterian U.S., United Presbyterian, Reformed Church in America, Protestant Episcopal.

[8] Differences cited in this article are those found statistically significant by the chi square test.

parish ministers and least strongly by the Protestant Episcopal clergy.

When factors other than denominational affiliation are considered, few differences are observed. The ideological dimension of the master role held by ministers serving churches in different regions of the United States does not differ significantly. The functional dimension does differ. Midwestern ministers are more likely to stress the functional concepts than do ministers in other regions. The ideological dimension does not differ significantly by age of the minister. However, in the functional dimension, men over 45 years of age are more likely to have the service concept of the master role. It would appear that clergy share a common socialization to their master role to a greater degree than present day assumptions and folklore about the ministry would seem to suggest.

4. Criteria of Effectiveness and Success

In American culture, most professions and many occupational groups have evaluative symbols that describe their effectiveness or success in fulfilling their master role. The clergyman shares in this aspect of our culture. He evolves an image of how to be effective and successful in his profession through the dealings he has with parishioners, through his experience as a religious functionary in the church, by the career pattern he is able to follow in the denomination and in response to the supervision and guidance he receives from denominational boards and officials. His image may also be affected by comparisons with that of other professions, the memberships he has in secular groups and associations, and the social status he is accorded in the community.

Effectiveness and success, on the one hand, are dimensions of his master role that are both internal and external to the church culture. They reflect the values of the church and they appear to reflect generalized values in American culture. On the other hand, the ideological and functional dimensions focus on criteria that are more or less internal to the specific culture of the church. These latter dimensions involve theoretical values and stated norms in the church. The former dimensions involved functional values and working norms. The relationship of effectiveness and success to the ideological and functional dimensions is important for the parish minister. The minister's concept of effectiveness and success should be conditioned by the theological and functional dimension of his master role. If this is the relationship, then stated norms become supportive of working norms at the parish and community level. If this is not the relationship, then a basic ambiguity exists in the minister's self-image of his master role.

The responses to the effectiveness and success questions have three foci: personality and character structure of the minister, practitioner skills, and denominational relationships. In the analysis that follows, all categories in each dimension are ranked from most frequently mentioned to least mentioned. The highest ranking characteristic of effectiveness was mentioned by 62 per cent, the lowest ranking by 6 per cent. The highest ranking characteristic of success was cited by 43 per cent, the lowest by 3 per cent.

Considering personality and character structure, character is ranked first under effectiveness but it is ranked fifth under success. "Integrity," "sincerity," "trustworthiness," and "sense of responsibility" are words used to express this category. An outgoing personality was ranked second for effectiveness and it was ranked third by clergy in their success criteria. Spiritual life was ranked fourth when effectiveness is considered and sixth when success is considered. Intelligence was ranked eighth for both effectiveness and success. Self-understanding or mental health was not mentioned for success but it was ranked fifth for effectiveness. A service orientation was ranked fourth for success, but it was not cited for effectiveness.

When the practitioner roles are considered, general ability in performing the practitioner roles is ranked first for success, but it is given seventh rank for effectiveness. The traditional roles (preacher, priest-liturgist, teacher) are cited under effectiveness only and are ranked ninth. Under effectiveness, pastor is ranked third and administrator tenth. A comparable category under success is ranked tenth. Organizer is given a ranking of sixth for effectiveness, but it is ranked eleventh for success. A few cited public relation skills with a rank of twelfth under success.

Denominational relations were not mentioned in responses to the effectiveness question. The wording of the question was not exactly comparable with the success question at this point. Three categories were mentioned in responses to the success question. Cooperation with denominational programs was ranked second. Politics in denominational office-seeking was seventh, and getting along with denominational executives and other ministers was ninth.

The differences in the rank of specific categories highlight the conflict of criteria to which the clergyman is subject. Character is given the highest rank for effectiveness, whereas ability in performing the practitioner roles is ranked first for success. Character was mentioned more than four times as frequently in effective criteria as it was for success criteria. Spiritual life was given a middle rank in both criteria. Intelligence was given a low rank in both the effectiveness and success dimensions. Cooperation in denominational programs was mentioned as often as a success criterion as the clergymen's own self-understanding was as an effectiveness criterion. Administration, a practitioner role to which the parish minister devotes forty per cent of his time, is ranked at the bottom for both criteria.

The effectiveness and success criteria give insight about how the minister thinks he is evaluated. The contrast between the top ranking criteria of each is illuminating. For effectiveness, the three top ratings are: character, an outgoing personality, and skill as a pastor-counselor. For success, general ability in the practitioner roles, cooperation in denominational programs, and an outgoing personality are rated first, second, and third respectively. The dominant criteria appear to have secular rather than theological overtones.

The success and effectiveness criteria do not differ significantly in relation to the minister's theological and functional dimensions of the master role. Ministers holding different concepts of the theological dimension of their master role do not differ from one another with respect to their concept of effectiveness and success. The ministers holding the mediator concept in the theological dimension would not differ in their concept of effectiveness or success from the ministers holding the servant of God concept. The same lack of relationship was found between these two criteria and the functional dimension. Ministers may differ in their concepts of effectiveness and success. Factors other than those considered in this article may explain these differences, but it is quite apparent that the stated norms of the church do not affect their image of effectiveness and success in their master role.

5. Incipient Role Conflict

Present knowledge about the social psychology of the clergy is inadequate to permit definitive statements to be made on the relationship between a minister's belief about himself in theological or functional terms and his effectiveness and success in the profession. The research reported in part in this article is suggestive and exploratory, but inconclusive on this point. It does indicate a need for a serious study in depth of the doctrine of the ministry as it is related to his personality and character structure and his skill as a practitioner of religion. Incipient role conflict may result if the normative dimension of the master role is not dominant in relation to the effective and success criteria. The lack of relationship between the minister's ideological perspective about himself and his working norms points to implications that require careful study and evaluation. The recruitment of the clergy, the concept of his vocation, the minister's mental health, the professional training of the clergy, and the relationship between the clergy and parishioners are some of the areas where further research may indicate a need for restructuring the concept of the minister's work in our society.

Preaching and Personality

By Earl H. Furgeson
Professor of Preaching and Pastoral Theology,
Wesley Theological Seminary,
Washington, D. C.

The personality of the preacher, in its hidden as well as its open aspects, is a decisive factor in the form, content, and effectiveness of the sermon.

Frederick W. Robertson, who antedated Freud, observed in one of his sermons that it is more true to say that our opinions depend upon our lives than to say that our lives depend upon our opinions. "It was the life that formed the creed, not the creed that formed the life." This truth, formulated before the psychology of unconscious motivation had become a generally accepted hypothesis, is a reminder to preachers (and the teachers of preachers) that the sermon is always the lengthened shadow of a man. That the personality of the preacher, in its hidden as well as its open aspects, is a decisive factor in the form, content, and effectiveness of the sermon is a truth which is easily overlooked by those who derive their homiletical principles too exclusively from oratorical or rhetorical or biblical considerations. The psychology of preaching, or the study of the sermon as a function of the personality of the preacher, is an area of homiletical research relatively untouched, but it is as important as it is unexplored.[1]

Attempts have been made from time to time to identify and classify the types of preachers. Halford Luccock, a penetrating observer of preachers and preaching, gives us four types, which he labels with his usual wit and wisdom: the jocose, the bellicose, the lachrymose, and the comatose.[2] Eric Waterhouse, in a context less humorous and less psychological, classified preachers as: literary, teaching, dramatic-oratorical, and "suggestion" types. He defended the idea that there is not much difference between one man and another, but what difference there *is* is very important. "The great preachers," he said, "owe their success to what they are rather than to what they say."[3] The Niebuhr report on theological education pays some attention to the personality of the preacher.[4] The report identifies ten kinds of persons who seek theological education and suggests that "there is a great diversity in personality orientation [and] motivation" among these applicants. Seminary professors will undoubtedly testify that the mature students, the guilt-ridden, the "holy Joes," the manipulators, the crusaders, and the "narcissistic self-pollinators" make a different approach to the subject matter of their courses and represent different levels of psychological and emotional maturity.

As to the emotional maturity of the clergy, the identification of unusual types should not be permitted to obscure the fact that the clergy compare favorably in mental health with the members of other professions. While positive proof of this does not exist,

---

[1] The late Dr. Rufus Bowman of Bethany Biblical Seminary was a pioneer in this area. See his "Personality and Preaching," *Pastoral Psychology*, Nov. 1954. He had the unique distinction of being president of a seminary which accepted the principle that "a Seminary should be as therapeutic as its students are sick."

[2] "Simeon Stylites," *Christian Century*, November 29, 1950.

[3] Waterhouse, Eric, *Psychology and Pastoral Work*. (Nashville: Abingdon-Cokesbury Press, 1949), ch. IX.

[4] Niebuhr, H. Richard, *et al. The Advancement of Theological Education.* (New York: Harper, 1957), ch. VII.

informed opinion among psychiatrists supports it, and, if it is any comfort to the reader, let him meditate upon the fact that the oustanding manifestations of mental pathology in public life in our day have presented themselves from the field of politics in the form of dictators abroad and demagogues at home. Despite the fact that there are currently before the listening and viewing public many manifestations of so-called religion which would be identified by any competent alienist as pathological, it is nevertheless true that the established churches and the recognized denominations take a serious view of the matter of providing competent leaders for the ranks of their clergy. The churches are, if anything, more self-conscious about the problem than many others who attempt to serve the public.

The generally accepted opinion that there are among preachers identifiable psychological types, extends to any observer an invitation to record his observations and, if one may claim a certain liberty of prophesying, to make some educated guesses on the relationships between a preacher's sermonizing and his personality orientation.

In the first place, there is a recognizable affinity between some homiletical forms and a psychological pattern of overt or covert hostility. Who has not heard sermons which seemed like "long rows of hooks to hang one's grudges on"? What congregation, at some time or other, has not suffered through some of those negative and denunciatory discourses which magnify the condemnatory and punitive aspects of the subject? In view of the fact that the gospel is supposed to be the *good* news of deliverance, what can account for the preacher's preference for carping criticism? How shall one account for a homiletical talent which turns to throwing stones instead of placing stones one on top of another to build something—except by assuming that the preacher's own unconscious, unassimilated hostility is intruding itself unfortunately into the picture? The hostile minister may be "as minutely venomous as a wasp or as sweepingly violent as a whirlwind," or he may release his fire, like a revolving gun turret, upon whatever subject offers a plausible pretext for ventilating his repository of grievances. It is said that Billy Sunday was once advised to tone down the intensity of his pulpit polemics on the ground that nothing is gained by rubbing the cat the wrong way, to which the incomparable Billy replied, "If the cat doesn't like it, let the cat turn around!"

Forgetting that the heart of the gospel is the loving, forgiving grace of God and that "God sent not his Son into the world to condemn the world," the preacher who has a personal problem of hostility to reckon with will betray his trust and preach a gospel of condemnation, exalting, not the things he loves, but the things he hates. Here, for example, is a preacher who delivers a Thanksgiving sermon based on the healing of the ten lepers. The sermon deals in a condemnatory and sarcastic manner with the nine lepers who did not return to give thanks, and by implication it deals with the present (and absent) members of the congregation who can be identified with the nine ungrateful lepers. A hostile rebuke for the sin of ingratitude exhausts the propositional content of the homily. Now, the biblical account provides, in addition to a reference to the nine ungrateful men, an account of one man who was grateful, who found joy in expressing his gratitude, and who by his faith was made whole. Why does the preacher overlook him? Why is he charmed by the negative aspects of the account? The answer is certainly to be found in the preacher himself, and a psychotherapist might locate the cause of the preacher's choleric tempers in a large quantity of unconscious, unresolved hostility which is displaced upon other people through the medium of the sermon.

The paranoid pattern, in its religious manifestations, has many forms and ramifications. It produces a whole company of restless souls whose divine calling it is to "improve" other people, a company of crusaders, reformers, "prophets." The Pharisaical moralists of the New Testament and Dostoevski's Grand Inquistor come to mind in this connection. To recall that there are neurotic forms of virtuosity is, of course, not to deny that virtue has also its mature and life-giving manifestations. Not all prophets are fiery mavericks although some are, and it is not so much the issue as the man that makes the difference. John Watson, the Scottish preacher affectionately remembered as Ian

Maclaren, told those who listened to his Yale Lectures on Preaching that:

> It seemeth to us, when we are still young, both clever and profitable to make a hearer ashamed of his sin by putting him in the pillory and pelting him with epithets. Such is the incurable perversity of human nature that the man grows worse under the discipline . . . As we grow older and see more of life it seems easier to put a man out of conceit with his sin by showing him the winsome and perfect form of goodness. . . . He that scolds in the pulpit, or rails, only irritates; he that appreciates and persuades wins the day.[5]

For the fulfilment of this sound advice there is one obvious requirement: A preacher whose personality and temperament permit him both to give and to receive appreciation. The price of this is the cost of coming to terms with one's own unconscious hostility.

At the opposite pole from the paranoid pattern of displaced and projected hostility is what might be called "the religion of structuralized helplessness," the homiletical forms of which are usually associated with themes of self-denial, self-surrender, and "selflessness"—an erroneous homiletical term which invites a wealth of psychological speculation. Sermons of this type sometimes praise self-surrender as the fulfilment of love and identify "self-love" as the essence of original sin. Without making any distinction between neurotic self-love and legitimate self-respect, preachers in this school make implacable warfare on the whole self and tend to annihilate the responsible and creative self along with the anxiety-ridden neurotic self. Of themselves, they say they can do nothing. The very thought of assuming personal responsibility for their acts or attitudes impresses them as an act of insubordination against the Holy God; they are "called" or "guided" in all they do. Quoting the mortification passages in Calvin's *Institutes,* they say, "We cannot think of ourselves as we ought to think without utterly despising everything that may be supposed an excellence in us." Or, following Luther's *Commentary on Galatians,* they condemn "that pernicious and

---

[5] Watson, John, *The Cure of Souls* (New York: Dodd, Mead, and Co., 1896), p. 57-58.

pestilent opinion of man's own righteousness," and, bidding man to "shed the filthy rags of his own good deeds," they remind him that man is "a sinner, unclean, miserable, and damnable."

The subversion of the doctrine of salvation by grace into forms of self-alienation in which the individual self is annihilated in order to permit the individual to become possessed by the Transcendent God who assumes responsibility for the self-alienated individual will undoubtedly be viewed by the psychologist as one of the devious theological rationalizations of the guilt-ridden personality. If total self-alienation is the necessary precondition for the operation of divine grace and if this grace is proffered only on the additional condition that the individual remain obedient to the Divine Authority through the punctual performance of his ritual obligations, then it is difficult to see how religion can meet the Freudian criticism that religion is a pathological mass compulsion neurosis.

Clinical examples of the helplessness pattern are not difficult to locate in the homiletical workshop since this is a common pattern. The subject of such sermons is usually "The New Birth," or "New Life in Christ" and the propositional content usually develops the theme that man has no merit in himself and cannot change himself. He must "let go and let God." Following upon his complete surrender the "born-again person" has a new personality, a new ability to keep God's commandments, new power and victory over sin, and a new relationship with his fellow man. Self-surrender is the condition of receiving these supernatural gifts and the surrender of individual responsibility is paradoxically the key to making the individual responsible. This is all the miraculous free gift of God won for us through the atoning sacrifice of God's Son on the cross. "Jesus paid it all; he put the money in the bank and all we have to do is write the check," is the way one preacher put it.

It would be folly to deny that significant changes have been wrought in the lives of those who have died in order to be born again. In one meaning of the phrase, "dying to be born again," lies the principle governing all growth including growth in grace. William James inclined toward the opinion that the Lutheran justification by faith and the Wesleyan salvation by grace represent, "if not the healthier-minded, yet on the whole the profounder religious instinct."[6] Also, he found the pattern of "being nailed on the cross of natural despair and agony, and then in the twinkling of an eye . . . miraculously released"[7] more "interesting" to study psychologically than the pattern of conversion by gradual growth.

On the other hand, the accumulation of case materials over the half-century since James wrote makes it abundantly clear that the "new birth" conceived as he conceived it and propagated as some preachers have propagated it may produce pseudo or regressive "conversions" as readily and as richly as it produces conversions which represent a genuine healing of the divided self. The reason for this is that the self-alienated individual may find in this religious pattern a structure in terms of which he may consolidate his helplessness. A typical case will help to make this clear.

A candidate for religious orders personally known to me spoke enthusiastically of the manner in which his conversion had brought him "out of the gloom and into the gleam." He had been resentful, but "God took away my resentment." He had felt self-conscious and isolated, but God took away the isolation. He had been "selfiish" and the victim of "neurotic tendencies," but God gave him the power to face himself and be rid of his limitations. "God is on the winning side and self is having less of its own way," he said, "and so long as I love God I will be able to love my fellow men." This last remark impressed me as a curious reversal of the New Testament teaching that "If a man love not his fellow men whom he has seen, how can he love God whom he has not seen?" So, I asked, "Could you carry on these improved relations without God if it should be necessary to do so?" He answered, "If God loses I want to lose with Him, and I mean that like I mean nothing else. Whatever His fate is, that's my fate."

The psychological report on this same candidate, a report

---

[6] *Varieties of Religious Experience.* (Everyman Edition), p. 223.
[7] *Ibid.*, pp. 203-204.

prepared by a competent clinical psychologist after a battery of projective tests, included the information that ". . . The boy appears acutely ill and is barely holding on at present . . . He is an extremely immature, infantile person who makes contact with people but poorly, and even then, on a superficial, very dependent level . . . He sees himself as a little boy needing his mother, naked and exposed to the cruel world about him . . . At times he has some desire to be independent but just cannot accomplish it." The psychologist suggested that it was probably his symbiotic religious concepts which prevented him from going to pieces altogether—a fact of some importance in the interpretation of the pathological forms of religious experience.

The hostile and the helpless; the paranoid and the schizoid; the love-deprived made angry, and the love-deprived made hungry are probably not the only clerical personality types which produce distinctive homiletical forms. Of the most promising, and one would hope the most prevalent, clerical type we have said nothing, that is, the mature love-satisfied preacher who follows what might be called a love-made-vital pattern. It does not fall within the scope of this study to include an investigation of this type, although it is probably unfair to exclude by definition the one pattern which offers greatest promise for a mature and relevant interpretation of the gospel. Any expansion of the theme, however, even in this direction, would only serve to support the thesis already suggested, namely, that the sermon is always the lengthened shadow of a man. As Beecher said of the Bible, "A Bible alone is nothing. A Bible is what the man is who stands behind it . . ." As with the Bible, so with the sermon—both are in a prominent degree what the preacher makes them. We have noted some sermons which reflect what Paul Tillich would call "a limited self-affirmation" on the part of the preacher. These sermons grow out of the unconscious needs of the preacher's own personality, and they communicate, in so far as they communicate at all, with the corresponding needs of the listener. The pathological forms which are based on a limited self-affirmation have the unfortunate result of limiting the being of both the preacher and the listener and they strengthen this limitation through the power of religion. Such an unintended consequence magnifies once again a basic but neglected principle in homiletics: "The making of a sermon is the making of a man."

Self-Understanding in Pastoral Counseling

By Dean Johnson
Director, Marriage Counseling Service,
and Associate Professor of Social Welfare,
Florida State University,
Tallahassee, Florida

The counselor himself is the most effective counseling tool he can possibly have, provided he can come to understand and accept his own subjectivity.

For many years there has been common agreement that because of the unique position occupied by the minister he has tremendous opportunities for counseling with his parishioners. It is obvious that these opportunities come about, in part, because the minister is widely known, constantly goes into homes, and is a key person and confidant in many of the crises experienced by his parishioners. Moreover, one need feel no particular reluctance in seeking the counsel of his pastor, whereas one might feel that a certain stigma is attached to seeking the aid of a counselor in such professions as psychiatry and psychology. Furthermore, a minister whose sermons and other public addresses are attuned to the personality needs and frustrations of people may regularly stimulate the desire of his hearers to obtain help for their problems.

Until comparatively recently not a great deal of recognition has been accorded the need for specific training in the field of pastoral counseling. It is true that The Council for Clinical Training, Inc., had its beginnings as early as 1925 and, since its incorporation in 1930, has steadily expanded its work, the heart of which is supervised pastoral counseling. Most of the programs in clinical pastoral training operate in such settings as mental hospitals, general hospitals, and penal and correctional institutions. The Council began its work at a time when few, if any, courses were being offered by theological seminaries to help men prepare for counseling. The Institute of Pastoral Care has also provided training in clinical pastoral work and, at the present time, is offering a number of six to twelve-weeks' summer courses in clinical pastoral education.

A study of the catalogs of twenty-seven theological seminaries recently revealed that all but one of the seminaries offered some help in preparation for counseling. Eleven of the schools offered opportunities for clinical courses or clinical experience. Apparently there is a growing recognition on the part of theological school administrators of the need for counselor training in their curriculum. Such recognition is not confined to the theological school. Dr. Murray H. Leiffer of Garrett Biblical Institute, Evanston, Illinois, found in a recent study that 87% of the laymen involved in the study believed that skill in counseling should be a part of the total training of a minister. It seems probable, then, that many ministers who are now studying for the ministry in theological schools have opportunities for training in counseling which were not readily available prior to the present decade.

Didactic training of counselors in the various professions has emphasized the need for the counselor to understand the counselee and his problems. In addition, techniques of counseling have been studied. Admittedly these are important matters and should be included in the training of every counselor, but such training is not enough. One may know a great deal about the person with whom he is counseling and he may be very well versed in the techniques of counseling; yet fail miserably as a counselor for one reason: he does not understand himself.

In one sense, some kinds of counselor-training come danger-ously close to encouraging a lack of self-understanding on the part of the counselor. The word "objectivity" has been grossly over-worked in the field of counseling, the assumption often being that the counselor not only *should* be objective, but also that he *can* be objective. But this over-emphasis on objectivity overlooks the fact that the counselor is a human being, with human emotions, and with life experiences not entirely dis-similar to those of his counselee. Complete objectivity is, there-fore, impossible. The counselor reacts to emotional stimuli sub-jectively and so cannot maintain complete objectivity even if that state were desirable.

The counselor himself is the most effective counseling tool he can possibly have, provided he can come to understand and accept his own subjectivity. He can never help the client by being so objective that he is detached emotionally from the relation-ship between counselor and counselee. It is only as he can effec-tively use his subjectivity that the counselor can feel, sense, and anticipate the reactions and emotions of the counselee.

The self-understanding of the counselor, then, is of primary importance for effective counseling. For one cannot fully utilize his own subjective reactions unless he has understood and ac-cepted those reactions and, as long as he has only a minimal understanding of his own subjective reactions to emotional stimuli, it is quite probable, if not certain, that he will get in his own way in counseling. It is only as he is able to "get himself off his hands" through the understanding and acceptance of his own motivations and the dynamics of his own reactions that he is freed enough from his own emotional blind spots to really understand the counselee and function adequately as a counselor.

Whether the counselor be a minister, psychiatrist, social worker, or a member of any other of the "helping" professions, if he continues a counseling relationship with another person over a fairly long period of time, he may observe his counselees reacting in a manner not consistent with the reality situation. The psychoanalysts who first observed this phenomenon termed it "transference." These reactions toward the counselor are not appropriate to the actual situation and are as if the counselor were an important person in the client's past. Usually the counselee does not know what the sources of his reactions are, nor does he know why he feels toward the counselor as he does. Such phenomena may not be observed by the counselor who sees the counselee only two or three times, inasmuch as these reactions seem to flourish and grow in the close interpersonal relationship which evolves when counseling sessions are spaced over a long period of time.

It may be helpful here to distinguish between reactions that are based largely on unconscious displacements from early life experiences and those which are based primarily on the reality situation of the present. In the latter case, the attitudes and behavior of the counselee may reveal his conscious appreciation of the counselor as he really is, but transference phenomena may involve the unconscious projection of the counselee's attitudes toward some important figure of his early childhood onto the counselor.

Reactions which are not reality-based have doubtless been observed by any minister who counsels with parishioners. For example, a husband who has become involved in an extra-marital affair may come for help to his minister and he may carry into the relationship with the minister the assumption that his pastor has the same devaluating attitude toward him that he has toward himself. He may, therefore, react toward the minister on the assumption that the minister considers him "unworthy," "bad," and "no good." Or, a parishioner may seek help from his minister but carry into the counseling situation the same kind of "cover up," "fake good" attitudes utilized with a parent in early childhood, thus reacting toward the minister as if the minister were the parent. Yet the reality situation of the present does not require such attitudes nor, indeed, are these attitudes helpful. It is important to note that the counselee does not know that he is reacting out of unconscious motivations.

Now let us go one step further and see that precisely the same kind of reactions we have discussed with regard to the counselee may also be seen in the counselor. He, too, may react on the basis of unconscious needs and motivations. Such phenomena, referred to by psychoanalysts as "countertransference," occur when the counselor transfers on to the counselee emotional attitudes related to some important person in the counselor's past, such as a parent. Lorand's admonition to psychoanalysts applies almost equally well to the minister-counselor:

> The analyst must do double duty: On one hand observe his patient, weigh and understand what he says, and from his productions and behavior draw conclusions about his unconscious; at the same time, he must be aware of and control his own attitudes toward the patient.

It is obvious that if the minister is able to understand his own (formerly) unconscious motivations and emotional needs, he should be better able to understand and accept the non-reality based reactions of his counselee. But if his own "neurotic" traits and unconscious conflicts remain unknown to him he may find himself emotionally involved with a counselee to the extent that in his work with the counselee he actually tends to seek unconscious satisfactions. And if he cannot recognize his own unrealistic feelings, he will not be able to control them. On the contrary, he may react toward the counselee in a way which essentially treats the counselee as if he were a projected part of the counselor. If such an occurrence takes place, the counselor may attempt to reform the counselee because the counselor feels that something within himself is bad and needs to be reformed. Or if basically the counselor feels unloved and insecure, any bit of appreciation expressed by the counselee may on the one hand be magnified all out of proportion to the reality situation, and on the other hand be completely rejected in a manner inappropriate to the reality situation. Sometimes counselors react to their counselees with strong sympathetic feelings due to an over-identification with the counselees.

A counselor may be particularly vulnerable at this point if in early childhood he felt that he was getting a "raw deal" and that people were treating him unfairly. The resultant long-felt self-pity may precipitate the over-identification with the counselee and, in being overly sympathetic with the counselee, the counselor may be really pitying himself. And, interestingly enough, many times excessive sympathy may be almost the exact opposite of the attitude which would be most beneficial to the counselee.

In a similar way, a counselor who does not understand the basis for his own reactions may react toward counselees with resentment, hostility, or demanding, authoritative attitudes. This is probably the basis for Wood's statement:

> The minister must understand his own motivations. He must know whether the counseling is done, first, foremost, and always, with the well-being of the persons counseled as the only major interest.

Some other of the "helping" professions have strongly emphasized the need for the self-understanding of the "helping" person. Such recognition came very early in the development of psychoanalysis with the result that a training analysis has been considered essential for every person entering the profession. Not only is the training analysis supposed to be a practical means of providing the analyst with a knowledge of the psychoanalytic method, but it is also designed to give the analyst an intimate knowledge of the dynamics of his own personality.

The training analysis tends to dissolve the analyst's emotional blind spots and to make available to his conscious reasoning powers the motivations within him which were formerly unconscious and therefore unrecognized. As a consequence, the analyst, having come to terms with himself, is now better able to understand the patient and meet the patient's needs therapeutically because he now has far better control over his own needs.

At the present time there seems to be a trend in social work toward emphasis on the value of personal psychoanalyses for case workers whenever possible. This trend has probably come about as a result of a very gradual progression in the recognition and acknowledgment of transference phenomena as an important factor in case work treatment ever since Jessie Taft began talking and writing about it in 1924. In this vein Hamilton (1951) states:

> Casework in America has been deeply affected by psychiatry, particularly psychoanalytic developments, and so it is predisposed to

adapt psychoanalytic principles for its own professional purposes. Whether such adaptation should be called psychotherapy or case-work therapy or simply casework, the fact is not altered that psycho-dynamics are increasingly used in the treatment of problems of human relationship.

The recognition of the importance of the possible non-reality based reactions of both the caseworker and the client prompted Odmark (1946) to state that if the application of therapeutic techniques is to be successful:

> The caseworker must be genuinely interested in people, clear in her understanding of her own emotional attitudes and subjectivity, and absolutely without self-consciousness or a need for personal power. It is rare to find caseworkers with all these innate qualities, and for this reason, psychoanalysis of the caseworker seems invaluable.

All this merely serves to indicate the trend in social work toward emphasis on the caseworker's need for self-understanding. There are, of course, comparatively few social workers who have had a personal analysis, just as there are comparatively few psychologists and psychiatrists who have chosen psychoanalysis as a means of obtaining greater self-understanding.

In recent years an increasing number of ministers have turned to the psychoanalysts for help in obtaining a more adequate understanding of the dynamics underlying their own reactions. But obtaining one's personal psychoanalysis is usually expensive in terms of time and money. Many ministers do not have such opportunity and many others could not avail themselves of the opportunity because of time and financial limitations.

Although a personal analysis may be the most promising method for obtaining greater self-understanding, it is not the only one. Other opportunities for deepening the minister's self-understanding may, for some, be more readily available.

Perhaps the most important step in the direction of deepening one's self-understanding depends upon the minister's ability and willingness to carefully examine his real motives. Doubtless it would be profitable for professional persons of all disciplines to attempt such an evaluation. Why, for example, does a man enter a certain profession in preference to all others? It is not uncommon for a man to choose such a discipline as psychiatry, psychology, social work, or counseling for his professional vocation on the conscious basis that he wants to help other people. This, indeed, is one of his wishes, but he may also have some unrecognized reasons for his choice of profession. It is not at all uncommon for one to discover in the process of his training that one of the formerly unrecognized reasons for his choice of professions was to obtain help for himself.

A counselor remarked that prior to his supervised counseling training he had firmly believed that his whole purpose in entering the profession was to provide help for other persons because he liked people, but that in the process of counseling under supervision he discovered that his underlying (formerly unrecognized) motive was to obtain the appreciation, respect, and admiration of others. He then began to recognize that the reason for this lay in early childhood experiences in which he felt unloved and rejected. As a result of his deepened self-understanding he became an excellent counselor because he no longer used the counseling situation for his own unrecognized purposes. Moreover, his understanding of other persons who were constantly reacting in a non-reality based manner was greatly enhanced.

Cope reports that, as a minister, he has for a considerable period devoted himself to an attempt to understand better what people are really like inwardly and to gain a more thorough knowledge of unconscious motivations and the real sources of failures in life:

> As my understanding grew, the emphasis in my sermons changed, with the result that people came to church expecting more than to audit a carefully prepared sermon. As the theme 'wholeness' became more articulate, and as it was emphasized that the good life involved more than intellectualizing about means and ends, an increasing number of people, in and out of the church, asked for an opportunity to talk over problems which confused them.

Similarly, a minister who had been studying the dynamics of human behavior and in the process had joined in group therapy sessions over a period of some ten months reported that he was now much more comfortable in his preaching because he had come to understand that he had previously used the pulpit for exhibition purposes and that with greater understanding of himself this was no longer necessary. He had been relieved of self-consciousness to such an extent that he could speak more freely and frankly and more to the real needs of his people.

Another minister reported that prior to his study and therapy he had constantly scolded his congregation. He now recognized that what he had actually been doing was using the congregation as a projected part of himself for he felt that he really needed to be scolded.

Still another minister said that he had emphasized counseling in his pastoral work, thinking that he had done so because of the need of the people and because of his love for people. He now recognized that his deeper and previously unrecognized wish was to obtain power over other persons. With this new understanding of himself he was a more effective counselor and minister because it was no longer necessary for him to exert power over other persons in such ways as remonstrating with his counselees, advising them, and in some cases causing them to feel more guilty than before. In short, he was now able to recognize not only in theory but also in practice the counselee's right to self-determination and to self-resolution of his problems. He no longer needed to "play God" and be the all-wise superhuman "fountain of wisdom" he once tried to be.

Admittedly such attempts at self-evaluation are difficult. It is doubtful that any person by himself can fully evaluate the dynamics of his own reactions, but some achievement in this direction is better than none, and the counseling situation affords him an excellent opportunity for self-study. How does he react when a counselee reports that he has engaged in some activity which the counselor considers immoral or reprehensible? Is it possible for the counselor to accept this material as genuinely as he accepts other material produced by the counselee? How does he react when, after several interviews, a counselee says that he wonders whether counseling is going to be of any assistance to him after all? Does the counselor feel hurt? Does he take this as a personal affront? Does he react with indignation or with hostility? If he has such reactions, he cannot possibly be of assistance to the counselee because the counselee will sense the inadequacy. The important question for the counselor is, "Why do I have such reactions, and how can I overcome them?"

As previously stated, it may be impossible without professional help for the counselor to find the answers to these questions. If he cannot find them, he will do well to engage the help of a well-trained counselor or psychiatrist. As a matter of fact, there is much to be said for the thesis that the minister-counselor should constantly have available a psychiatric consultant with whom he can discuss at least the more severe counseling cases. If he has such a consultant, it is not difficult to establish the kind of relationship with the psychiatrist that will enable him to talk about some of his own reactions as well as those of his counselees. In this way, the minister obtains both supervision and a heightened understanding of himself. Some ministers feel that because of the nature of their profession they cannot seek help for themselves. This is unwarranted pride. As a matter of actual practice many psychiatrists frequently seek the counsel of their colleagues and some notable psychoanalysts contend that every practicing analyst should return to the "couch" for therapy every five years or so.

Another method which may be utilized by the minister-counselor for deepening self-understanding is that of taking advantage of opportunities for further study in the field of counseling. Several training centers now offer such opportunities and a number of ministers take sabbatical leaves or make other arrangements in order to increase their effectiveness. Obviously, one may read widely in the field but there is no substitute for well-supervised in-service training in counseling, for it is in supervision that the counselor is most likely to make progress in self-understanding. This is true because he and the supervisor have opportunity to talk over counselor and client reactions in every interview in which the counselor is involved.

A final suggestion is that the minister-counselor may discipline himself in the matter of making extensive notes on each counseling interview. Such notes should contain an adequate number of responses made by the counselor as well as those made by the counselee. The time required to read through one's records is well spent if the counselor does so with a view to deepening his self-understanding. He may question himself as he reads: "Why did I respond in that way? To what was I reacting? What was really behind it? What was my real purpose in asking that question? Was I being judgmental in doing so? Or, was I simply curious? Why did I feel so deeply emotionally involved with this client who seems so insecure? Is it possible that I, too, feel insecure and so have over-identified with the client in his insecurity? Why did I feel that my own tears were near the surface when this client said that nobody loved her or really cared for her? Can it be that I have some such feelings also?"

Perhaps the important matter is not how one goes about becoming more conscious of his own motivations and of the underlying dynamics related to his reactions. There are various opportunities available, as has already been indicated. The important thing, then, is not how it is done, but that it *be* done by some method, for the rewards are great indeed. To have established a lifelong pattern of reacting unconsciously on the basis of hidden motivations, and then to uncover them and get them out in the open where one can apply his rational, reasoning, mental powers to them is like being born again.

The Protestant Parish Minister's Integrating Roles[1]

By Samuel W. Blizzard
Professor of Christianity and Society,
Princeton Theological Seminary
Princeton, New Jersey

One of the main sources of distress, requiring much self-under-standing on the part of the minister, is the conflict in the various roles he has to perform. He must find some core of integration in his many tasks. Samuel Blizzard, in an article published in Religious Education, *Volume LIII, January-February, 1958, pages 374-380, gives a careful psychosocial analysis of this problem of integration. The research data analyzed in this paper were collected while the author was visiting professor of Social Science at Union Theological Seminary, New York, with a grant from the Russell Sage Foundation.*

There is much confusion in contemparary usage about the role of the Protestant parish minister. In part the lack of clarity is related to the use of similar nomenclature to describe the clergyman and his professional behavior. The purpose of this paper is to ferret out the various usages and connotations and

[1] A shortened revision of a paper presented at the Biennial meeting of the American Association of Schools of Religious Education, Cincinnati, Ohio, December 28, 1957.

to develop a system of analysis to distinguish between them. Three types of roles are identified here: the master role, the integrative role(s), and the practitioner roles.[2]

I

The minister plays many professional roles. The clergyman *qua* clergyman plays a master role (to be discussed in detail in another article) that distinguishes him from those in other professions (lawyers, physicians, social workers) and occupations (policemen, salesmen, plumbers). The master role not only identifies him as a minister but it also identifies his occupation in relation to other roles he plays.

In addition to those roles that are identified as occupational, the clergyman plays many non-occupational roles. He is a citizen, a community resident (unless he is a member of a religious order), he has kinship roles, he may be a family man (unless he is single or has taken a vow of celibacy), and he has a social status role.[3]

It is assumed that his non-occupational roles are in a sense subservient to the master role. As citizen, the minister is not free to act without regard to his role as minister. As family man, the minister, his wife and children are not free to act without considering his master role. The traditional community image of the p.k. (preacher's kid) and the social-control function of gossip in relation to the minister's wife underline the interlocking nature of the master role and the subservient non-occupational roles.

II

Ministers have different orientations to their master role. In their professional relations with people and groups their be-

[2] This analysis of parish ministerial roles is an expansion of the system of categories used in earlier, preliminary reports. The informants whose roles are reported are the 1,111 college and seminary trained clergymen who cooperated in an action research project conducted under the auspices of Union Theological Seminary, New York, and the Russell Sage Foundation. For further information, see Footnote 3 on page 115.
[3] The social characteristics of the ministerial informants are included n a forthcoming report tentatively entitled, *The Protestant Parish Minister—A Behavioral Science Interpretation.*

havior may have different goal orientations. In this research the minister's goal orientation, or frame of reference to his work, is called the integrative role. It is the end toward which he is working in his professional relationship with parishioners, church associations, community groups, and the general public. It is what he is trying to accomplish with people in the professional practice of religion.

The minister is not of necessity aware of the behavioral functions of the integrative role. He may never have been analytic about his behavior from the perspective of the integrative role. He may or may not be conscious of the way in which it gives direction to his ministerial behavior.

We have now identified the master role, and the integrative roles. Brief parenthetic reference is made to the practitioner roles which are behaviorally oriented.[4] They are performed by the minister as a means to an end (or goal). Ministers may preach for different purposes. The intent of one minister in preaching (a means-oriented practitioner role) may be to be persuasive to the non-believer, or to evangelize (a goal-oriented integrative role). Another may preach to instruct the believer, or to edify or to educate; another may preach to bring judgment to the community, or to be prophetic.

III

Clergymen may be identified by the differing ways in which the goal orientation of their role behavior is structured. In this research fourteen integrative role categories are used for the analysis.[5] The general practitioner evidences no identifiable dominant integrative role. Five of the roles appear to have a traditional orientation: believer-saint, scholar, evangelist, litur-

[4] The practitioner roles are briefly described and analyzed in an earlier article: Samuel W. Blizzard, "The Minister's Dilemma," *The Christian Century*, April 25, 1956.

[5] The integrative role analysis was developed jointly with the Rev. George A. Lee. Coding of integrative role orientation of each parish minister informant was supervised by Mr. Lee. Harriet B. Blizzard gave invaluable aid in many ways. The author gratefully acknowledges this assistance, and accepts full responsibility for the interpretation of the research reported in this article.

gist, and father-shepherd. Eight of the integrative role categories appear to have a contemporary orientation: the interpersonal relations specialist, the parish promoter, the community problem solver, the educator, the specialist in a subculture, the representative of the church-at-large, the lay minister, and the church politician.

The brevity of this article does not permit a full discussion of the methodology for identifying the integrative roles of informants.[6] The integrative roles require analysis in depth and are derived by a content analysis of themes. These themes tend to recur in an extended discussion. It was not possible to identify these roles by direct, structured questioning. The full and intense responses from informants in the present study permit the identification of minister as he gives goal direction to his professional behavior in the master role through the practitioner roles.

Four indicators were used in the content analysis procedure to identify each informant's integrative role(s). First, the key statement—the minister's summary in intense and expressive language of the essence of what he is really trying to do in his job. Second, the frequency with which he mentions a certain role and fails to discuss other roles. Third, and fourth, the peer and mentor referents he identifies or associates with his way of doing things.

The major purpose of this article is to identify and describe briefly the various integrative roles. The proportion of ministerial informants using a given role primarily is indicated.[7] Each informant was scored on all the integrative role patterns. However, for brevity those in a secondary and less dominant relationship are not included in this report. There is no attempt to analyze them in relation to such variables as denomination, size

---

[6] A fuller discussion on the methodology of the project is included in the forthcoming report—*The Protestant Parish Minister*—A Behavioral Science Interpretation.

[7] The proportion of ministers in each integrative role category is preliminary and is subject to further checking before final percentages are published.

of church, regional location, community type or social characteristics of the clergy informants.

IV

The *general practitioner* does many things for different reasons. His goals are relative and his ministry is not dominated by
one specific integrative role. He holds three or more integrative
roles with the same relative intensity. He balances off and is
discriminating. He makes a conscious effort to include the many
aspects of the minister's work in some workable scheme. About
one minister in fourteen is a general practitioner.

V

Traditionally, the *believer-saint* integrative role pattern has
been normative for the clergymen. The believer-saint is an ex-
emplar for others to follow because he is dependent upon God.
He conceives himself primarily as a "man of faith" who humbly
seeks God's will. Some of the qualities of character structure that
reflect this integrative role are: (1) prayerfulness, (2) submissiveness, and (3) permissiveness. The believer-saint was a primary
integrative role orientation for one in fourteen informants.

The believer-saint may refer to himself in the following
phrases: "The minister cannot go with anyone else beyond his
own spiritual experience." "The minister's first task is to be sure
of his own health of soul." In a peer referent he may explain:
"I seek to know people who are interested in finding the will of
God." In a mentor relationship he may report: "It was through
[this professor's] saintly personality I came to understand the
incarnation."

Traditionally the ministry has been one of the learned professions. In many Protestant denominations the robe of office
is an academic rather than an ecclesiastical garment. The clergyman's office is called a study. His scholarly life is characterized
by a patient examination of the Scriptures, a perspective on
church history, and full knowledge of the doctrine of the church
and its interpretation. The minister is supposed to go beyond
a simple acceptance of Christianity into a search for truth. The

minister is expected to know the technical facts about religion regardless of the educational level required by a particular denomination. The more broadly oriented scholar type is interested in a general study of society and culture, but this is a peripheral interest for many. The minister whose integrative role is that of *scholar* may see it as an end in itself. He will go beyond the clergyman who sees scholarship as a spiritual discipline or as a means to a more effective performance of the practitioner roles. Very few (one in seventy-five) of the informants had *scholar* as a primary integrative role.

Ministers whose integrative role is that of *scholar* refer to themselves as follows: "The Minister has been set aside by his people to have time to study and contemplate in order to better interpret God's will to those who are his members and constituents for intensive study." In a peer referent he may suggest: "I like to associate with professional leaders and teachers who have had formal schooling and education." He may identify with a mentor because of his "scholarly interpretation of the Scriptures."

VI

The *evangelist* integrative role pattern suggests a functional orientation within a normative frame of reference. The minister is dedicated to a "call" to proclaim the Word. He feels compelled to preach the Word and to save souls. This type of minister's faith is like a rock, it is unshakeable. Often he deals in "blacks" and "whites," feeling that "shades of gray" would compromise his position. Hence this role pattern may harbor in some a type of authoritarianism. One-twelfth of the clergy in this project have evangelism as a primary integrative role.

The evangelist feels that "the only program [his] church has is the salvation of souls." Or he may offer this key statement: "There is no substitute in the parish ministry for telling people through your actions and words about Jesus Christ." "In my ministry I am concerned about the problem of conversion, how to present the church to the people in it and to others seeking admission." As peer or mentor referents those who have this integrative role may cite either fellow clergy who have conducted evangelistic meetings for them or a national big-name evangelist.

The *liturgical* integrative role pattern focuses on a definite concrete ritual. The liturgy is essential for the church to exist and is seen as a near perfect blending of belief and action. Identification with this role as integrative may include an appreciation for the aesthetic. The beauty of worship is more important than the congregation. Liturgy for the purist is an end in itself; for the middle-of-the-roader it is the device by which the grace of God is mediated. Less than one per cent of the informants in this research are liturgists from the point of view of a primary integrative role.

A few expressions that represent the integrative role as the liturgist views it are: "[celebrating Holy Eucharist] is a parish priest's greatest privilege and when I am offering the Holy Communion and I am praying the prayer of the church, then I am supremely happy." "I derive the most personal enjoyment celebrating the Sacrament—in assisting clergy in such services."

One-fifth of the clergy in this project have as a primary integrative role the *Father-shepherd* pattern. The minister is a strong figure. Implicit in the Father-shepherd role is the fact that the minister is a man of unshakeable faith; in his presence God is near to man. This minister is like a comforting father to his children. As a shepherd of the flock he understands and protects them. The specifics in church work do not have to be accounted for by the Father-shepherd. Without doing any specific duty he performs an adequate service to his church in his own mind and in the mind of his parishioners if he is himself and is near when needed. People accept the minister for what he is and for the meaning that his presence puts into the routines as well as the crises of their lives. Thus the routine pastoral calling, cheering the sick and being with the dying, visiting the new born and the aged in his congregation all are part of a good day's work. The Father-shepherd speaks of his mentor as "a wise pastor and a great churchman," and as "a man of prayer, patience and poise." When he describes ministers oriented to this integrative role he may suggest: "He can break the bread of life for men and feed them . . . He can stand by a family facing disgrace and

know what it means to be God's man for them. He can sometimes say a quiet word to the sick and feel the very current of
God's power flowing through him. He can sit with anxious parents waiting the outcome of an operation on a child, and finding
them gaining calm because he is there."

VII

The minister who integrates his roles as an *interpersonal
relations specialist* is analogous to those who are Father-
shepherds, except that the latter is traditionally oriented and the
former is oriented to contemporary values. The interpersonal
relations specialist thinks that to truly "love people," as every
minister should, he must understand them. In understanding and
counseling members of his congregation and others the minister
gets close to their soul. The source of his understanding is his
identification with lay psychiatrists. He believes so much in the
effectiveness of this role that he undergoes therapy himself.
Hence the implementation of this role is more specific than that
of the Father-shepherd. Interpersonal relations deals with
specific interacting personalities instead of the diffuse "flock."
Through this type of integrative role the minister looks on all
the practitioner roles in the context of interpersonal relations.
The interpersonal relations specialist approach is taken by one-
sixth of the informants. As a peer referent one minister reported: "The most helpful person has been a psychology professor who is one of our members . . . I have spent an hour a
week for four months with [him] . . . as a result, I am less compulsive and more effective, both personally and professionally."
Key statements that identify this integrative role are: "Increasingly my ministry becomes a series of conferences with people
who have crucial problems. I feel the need personally to understand human personality (my own and others) better to relate
the various functions of a church to this understanding in a
creative way."

The *parish promoter* is a primary integrative role for every
seventh informant. Those who have this orientation apply the
skills of the secular organizer and promoter to the local church

system. The successful business man who organizes his personnel and promotes his program is the role model of this type of ministerial respondent. This minister seeks to run a smooth organization that measures its effectiveness by statistical standards of attendance, new members, budget, variety of organizational structures, and recognition by national headquarters for cooperativeness in the denominationally recommended program. The mentor of the parish promoter is seen in this admission: "Some of my best guidance comes from hard-headed business men." In identifying his peer referents another informant states: "I like to 'pick' the mind of other clergy especially. 'Have you done this or met this problem.'" Some key statements that portray the parish promoter are: "There are . . . some cliques in this church that have been prevented from dominating the entire life of the church. A pastor of a church of this nature needs to be adroit at knowing when to yield and when to give ground, but if he gives too much ground he will be on the run. How on earth do you develop leaders and still keep them in their place?" "The minister is primarily a leader of leaders in the organizational life of the church . . . he must recruit them, define their job, get them trained and give them a deep consecration for their task."

The *community problem-solver* integrative role, held in primary relationship by more than one-tenth, is related to the parish promoter role. In this case the minister conceives his interest and skill as an organizer extending out to community, national, and international issues. The minister may conceive his role as somewhat akin to the Israelite prophets of Old Testament times or he may be a crusader with a social welfare orientation. His choice of these two justifications will depend on the extent of his sacred or secular ideology. He may identify himself closely with the interest of labor, political or social welfare groups and causes. The community problem solver may admire a mentor referent because he has "strong Christian convictions on social issues which [he is] not afraid to express." As peers he may identify "community leaders in social and civic work." A key statement made by a minister with this type of integrative role orientation reported: "The crying need is that the church be more than the social club of middle class, successful people. It must find some ways to strike harder at [social] problems (crime, alcoholism, delinquency, war, secularism, immorality, neuroticism).''

VIII

The *educator* integrative role represents the primary goal orientation of one in twenty-five. The role of educator is seen as the most valid expression of the ministry by those in this pattern. Religious education is viewed as the major program of the church. Within this area there are plans to be made, leaders to be recruited and trained and groups to be supervised. The educator must understand the basic philosophy of education, know the needs and abilities of children and young people, and possess certain special skills associated with an educational program. The minister-educator may hold a theological position that is somewhat independent of the educational method. His religious ideology may range from conservative to liberal, but it is important that he be committed to the basic goal of religious education. This goal is that faith be communicated appropriately and comprehensively at every age level. To implement this goal a full program involving all resources of the church is in order. Some key statements give further meaning to the educator as an integrating role. "I enjoy most the aspect of Christian education including the pulpit, church school, home visits, classes, youth and adult programming." "We must instruct all persons—individually, at group meetings, at services, counseling, etc. We must teach through sermons, through special confirmation classes, reaching non-church people through personnel and contact."

The *sub-cultural specialist* is a primary integrative role for one in fifty. This role helps the minister see his work from the perspective of whatever group that he chooses for his ministry. It may be the rural ministry or the inner city, or the suburbs. He may consider himself a specialist in ministering to laboring people or to an ethnic group. The sub-cultural specialist will have strong motivation and interest. Being a rural minister or a minister in an inner city area will be a way of life for him. He will think of it as requiring special skills that are not required in other ministries.

A few key statements will illustrate this type: "I chose the rural ministry deliberately. I feel that many of my seminary professors, classmates and other friends and relatives think I am wasting my time up in the north woods and getting nowhere." "I believe my work in the city church is most effective . . . I would not want another type of ministry." "I work five days a week in the ———— factory. I do my pastoral work, studying, etc. evenings and Saturday. I accept from my church the difference between my factory earnings and the cash salary in my call. This way I am closely identified with the factory workers who are the core of my parish."

The *"lay" minister* approach to an integrative role is a reaction to the uniqueness of the minister in a sacred role. It involves an implicit anti-clericalism. There is a conscious effort to identify with lay people. The minister is afraid of being a stuffed shirt; he wants to "be just like everyone else." He sees himself as practicing the doctrine of the priesthood of all believers. The minister is just like other believers except that he devotes more time to the church and may have more training. He avoids clerical garb and may dress like the lay persons in his parish, even when officiating at church functions. He can do "a man's work" and can speak in the language of the man of the street rather than merely in technical religious language. About one in twenty-five is oriented to this integrative role on a primary basis.

The clergymen whose integrative role is that of the "lay" minister describe themselves in the following key statements: "I have fought to overcome the professionalism in the ministry, the loss of Protestant understanding of Christian vocation, the priesthood of all believers." "We are all laymen. The minister is a more educated layman. The minister may not be a more dedicated layman; he must be able to communicate with people where they are . . ."

The *representative of the church-at-large* is an integrative role for one informant in fifty. This type is oriented to the community rather than strictly to the local congregation. This minister is warm-hearted and mixes well with people; he is a Christ-like Rotarian. In his attempt to be a servant of the whole community he may express his ideology in cliches and shop-worn phrases. He wants to be "like Christ" or the "friend of man" in the Edgar Guest tradition. Since there are no parish limits to his pastoral work, he may appear to lack focus and have a diffused ministry. He may "minister" to a person who happens to occupy a seat next to him on a bus, plane, or train. He may hear "confession," marry and bury the churchless and the excommunicated of the community. The representative of the church-at-large may speak of his mentor as a "tried, trusted and accredited friend at large." He may honor a peer who ministers to a fashionable congregation but who insists on ministering to those on the wrong side of the tracks. When describing his own ministry he refers to "my work as a friend, a fellow traveler—along life's road—together we can learn and grow and pray and sing and find a greater purpose and joy in life." Or he may report: "I make a particular point of calling most on the outcast and poor in the community, for it is here that the greatest needs, emotional, physical, psychological and spiritual seem to exist, and once you get to know these people, they seem to be the ones who will most readily come to you and ask for help."

The *church politician* is a primary integrative role for only one in a hundred. This minister is a system follower or the organization man. As an integrative role it is a product of an explicit or implicit hierarchical system. The minister feels that his purposes are best forwarded by conformity to this system. He will stress cooperative work or connectional work. In a sense denominational matters are part of every minister's work, but for some this is dominant and intergrative. They feel that it has its own built-in security system. Their professional creed is: "take care of the system and the system will take care of you." It does not depend on knowledge, skill, or understanding on the part of the minister, but simply upon his ability to obey orders and glory in following them.

IX

The integrative role analysis explores one possible way in which the parish minister gives purposeful focus to the many dimensions of his work. It gives meaning to some of the ambiguity associated with the minister in contemporary society.

This analysis suggests that four integrative role patterns are primary for almost two-thirds of the parish ministers studied. These role patterns are oriented to the world of people rather than the world of ideas. The father-shepherd, the interpersonal relations specialist, the parish promoter, and the community problem solver patterns may have varying ideological undertones but essentially they involve interpersonal, intragroup and intergroup relations. Two role patterns are primarily integrative for more than one-sixth of the informants. They are the believer-saint, and the evangelist. Both of these integrative roles are ideologically oriented.

The remaining eight integrative roles are held primarily by one-fifth of the ministers researched. Aside from the general practitioner, no one of the residual is a primary integrative role for more than one in twenty-five. This is notable since the educator, the sub-cultural specialist and possibly the liturgist is strongly recommended by church executives and theological educators. Analysis of integrative roles held in a secondary relationship may indicate greater utility for them.

Role ambiguity raises many problems for the contemporary Protestant parish minister. This article has explored one avenue by which intrapersonal aspects of it may be systematized and role conflicts resolved. Further research and self-examination by parish clergy is required to evaluate the integrative role in relation to role conflict.

PART FOUR

THE MINISTER AND HIS FAMILY

THE very title of this section underlines the fact that the book is
developed from a *Protestant* point of view. The Protestant Reformation, according to Roland Bainton, made its most profound
impressions upon the home. He says that Luther's deepest
influence was in the home. (Roland Bainton, *Here I Stand*.
New York: Abingdon Press, 1950, p. 384.) Emotional immaturity
or maturity inevitably involves one's relation to his family of
orientation, i.e., his parents and siblings. The research of Ter-
man and others indicates that marital unhappiness is predom-
inantly related to emotional involvements with one's parental
family. On the other hand, the fact that the minister is usually
expected to be a *married* minister among Protestants tends to
focus many of his emotional problems of living upon his relationship to his wife. As the research of Hiltner will also show, it
is impossible for the minister to make a decision to end marriage
distress by divorce without involving his vocation.

157

Consequently, any discussion of the mental health of the minister must take into consideration the role he fulfills as a married man, as a father, and as an exemplary "manager of his own household well," to use the phrase of the Pastoral Epistle.

The Minister as a Family Man

By JOHN G. KOEHLER
Minister,
Calvary Baptist Church,
Providence, Rhode Island

John G. Koehler conducted a questionnaire survey of 150 American Baptist ministers with the intention of getting a view of their relationships to their families. A remarkable response of 79% returns indicates that his findings are not only significant, but that he has also touched a center of deep concern in the personal adjustments of ministers.

"I will be fair to my family and will endeavor to give them the time and consideration to which they are entitled." So reads a code which the Disciples of Christ formulated for their clergy.

In recent years extensive studies have been made of the amount of time a minister devotes to his professional responsibilities. The purpose of this article is to call attention to the amount of time a minister spends with his wife and children; how they feel about him as a family man. Many a Protestant minister would readily acknowledge that often he becomes so engrossed in his "church" work that he nearly forgets his "home" work.

Manuals for ministers have little to say on this important

subject. Much more has been published about the pastor's wife and her role in the family circle.

In an effort to learn how his fellow ministers were measuring up as family men, the writer mailed a questionnaire to 150 American Baptist Convention ministers' wives whose husbands serve churches large and small in village, town, and city. A third of the mailing covered all the parsonages of one specific State Convention. Another third was directed to women whose husbands were officers of state or national Ministers Councils. The remaining third represented pastors of large parishes or those who carried significant responsibilities in community, denominational or interdenominational bodies.

In less than four weeks 119 returns were received. Judging from the unsolicited comments and the high percentage of returns (79%), "the minister as a family man" is a subject of genuine concern to pastors' wives.

One of the questions asked was, "Think back over the week just past. How many hours was your husband at home with his family (exclusive of sleeping)? This should include mealtimes, family outings, helping with the children or housework, watching TV with the family, family devotions, etc." The replies indicated that six ministers had spent less than 10 hours, eleven from 11 to 19 hours, twenty-three from 16 to 20 hours, fifteen from 21 to 25 hours, fifteen from 26 to 30 hours, ten from 31 to 35 hours, eight from 36 to 40 hours, four from 41 to 45 hours, and three 46 hours or more. Over twenty respondents did not answer this query. Half the replies fell between 16 and 30 hours a week; the median was about 26 hours.

Did the size of a church's active resident membership make a difference in the number of hours a minister spends with his family? Evidently not. In the churches (29) of under 200 members, the minister averaged 27 hours at home. In the churches (21) of 1,000 members or more, it was 22 hours.

Did the number of children who were still at home have any bearing on the time a minister had shared with his family circle? Eighty-five of the 119 returns indicated that there were still children at home. Where there was one child in the home (20),

a minister averaged 25 hours; where there were two children
(31), 24 hours; where there were three children (25), 25 hours;
where there were four or more children (9), 19 hours.

According to these limited findings a minister spends about
25 hours a week at home regardless of the size of his church membership or the number of his offspring still at home.

Linked with how many hours a week he was at home was a
question which called for a subjective answer by the minister's
wife. "Is your husband away from home so much that you wonder
whether the family is becoming a matriarchy?" Fifty-two answered
without hesitation, "No." Another 42 leaned toward an affirma-
tive reply, ranging from an outright "Yes" to "I once did" or
"Sometimes" or "I've been concerned about it." A few lined
up with the "shepherdess" whose sense of humor prompted her
to write, "We are all away so much that probably the house
wonders whether it has a family."

It is one thing to know how much time a minister spends at
home. It is something else to find out how he spends it. Is the
minister's time with his household scattered like buckshot, a
little here and a little there, at odd hours of the day or evening,
nothing that can be counted on by the family?

This subject was introduced by asking, "Does your church
encourage its minister to take a regular day off?" Less than 50%
of the churches appeared to encourage their ministers in this
regard. A few of the wives were startled that any church would
even think of such a practice. One put it, "Church people don't
know whether the minister does or does not take a day off."

Maybe the matter of a regular day off should enter into the
discussion when a pulpit committee is calling a minister. Perhaps
the minister is at fault. If he fails to stress the importance of a
regular day off for his family and himself he can scarcely expect
the church leaders to think of it.

In some cases where the church encouraged a regular day off,
the minister had not taken one in the previous four weeks. In
other cases where the church had not given any encouragement,
the minister had taken some days off. So it requires more than

encouragement on the part of the church to discipline a minister to reserve one day in seven for his wife and children.

"In terms of the last four weeks," the questionnaire asked, "how many days off have you and your husband taken together?" About 50% reported not one day off in the entire period; twenty had taken one day, two a day and a half, sixteen 2 days. Only two had taken one day off each week with their wives.

One minister's wife suggested, "His time should be so budgeted that it will reflect that his concern for family is equal to his concern for parishioners. Too many ministers have a queer 'conscience' that makes them feel guilty if they spend time relaxing at home. Time at home is so rare that they try to force recreation, family conferences, family devotions, instead of enjoying a more relaxed and natural sequence of family living."

Another replied by citing a personal experience. "For the first seven years of our ministry my husband was 'too busy' for regular days off. It was his physician who asked him if he were trying to save the world in the first ten years of his ministry and die or become disabled at an early age, or if he might consider pacing himself and being around to contribute his energies for four decades. My husband took stock of himself and his job and made the decision. He works like a beaver six days a week, arranges to be home for meals whenever possible, and plans the one day as a 'date' with me or with the family unless emergencies keep him. I answer the phone on the day off and I am sure that one day I shall be candidate for some sort of degree in being downright 'cagey' about his whereabouts. After all, I can always reach him in the event of an emergency—and I do."

A third woman suggested, "Anything that is worth while takes planning, and for a minister to be a family man takes very careful planning." Still another minister's wife wrote, "I get hold of his engagement book, compare it with mine, and plan a month in advance on the 'blank spaces.' Planning together, working together helps to bring about those enjoyable times when we can be together as a family."

The questionnaire asked, "What social ties do you and your husband have together outside the usual church functions?"

Sixty-two women answered, "None." In a few instances there was an accompanying word. One declared, "We belong to no outside social organizations because of Christian principles." But another demurred, "We truly miss such outside social ties." Between these two points of view were such comments as, "We have a great deal of social life in the church; are included in private affairs as well as church groups, almost more than we can do"; and "Were we to have outside social ties we would have less time with our family."

Very few listed outside social ties. For example, nine included P.T.A. as a social event. The largest number, sixteen, put down symphony or opera, possibly of the Community Concert type. Ten mentioned "eating out"; eight spoke of a group of friends with whom they met. Masonic functions accounted for seven, and Service Clubs for five (one wife called attention to the fact that these were only annual affairs). It is safe to generalize that the minister and his wife are not noted for their social ties outside the church fellowship.

This was further demonstrated by the response to the question, "Were two things scheduled at the same time—one a church function, the other a community activity which involved a member of his family—which would he be apt to attend?" Fifty per cent replied "the church." Others could not leave it there without adding, "The church, and I am in agreement with him." "If he didn't attend the church appointment, he would not be a man of God, and mine is!" "Are you kidding? It would have to be an outstanding event, or his deacons would say NO!" "His one REAL interest is the church." A couple of the wives asserted their independence at this point, saying, "This is my pet peeve."

Of the remaining wives, twenty-one did not rule out the possibility that their husbands might choose the church function, though they qualified it by saying, "It would depend on the importance of the church or community activity." And there were twelve who thought that their husbands would attempt to attend both affairs. Four believed that the husband would probably attend the "family" community function by carefully planning his over-all schedule. Still another woman was sure that the minister in her life would attend the function he felt was the more important or the one to which he had made the prior commitment.

Most of the wives regretted that their husbands were not spending more time with the family. However, they saw some positive values in parsonage life. "I think that most ministers are more of a 'family man' than are the men of other professions. They have fewer hours at home with the family, but ministers tend to make more of these hours." "Ministers and their wives are peculiarly lucky in that they work as a team much more than any other couple, and for this reason, are much closer to each other. In spite of being in demand I think ministers as a whole are with their families more than a great many men are. All executives, public figures and professional men have to spend much time outside their homes as do ministers, and the families have to understand and be proud that the father is in demand."

It would be helpful if there were some way of comparing the average time a minister spends with his family with that which is spent by other professional or community-minded men, not to overlook laymen who conscientiously devote many hours a week to church boards and committees. Perhaps the minister would not be too far out of line. There is one situation which is peculiarly that of the parsonage family. The father is always working on week-ends, a time when most other families are able to let up and do things together.

John C. Wynn in his book, *Pastoral Ministry to Families,* states that if a minister "devotes all his time and his energy to making a success of his profession, life in the manse must suffer. It is possible for him to gain a church and lose a home. The fitness of a pastor to assume the cure of souls is roughly proportionate to his quality as a husband and father . . . His sense of values needs constant, prayerful review lest he subjugate family welfare to administrivia under the mistaken assumption that these comprise the Kingdom of God."

The writer submitted the findings contained in this article before a theological club, a gathering of ministers' wives, and a series of five workshops at a ministers' conference. The discussions of these people as well as the answers to the questionnaire leads the author to draw several conclusions.

1. Ministers seem to spend, on the average, about 25 hours a week with their families. This is less than a quarter of their waking hours. Both the amount and the proportion of time seems small.

2. It seems strange in view of the Christian understanding of the family that a minister with children at home spends no more time in the parsonage than the pastor who is childless or whose children have left home.

3. The minister probably shares with other professional men, like the physician, the need to plan his home time and family activity if he is to have it at all. It is unlikely that he will merely drift into good practice.

4. Many ministers seem to feel guilty about taking time off with their families. Does this suggest more a theology of works than one of faith? Perhaps the man who is indispensable for too many hours a week is "playing God" more than he realizes!

5. As a whole, the ministers' wives complain far less about the *amount* of time their husbands are at home than about their inability to *count on* the time agreed on.

6. A minister and his family may enjoy many happy occasions within the church circle. However, the minister may become narrow who shuts out other forms of sociability in the community at large.

"What can be done about it?" The following are a few of the suggestions which have emerged from group discussions on this subject.

1. Get the story across to the clergy. Many ministers feel guilty about not spending enough time with their families. They need to know that other ministers face the same situation. Perhaps local ministerial bodies could encourage their men to find creative ways of dealing with this issue.

2. Get the story across to the ministers' wives. They, too, need to know that other ministers' families face this problem. Significant gains can be made only if the "parsonage partners" work on it together.

3. Get the story across to the seminaries. The writer has cor-

responded with some of the theological schools of his denomination. He was encouraged to learn that in the past few years the curriculum of these institutions has begun to recognize the need for alerting the theological student to his eventual role as a family man.

4. Get the story across to the church laymen. These men and women appreciate the importance of reserving time for the family circle. They can encourage their minister to take a regular day off. They can see to it that one or two nights in the church's weekly calendar are cleared so that the pastor may be with his own household.

Wilhelm Pauck[1] writes, "Nothing shaped the social status of the Protestant ministry as decisively as the fact that they were permitted and indeed encouraged to marry . . . Ministerial households often exemplified the practical application of the Reformers' new understanding of the Christian religion, namely, that the faith in Christ must be practiced in mutual love and service in the natural, social setting of human life and in the ordinary, secular pursuits. Thus the married ministry came to demonstrate that family life together with the manifold social activities it engenders can be a more effective vehicle for religion and the service of God than asceticism, celibacy and other-worldliness."

The Protestant parsonage still plays an important part in the work of God's Kingdom. Let each minister examine anew his role as a family man.

---

[1] *The Ministry in Historical Perspectives,* edited by H. Richard Niebuhr and Daniel D. Williams (New York: Harper & Brothers, 1956), p. 146.

Role Attitudes of the Minister's Wife

By Wallace Denton, Ph.D.,
Counselor, Midwest Christian Counseling Center,
Kansas City, Missouri

*Wallace Denton reports here on the results of an intensive inter-
view-type research into role attitudes of the minister's wife which
he did in partial fulfillment of his requirements for a doctor's
degree at Teachers College, Columbia University. He enriches it
further with his observations as a counselor of many ministers and
their families.*

Someone has said that nothing is so persuasive as an idea whose
time has come. The clergyman's right to marry was one such
idea, though a married clergy was only one aspect of the larger
idea embodied in the Protestant Reformation. Maurois says
that Mrs. Thomas Cranmer, wife of the first Archbishop of
Canterbury subsequent to the break with Rome, was forced to
live in such retirement that she had to travel in a box with
ventilating holes in the lid.[1]

The minister's wife came to this country with these battles
won. She faced new ones in a new country. Mrs. Cranmer's traveling box replete with ventilating holes may now strike readers

[1] Andre Maurois, *The Miracle of England*, trans. Hamish Miles. (New
York: Harper & Brothers, Publishers, 1937, p. 211.)

167

as an unbelievable anecdote. However, one occasionally gets the impression that the numerous and high expectations placed upon the modern minister's wife still handicaps her, much like the traveling box.

A woman's decision to marry a minister is a decision to accept a role which can offer deep personal satisfactions. It may offer despair! To marry the minister of a church is a decision to marry more than a man. It is a decision to become a part of a role with a long tradition. To a greater or lesser degree it dictates that she shall be a part of her husband's work. She can extricate herself from this role only at a risk to herself and her husband's ministry. An understanding of her role inevitably has relevance for her mental health.

A survey of the literature on the minister's wife points up several needs. One of these is for a study of her attitudes toward her role expectations. It is the purpose of this chapter to explore some expressed attitudes of the minister's wife with reference to her role expectations and some implications of these for her mental health.

The data and conclusions presented here are drawn from research conducted for a doctoral dissertation,[2] several years of intensive counseling with numerous ministers' wives, and seminars conducted for the wives of pastors in which their roles were explored. In all of these investigations and contacts, role expectations of the minister's wife were the central focus. They were conceived in a framework covering the major areas of her existence: her husband's work, her family life, and the church and community. These areas will be briefly explored.

1. Attitudes Toward Her Husband's Work

ASSISTANT PASTOR?

One of the primary aspects of the minister's wife's role is her participation in her husband's work. This is done in a manner and to a degree probably experienced by few other wives.

[2] Wallace Denton, "Role Attitudes of the Minister's Wife." Unpublished Doctor's thesis, Teachers College, Columbia University, New York, 1958.

"I think the minister's wife is a kind of 'little minister'," remarked one wife to the writer. The "little minister" type of wife is a rather descriptive term for a few wives. She is engaged in all types of church activities, teaching, speaking, visiting, counseling, and doing certain administrative aspects of the work such as making the quarterly report to the state headquarters.

However, the assistant pastor type of wife appears to be passing. A rebellion against this type seems to be taking place. Remarks as the following are frequently made:

> I feel the minister's wife has enough to do being a wife without being the unpaid assistant of the pastor. She shouldn't be expected to do any more than the banker's wife or farmer's wife.

> The minister's wife is only a layman. I think she and the congregation should remember this. She should not take on responsibility that is the minister's. I do think she should be as active in the church as one of the other active wives.

The average wife participating in the writer's research both felt and appeared to be no more active in the work of the church in a direct manner than any other active wife. However, what she did was different from that of other women by virtue of her role as the minister's wife. Her primary contribution to her husband's work was on the homefront. Here she shared in his work by hearing him out, discussing ideas with him, and providing the type of atmosphere at home to which her husband might retreat as a kind of refuge from a busy and frequently hectic schedule.

Many ministers' wives frequently speak of "staying in the background" with reference to their husbands' work. One third of the wives in the research project described their "place" as being in the background. This refers to a behind the scenes type of role. There seems to be no question in the minds of these wives but that this was their proper sphere. However, they were not cowering in the background. Possibly the ability of the wives to accept this role with aplomb is partly attributable to the fact that her role frequently places her in the limelight. Thus some of her needs for recognition are met. As one wife remarked, "I wouldn't be telling the truth if I said I didn't enjoy the special attention I get as the minister's wife."

The literature on the minister's wife frequently admonishes her to occupy a background position. Possibly the accumulated wisdom of the years has indicated that less conflict is engendered and the church program operates more smoothly when the roles are delimited by defining the position of the wife as being "in the background." That is, from the standpoint of role theory, this may be an attempt to draw the lines of demarcation between her role and her husband's, thus avoiding some of the conflicts of overlapping roles.

This suggests the matter of the wife who is trained to be a professional church worker, such as a director of religious education, and who then marries a minister. The experience of those who work with ministers and their families indicates real conflict can come from such a union. The conflict arises out of a conflict of roles. That is, she has spent years developing a concept of herself as a professional church worker and leader. This has also been the goal of her education. Then rather suddenly she becomes a minister's wife, whose ascribed role appears to be in the background. Furthermore, her training has roughly paralleled her husband's thus equipping her to perform some of the functions commonly done by the pastor. The husband is sometimes threatened by such a wife. This wife's problem may not become apparent until the arrival of children. Confusion may then arise as to where she derives her major identity—the church or home. Therefore, what appeared to be an ideal marriage also carried with it certain built-in pitfalls.

LONELINESS

In a realistic sense the minister's wife shares the symbolic role of her husband, and as such is partly an embodiment of the community conscience. This has the effect of setting her apart, of isolating her. Approximately two-thirds of the wives in the author's research discussed feelings of lineliness. "We're the loneliest souls in the world," voiced one wife. Herein lies a paradox.

She is surrounded by friends, many of whom are willing to go to great lengths for her happiness. Yet, she is lonely.

Loneliness has its genesis not in the absence of people, but in the absence of meaningful relationships to people. The loneliness of the minister's wife is partly attributable to an attitude expressed by many of them that there should be no close friendships among parishioners. Since church people provide the main social contacts outside the home for most of the wives, they simply have few close friends. That is, they have no one with whom they can really "let their hair down."

Certainly not all wives felt lonely. A few established deep, personal friendships among parishioners. Other wives simply do not have as much need for close friendships with anyone. In fact, they may actually avoid such relationships.

However, wives who experience loneliness are faced with a dilemma. They feel that close friendships within church frequently engender jealousies and leadership problems. But aloofness aggravates feelings of loneliness. Some cope with it by apparently burying themselves in activities. Others seek friendships outside the church. Most seem to continue in their loneliness.

BREADTH OF HER ROLE

In addition to sharing the symbolic role of her husband, the minister's wife also shares the breadth or extensiveness of his role. That is, at all times and places she is the minister's wife. Like the Psalmist, she has no place to hide. (Psalms 139:7-12.) The sales clerk can retreat to the powder room and be "another one of the girls." It is difficult for the minister's wife to find such a retreat in which she can lay aside this role temporarily and assume another. On the matter of the extensiveness of roles, Sargent notes that a boy may be a clown in one group and a leader in another. On the other hand, "a man of the cloth plays his ministerial role in all or practically all of his social contacts . . ." So it is with his wife.

All of this raises the question as to what degree her role inhibits her from expressing her own individuality. This writer had difficulty seeing the minister's wife as a person in much of the literature about her. For the most part she appears to be a faceless appendage to her husband. A role is carefully delineated and the feeling tacitly communicated to her that the "good" minister's wife will fit herself into the role.

An interesting contrast to this concept is found in actually talking with the average minister's wife. Half of the wives interviewed for the dissertational research noted earlier spontaneously mentioned the necessity of "being one's self." The large number referring to this probably reflects their recognition of certain pressures which could lead to a denial of their own selfhood. Not only did these wives talk of being one's self, but they communicated the distinct feeling that they were individuals. With few exceptions, these wives were not faceless adjuncts to their husbands. In fact, some wives mentioned their husbands encouraging them to express their own individuality.

One wife offered this advice to a girl considering marriage to a minister:

> Do not be discouraged if you cannot be the "firstest with the mostest" in everything. A girl saddled with feelings that she has to be the most talented, most scintillating, most everything, is so busy flagellating herself that she doesn't have time to be her own sweet self.

Such an attitude, if accepted and acted upon, should vitally contribute to good mental health.

A SENSE OF MEANING

The role of the minister's wife seems to offer deep personal satisfactions for the average wife. In talking with her one gets the feeling that whether on the homefront or in the background, this is her ministry, too. It is a service which has meaning and gives a sense of direction to her life. Thus, while frequently voicing loneliness, she is likely to have a sense of purpose not possessed by most other wives. Meaninglessness is not so likely to be her lot. Inasmuch as a sense of purpose is one requisite of good mental health, the minister's wife is fortunate that she can share and participate in her husband's work. This underlines the fact that some of the limitations of her role also contains the potentiality for some of the most important assets of her role.

Any attempt to focus on the minister's wife and her husband's work to the exclusion of other aspects of her life is a purely arbitrary one. She lives and moves in an atmosphere which at once includes the home, church, and community. Granting this, let us shift the focus to her family life.

2. *Attitudes Toward Family Life*

The number of anecdotes and jokes about the minister, his wife and children probably reflects, among other things, a type of curiosity about members of the parsonage. A lively interest on the part of laymen is rather easily aroused by a discussion of the more personal dimensions of life in the parsonage. What attitudes does the minister's wife have about living there?

PRIVACY

Out of the very position of the minister in the community as one of its leading citizens rise ambivalent feelings on the part of the minister's wife. There are the satisfactions which come from public recognition, but this necessarily entails a certain invasion of the privacy of the minister and his family. Examples in which the privacy of the parsonage are rudely invaded are replete in the literature on the minister's wife. These bold intrusions, such as people who fail to knock, apparently do not now occur with any frequency in most pastors' homes. There is a more subtle invasion. The writer's research indicated more than two-thirds of the wives agreed that life in the parsonage is "fishbowl" living. How they responded to this varied. Fifteen per cent of the wives mentioned the lack of privacy as the thing they disliked most about being a minister's wife. One wife said that she and her husband frequently watched television at nights with the lights out and the shades drawn so as to appear absent from home.

While recognizing that their lives are to a degree public domain, most wives seem to adapt with minimum conflict to the situation. Younger wives tend to find it more annoying. Age apparently brings adjustment, or else they learn to deter it. One wife quoted a well-known political figure as saying that "after

being in a goldfish bowl a while you become like the goldfish—
you just don't give a hang." Probably it is well to note that what
passes for idle curiosity on the part of parishioners may in fact
be concern.

The degree of privacy which the pastor's wife and family has is
determined by several factors. Among these are the type of community, the location of the parsonage with respect to the church,
and the manner in which the wife handles the situation. The
degree of privacy is related to the size of the city in which the
church is located. The larger the city, the more anonymity the
pastor enjoys. Then, too, privacy is facilitated by the parsonage
being located away from the church. There seems to be a trend
away from locating the pastor's home next to the church. Finally,
some wives seem to unconsciously encourage, or else are unable
to discourage invasions of her home.

REARING A FAMILY

The minister's wife has some rather clear-cut attitudes about
rearing a family in a parsonage. She probably will discuss both
its assets and liabilities. The most frequent disadvantage mentioned to the writer by more than half of the wives was that
too much attention was showered on the children. Another disadvantage noted by a third of them was that more was likely to
be expected of their children than others. Yet, this pressure was
not usually overwhelming. All the wives were unanimously against
saying, "You cannot do that because you are the minister's
child." One wonders to what degree they are able to keep from
tacitly communicating this to the child.

The assets of life in the parsonage mentioned were the development of social skills through contacts with many people, the
intellectual stimulation of good books, the contacts with interesting visitors from home and abroad, moral and ethical training,
the advantages of good music, travel and other culturally broad-
ening experiences. Research and other contacts with them indicated that they want their children to live as nearly normal lives
as possible. The type of community, location of the parsonage,
and manner in which parents cope with outside influences determine the degree to which this can be achieved.

FAMILY TIME

Life in the parsonage is rather limited in family time. The most frequent complaint the minister's wife voices is probably the lack of time for the whole family to be together. In fact, when asked what she dislikes most about being a minister's wife, her answer is likely to be the lack of family time. Relatively few ministers consistently take a day off to spend with the family. Many who do take time off spend it at meetings away from the church rather than with the family. One wife undoubtedly voiced the opinion of many when she said, "At times I feel that surely Mrs. Jones' problem isn't any worse than mine, and why can't he spend some time with me." Those wives who find the lack of time a less pressing problem usually appear to be vitally engaged in work outside the home.

3. Attitudes Toward Church and Community

The minister's wife lives and moves in the larger context of her church and community. In spite of various expressions of discontent by different wives, the predominant attitude is strongly positive. The average wife is likely to talk with pride about her church and ways in which its members have helped and supported her.

She also perceives this as a mutual feeling on the part of the church. She tends to feel the church has a sense of pride in her. Some mention parishioners introducing them with pride, "This is our minister's wife!" In fact there may be a tendency to place her on a pedestal along with her husband. This elevated concept of her is more likely to exist in smaller towns and communities.

COMMON EXPECTATIONS

One of the commonest expectations by the church of the minister's wife seems to be that she shall be a friendly person. There also seems to be an expectation that in most matters, such as dress, she will be conservative. At times, though, it appears the wife may place more restrictions on herself at this point than the church. Ten per cent of the wives in the writer's research voiced the feeling that their freedom was impinged upon by expectations of the church.

The psychic satisfaction of being a minister's wife can be deeply rewarding. When asked about the satisfactions of her role, the minister's wife frequently mentions the joys of being appreciated, of being wanted and needed by the people. She may even admit that at a dinner it is nice to be seated at the head of the table.

One of the expectations by the minister's wife of the church is an adequate salary. Research indicated most wives apparently felt the salary was at least adequate. Ten per cent felt the salary was wholly inadequate. All could use more! Though discounts to ministers are common, the younger minister's wife is likely to say she would rather have an adequate salary and pay the full price.

One wife quoted a psychiatrist as saying that when the monetary pay of a position is low, the psychic "pay" associated with it must be high, if the person is to continue to operate effectively with good mental health. This may partly explain how most ministers' wives are able to maintain relatively good mental health even though the ministry has a history of being one of the poorest paying professions. That is, they feel it has much to offer in psychic pay.

SOCIAL CLASS

One of the difficulties the minister's wife is likely to encounter in her church and community arises at the point of social class differences. By virtue of her role, the wife must relate to people of varying socio-economic backgrounds. Some of these are both above and below hers. Her plight is illustrated by the wife whose father had been a farmer in a remote area, and she married a minister who was now pastor of a church in an elite surburban area. Socially she felt extremely backward in this group and complained of not even knowing how to set a proper table.

Conversely, the minister's wife confronts the problem of moving down the social ladder, though this happens less frequently. Thus, the daughter of the owner of a large manufacturing concern who married a middle class minister was completely unequipped with the role expectations of her small village. Women of the church accused her of being a snob, because she always wore gloves when going to town or a meeting. Sarbin has aptly noted that "a person cannot enact a role for which he lacks the necessary role expectations; these must be acquired through experience."[4] Inasmuch as role expectations are learned, the younger minister's wife is more likely to experience conflict in enacting her role in a setting foreign to the one she has known.

While the average wife seems to have positive attitudes toward her church and community, the degree to which she lets them impinge upon her is partly a function of her own makeup. A few wives experience strong pressure from the church for certain types of behavior. The real focus of the pressure may lie within themselves. Some have too high, too idealistic expectations. Good mental health will require a working through of these expectations. Also, the hypersensitive wife is likely to interpret an expectation from one member as an expectation of the whole church. On the other hand, some wives note that the church can legitimately expect certain types of role enactments from the wife of the minister. This can be done, they feel, without losing their own identity.

By way of conclusion, the role of the minister's wife has built into it certain potentialities which can be an asset to mental health. But the role can be equally devastating. Most wives find the role deeply meaningful. However, the wife who seriously feels that she is trapped in a role with rigid expectation from the church, community—and possibly the husband and herself—is the wife who is likely to need and seek counseling. This person may feel whatever individuality she possesses being squeezed from her. This was the experience of one wife who related:

> I think I'd like to wear a sign around my neck and sit with the choir on Sunday morning up in front of all the people. On this sign I would want written in great big letters, "Me!, Me!, Me!"

---

[4] Theodore Sarbin, "Role Theory," *Handbook of Social Psychology.* Gardner Lindzey, editor, Vol. I, (Cambridge, Massachusetts: Addison-Wesley Publishing Company, 1954), p. 226.

The best therapy for a wife with this problem is frequently a healthy dose from her husband of love, attention, and time. Unfortunately, the minister is sometimes prone to forget that his own family is a part of God's Kingdom, and need "pastoral care." The Apostle Paul would remind him of ". . . the church in thy house" (Philemon 2). The wife of one overly busy pastor related this dream:

> I dreamed my husband had entered me at the Indianapolis Speedway. But the craziest thing about it was that I wasn't in a car. Just as real as could be, I was lined up with a number on my back. What is more, I had our two kids in my arms. Now I wonder what could make me dream a thing like that!

Emotional Disorders of Persons in Church-Related Vocations

By Edward E. Thornton

Professor of Pastoral Care,

The Institute of Religion,

Texas Medical Center,

Houston, Texas

Professor Thornton worked intensively in a family relations center in a metropolitan area. Many of his counselees were ministers and their wives. On a more intensive basis than either questionnaire or single interview, he did longer-term counseling of a multiple interview nature with disturbed and unhappy ministers and their wives. He gives an interpretative analysis of some of his work here.

The problem to which this research is addressed is, in general, to evaluate the factors involved in causing emotional disorder in persons who are in church-related vocations. In particular it seeks to isolate and evaluate occupational stress and marital difficulties as factors in emotional disorders.

The sample on which this research depends is the experience of twenty persons in a community counseling agency. Their ages range from twenty-one to sixty-four; the median age is twenty-five. Thirteen persons were enrolled in theological studies at the time of counseling. Since five of these were engaged in responsible church-staff positions, only eight (or forty per cent) of the total sample had not experienced the stresses of employment in the role of a church leader. Ages at which these people entered church vocations ranged from sixteen to fifty-seven, with the median age at twenty. Those who had had previous experience in church vocations averaged three years of such experience.

The sample includes thirteen men and seven women. Only seven were single (four men and three women). One woman was divorced; the remaining twelve were married. Four married persons had no children, six had one child, the others from two to four children. This says that the majority had completed the major identifications normal to adult status. Sixteen were in an urban, lower-middle social class group. It is worth noting that nine or forty-five per cent of these experienced upward mobility as a result of entering church vocation; eight or forty per cent experienced no change and three or fifteen per cent experienced downward movement. Six persons were reared in rural areas, but all six had settled permanently into urban modes of life. Only one was living in a rural area and this person had been reared in a city. Appropriate to this social class sampling, sixteen were Baptists, two were Methodists, one was Presbyterian and one was Christian in denominational affiliation.

According to the counselor's evaluation of case histories only one of the twenty persons came from a "happy" parental home. Six came from "very unhappy" homes in which acute conflict or divorce had occurred. One was an only child, but eleven or fifty-five per cent came from families of from three to seven children. The number of first-born (eight) is equal to the number of last-born (eight). Only two were "middle" children in the family constellation.

The counselor is a theologically trained person who functions in the role of "Counseling Director" in an independent, com-munity-sponsored counseling agency. He was perceived by each of the clients as a minister, however, and was related to some of them as part of the seminary community from which they also came.

The method of investigation was counseling in terms of the problems presented by the client. These problems included such concerns as early sex adjustment in marriage, homosexual fantasy in unmarried persons, academic failure, fear of mental illness, impending divorce and feelings of having committed the unpardonable sin. Information about a person's vocational choice and work adjustment was incidental to these other concerns in many cases. Since no effort was made by the counselor to gain data on vocational adjustment when this was not relevant to the person's primary problem, the counseling experience of these twenty persons is not uniformly valid in terms of isolating the factor of occupational stress in emotional disorder. Clients received from two to twenty-four hours of counseling each. The median number of hours was five. (Two had only two hours, eighteen had from three to six hours, two had ten hours and one had twenty-four hours.) Validation of one client's experience is available in the results of vocational testing administered by a clinical psychologist. Two clients have undergone extensive psychiatric treatment after counseling and have shared the insights gained in this experience with the counselor. Almost half (forty-five per cent) of the total sample have given progress reports to the counselor from six months to one year after counseling. Beyond this the validity of these findings must stand or fall upon the subjective perception of the counselor.

The findings will be presented under two headings: those whose emotional disturbances were due to *transient situational disorders* and those whose problems were due to *long-term personality disorder*. There were eight in the former, twelve in the latter group.

1. Transient Situational Disorders

One would assume that if occupational stress were a major factor in any person's disorder, it would appear in this group. Actually only one person had symptoms directly related to occupational stress. This person was threatened by the arrival of a younger, more adequate worker. Upon resolution of the inter-personal misunderstandings and after mutual clarification of job responsibilities, the client's symptoms disappeared.

Occupational stress played only an indirect role in the problems of three others in this group. Two of them were disturbed in the realization that graduation from seminary was imminent and the necessity of becoming breadwinner for the family was upon them. Both of them discovered in the process of counseling that their problem was not specifically related to their choice of the Christian ministry as a vocation but that it would have occurred in any other occupation. They were struggling against passive, dependent patterns of personality; they were afraid of competition and the strain of prolonged inter-personal relations. While more is expected of a minister than a bookkeeper, for example, the basic problem of taking a responsible, adult role in one's family and one's community would have been stressful for these persons in any vocational role.

For the remainder of those in this group the situations creating stress were marriage conflict and sexual maladjustment, unresolved parent-child conflicts, failure in courtship, and mental illness in the family. For none of these people was occupational stress a factor. This is not to say that difficulties in work relationships could not at a later time create the same kind of emotional disorder which they presented under the above circumstances. But it is to say that in the sample studied, occupational stress was an insignificant factor even among those whose disorder was due to transient situational stress.

2. Long-Term Personality Disorders

Twelve persons, or sixty per cent of the sample, were in trouble because of long-term personality disorders. As a group these people felt little anxiety about their personality disorder as such; they were anxious instead about the fact that their dreams were not coming true, their wishes were still unfulfilled. Most of them avoided close relations with others, were unable to express even ordinary aggressive feelings openly and were given to an active fantasy life, frequently with homosexual fantasy predominating. These persons tend to be cold, aloof, emotionally detached and fearful. They avoid competition. As children they were usually quiet, shy, obedient, sensitive and retiring. At puberty, they often became more withdrawn, and in mid or late adolescence attempted to handle their feelings of social inadequacy and moral impurity by religious fanaticism, making vows to God or developing a self-righteous or pharisaical pattern of relationship with others. Some of the persons in the group expressed in addition to the above traits much suspiciousness, feelings of being mistreated or persecuted, envy and bitterness, and self-pity. Many felt themselves unwanted and "as good as an orphan" in their parental homes. Many of the men recall vividly their shame in having been branded "sissy" or with other equally effeminate names. The presence of absentee or inadequate fathers and domineering, very religious mothers was common in their developmental histories. Still others were marked by long-term patterns of indecisiveness, helplessness and a tendency to cling to others. One was openly antisocial in sexual deviation. Others were marked by chronic, excessive concern with standards of conscience or of conformity and were overinhibited, overconscientious and had an inordinate capacity for work, lacking the normal capacity for relaxation.

Occupational stress was frequently presented by these persons as a source of their problems. For instance it was not uncommon for a young person to seek counseling because he was defeated in his effort to get married. He preferred not to marry, but felt marriage necessary to acceptance as a minister: "It will be hard to get a church if I'm not married and I'm almost ready to graduate from the seminary." Since he wishes to marry in order to fulfill the demands of his vocation, he can blame his sense of distress on being in a Christian vocation. Obviously such a conflict does not arise from being a minister, but from being a shy, socially inadequate and sexually immature person. The conflict conceivably could be less acute if one were entering another vocation, for in some areas the single person is less penalized for being a bachelor than in the ministry. But clients, themselves, usually recognized that their disorder was not vocationally rooted nearly so much as it was rooted in stunted personality growth.

Those who presented problems of homosexual fantasy frequently "blamed" them on stresses of functioning in a professional religious role. Uniformly the "temptation" was greatest when feeling inadequate as a minister. Feelings of inadequacy were stimulated by inter-personal ministries such as sick visitation, bereavement, calling or counseling. Moody feelings due to unsuccessful handling of hostile feelings also triggered temptation. Generally, however, homosexual fantasy became a problem before the person decided to enter a church-related vocation. Often the person put on the religious garb in the mood of one who would bargain with God and say: "If you will deliver me from this temptation, I will devote myself to your service." Regularly these persons were bitter against God for not living up to his end of the bargain. Other factors such as just having married or just having become a parent or just having had to face up to adult responsibility as a breadwinner usually attended the factor of occupational stress. Some clients felt that these factors were more important than occupational stress in causing homosexual feelings. Those who persevered in counseling discovered that their homosexual fantasies were designed as short-cut routes toward gaining the feeling of social and sexual adequacy, that they were secretly longing to draw strength from others rather than to cultivate it in themselves, that they were trying to relate to life generally in a passive, dependent role. Here again, occupational stress may be said to be an indirect factor in aggravating the emotional disorder, in that any kind of professional role requires a sense of personal adequacy. In less demanding roles a person might feel less sharply his inadequacy. But basically the disorders are rooted in long-term patterns of personality disorder.

Two common characteristics were apparent in the group of long-term personality disorders: (1) they have an inadequate self concept, (2) they have a distorted concept of vocation. These characteristics may be equally common to persons who do not present emotional disorders and they may be common to persons outside church-related vocations. Further research is needed at these points. But many of the clients involved in this sample felt that these factors were significantly related to their difficulties;

they made progress toward more adequate functioning in proportion as they came to grips with them in themselves. Thus we shall consider them briefly.

3. Inadequate Self Concept

Frequently in the course of counseling a person will label himself or the counselor will suggest a label which the client adopts for himself. Regularly the persons in this sample described themselves as "inadequate," "an orphan—deserving pity and indulgence," "a saint—overcome by 'the flesh,'" "a hero—an ideal person without a filthy mind," "the pharisee," "the outcast—forsaken by God," "a boy—blushing to admit I want a woman," "a wicked woman," "trash—the scum of the earth."

Behavior problems are rooted in self-concepts like these. A person who sees himself as the ideal husband, for instance, may deny his wife normal social contacts by being rude to friends who come in for an evening of conversation. He says: "I strive to be perfect and I'm afraid that their imperfections will rub off on me and I'll be tainted." Since an ideal husband is one who worships his wife, he must develop an elaborate set of rituals in helping her with the housework. This household help, however, may undermine the wife's self-confidence and breed emotional disorder in her personality. Marriage conflict will be sure to follow. Little improvement in the conflict can be expected until the husband sees how his picture of himself as "perfect" deprives his wife of the companionship she needs to feel secure. To experience himself as human rather than perfect will result in improved relationships at every level of life. But to experience one's self as human is to experience feelings of hostility and lust, to wish an escape from stress through alcoholic or other forms of intoxication, to acknowledge one's inadequacies, to crave companionship and to need to turn companions into comforters and protectors, to turn a wife into a mother, and to turn spontaneous children into conforming adults. Occasionally the counseling room becomes a safe enough place for a person to experience these feelings in himself and to assimilate them into a self-concept that is both honest and flexible.

4. Distorted Concept of Vocation

Distortions in the person's concept of vocation fit one or more of three patterns. (a) The concept that Christian vocation is superior to secular vocation. This assumes that the term Christian vocation is applicable only to full-time, paid, church-related vocations. The concept of Christian vocation as superior vocation enables the church worker to feel himself superior to those in non-church vocations. It is a piece of the larger cloth of the medieval two-story ethic, but it is very much in the fabric of some contemporary evangelical groups today. Alexander Miller[1] describes the two-story ethic by analogy with the medieval Benedictine Monastery in which a wooden screen was placed between the nave where ordinary Christians sat and the Choir with the Holy Table where the Monks sat.

This symbolized the double standard of the holy life: that there are two classes of men and only the separated can achieve maximum holiness. Those who are in secular vocations are involved in compromise with the evils of the political, social, and economic order.

(b) Closely related to the view that religious work is superior to non-religious work is the concept that a church-related vocation is a necessary or inevitable choice for one because he has always been "the good boy" or she has been "the good, sweet girl." John R. Mott said that to know a need and to have the capacity to meet the need constitutes a call. But these people act on the assumption that to need the approval of others as a "good boy" or "good girl" constitutes a call. Usually the "good boy" minister is one who has always been compliant with his mother's religious rigorism; he has been shy and withdrawn from his contemporaries; he frequently has suffered some organic inferiority such as obesity or bad eyesight; he has had little fun, has worked hard either to help support his family or to help in doing the housework of a demanding mother. In college, especially in church-related colleges, this person may become a Big-Man-On-Campus by virtue of his religious prestige. He has been branded by his

---

[1] *Christian Faith and My Job*, (New York: Association Press, 1946).

fellows as a religious zealot or fanatic long before he consciously makes his vocational choice. He may agonize over his "call to preach" but in honest reflection he may say: "I knew all the time that I could never be happy doing anything else."

Religious vocation for this person helps "to make me feel important and to help me overcome my timidity with other people." It may be a constructive factor enabling an extremely insecure person to break family ties and surmount the walls of partition between himself and others, but it may also be a destructive factor serving one's infantile need for short-cuts, the need to avoid normal competition for adult status and to postpone or escape the necessity of psychosexual growth toward marriage and parenthood.

(c) Others act as if vocation were a commodity to use in bargaining with God for special favors. This concept of vocation appears consistently among those who are suffering serious intrapsychic conflicts. One's commitment to religious work has the quality of a vow to God in return for which God is supposed to free the person from his deviant sexual wishes or his social isolation or his obscurity.

Divorced Ministers

BY SEWARD HILTNER
Professor of Pastoral Theology,
Federated Theological Faculty,
The University of Chicago,
Chicago, Illinois

Is the minister's "exemplary" function to be set above everything else? Or does the doctrine of universal priesthood imply that he can fail and acknowledge failure in marriage, as in other realms, since he is in God's eyes no better than other men?

It was almost ten years ago when the editor of *Pastoral Psychology* decided we should try to do something that would stimulate an appropriate type of public discussion of divorce among ministers. Over the past twenty years I have been consulted by a number of ministers who were divorced, or who were contemplating divorce, or who would have been contemplating divorce but for their being in the ministry. Simon Doniger and I wondered if it were possible to get some statements anonymously from ministers who had been divorced, that would shed light on the extent to which divorce among ministers is regarded as the same as or as different from divorce among other Christians.

At that time we published in *Pastoral Psychology* a list of five questions, asking any divorced ministers to write to me personally giving his own comment on each question. In addition, I was directly in touch with a few ministers. Several ministers wrote to me at once. But thereafter I found it exceedingly difficult either to have divorced ministers identified to me, or to have them reply when I wrote to them. Let it be confessed also that I was engaged in frying other fish as well; and the small number of net responses is probably due as much to that as to the reluctance of many ministers to comment.

Since 1953 this material has been set aside in the hope that it could some day be taken up on a larger scale. That time has not appeared. On looking over the available material recently, however, it has seemed to me that, although it is of no possible use statistically, some of the individual comments are of great importance and carry their own implications. In preparing this article, then, it is my hope that it will stimulate other ministers to write me their comment on the same five questions that will appear below. Perhaps eventually we shall have more comprehensive data.

I promised each of the men who answered the questions that the draft of any completed article would be sent to them for editing before publication. That has been done, and I am grateful to them for their time in reading the draft of this article, therefore, as well as for their contributing by commenting on the questions.

Because the number of respondents who gave answers to all five questions is so small, I am not identifying the respondents as Minister A, Minister B, and so on. I prefer to go too far in protecting the identity of each man. Thus, the first reported comment under one question is not necessarily from the same man as the first reported comment under another question.

This is in no way, shape, or form an attempt to discover why each minister was divorced. It attempts only to get comments on responses to him as a result of the divorce, or his own feelings on the extent to which his being a minister made a difference.

From here on we let these seven ministers speak for themselves.

1. Special Risks?

Our first question was as follows: *Out of your own experience with divorce, are you inclined to believe the minister who gets a divorce runs risks and confronts dangers different from those which would be encountered by other people?*

"The minister certainly does have to face up to many risks resulting from a divorce that other men do not have to face. Whether we like it or not, there is a sort of double standard, one for the minister and one for the non-minister, in the public mind. My former wife, before our divorce, used to tell our neighbors that I would never divorce her because a divorce would ruin me as a minister and that I was too proud to face that."

"Yes, the minister does run risks different from those faced by other ministers, or by other people who are divorced."

"Indeed a divorced minister encounters special risks and dangers, both personally and professionally. The very word 'divorce' still causes a chill to run up my back."

"Yes, a divorced minister does run risks and is confronted with dangers different from those of other people. However, I am not quite sure that I know what you really mean by the word danger."

"Yes. He is sometimes invited to take part in marriage counseling discussions; but when he is himself divorced, there may be questions both in his mind and in the minds of others. I was offered several positions in which I knew that members of the official board had disagreed about me owing to my being divorced. People tend to guess at the kind of trouble that brought on the divorce; and while they may be right or wrong, the content of the guesses usually involves the kind of thing they feel does not harmonize with the central purpose of the ministry. A minister's marriage is not a private affair. It is public."

"Yes, I believe that the minister does run special risks if he desires to stay in the ministry. The church I was serving was most understanding, and encouraged me to continue as its pastor which I did for a period. Later I declined to accept calls made to me when a minority was opposed to me on the grounds of my being divorced. Strange as it may seem, I believe I should have met less opposition in connection with those calls if I had then been remarried. I do want to testify that my ministerial brethren were considerate and helpful. The reason I feel the minister's risk is greater is this: he has seemingly been elevated to a lofty position of holiness in the thinking of many laymen, and the notion of his being divorced thrusts him down from their conception of his ivory tower. However, I think another reason, although an unconscious one, is that the divorce idea sometimes punctures the pride of lay church officials—to think that they should have chosen such a man as their shepherd. Some lay thinking seems to be along the line, 'Physician, heal thyself.' Or more often, 'If he hasn't been able to keep his family intact from this awful scourge, how can he guide the elect into paths of peace and harmony?' "

"Yes. There is probably no other profession where a divorce is as serious an obstacle to professional advancement. On the other hand, once the minister is in a parish, and the people have come to accept him, divorce and all, he is likely to be quite as effective as a marriage counselor, perhaps even more so, on the ground that people will think he knows what it is all about."

On the main point, these seven ministers are in agreement. Whatever the reasons, or the justification for them, divorce entails more risks for the minister than for others. Perhaps we may note especially the comment of the seventh minister immediately above, in indicating that eventually a divorced minister, if he makes it, may be able to help some people better than otherwise. The implication is plain, that, in this area, through choice or compulsion, ministers are felt to be successful; and those who are having troubles wonder whether the minister will understand. Let us hope this can be remedied without recommending wholesale divorce to the clergy.

2. *Delay?*

Our second question was: *When you were contemplating a divorce, but before a definite decision had been made, to what extent was your decision delayed because you were a minister?* Let the reader be reminded that the order in which the following comments appear is not necessarily the same as the replies to the first question above.

"In my personal experience, the decision probably should have been delayed longer than it was, as I now look back upon it. In general, I should say that while in theory a minister may have as much right as any other man to go through with it, considerations of the effect upon his congregation and possible reflections upon the profession in general ought to give him more than ordinary pause."

"I considered a divorce for a minister, specifically for myself, unthinkable at first. I saw myself as a hermit, off somewhere in the woods. I consented to the divorce only after receiving specific advice in that direction from church officers, physicians, and others."

"I did delay my decision, not because I doubted the need for a divorce, but because I was not prepared to do any other kind of work and I hated to give up the ministry. That caused me a great deal of anxiety, doubt and delay. I was afraid to seek direct counsel because I did not want to be told what to do."

"I delayed for a long time. I just could not see a minister getting a divorce in spite of the fact that this course was recommended to me by an ecclesiastical superior."

"I tried to forestall such a decision, and worked harder at it than I would have if I had not been a minister."

"Once I had reached a decision, I did not delay. But before the decision was reached, there was a very long delay owing largely to our having children."

"I was divorced before entering the ministry; so I cannot answer this question directly. However, had I been a minister at the time of the divorce, I believe the results would have been vastly different."

Here, again, the main line of testimony seems to be unanimous. Apparently every one of the ministers believes he delayed getting a divorce owing at least in part to the consequences this would have for his ministry. We note also that the men reveal quite different degrees of personal decision about their divorces, ranging all the way from the man who had this recommended to him by everybody to the man who did not want to consult anyone because he did not want to be told what to do. At least we can generalize this much: whatever benefit there may be to a cooling off period, these ministers have had it.

3. Discussion of Divorce?

Our third question was: *What policy have you followed concerning the discussion of your divorce? In the light of your own subsequent experience, has that policy proved the wise one?*

"I find this question very interesting and important. Frankly, I do not in any way inform people that I am a divorced person. I have not found it easy to inform new acquaintances of this part of my past. But if any person chooses to bring it up first, I am always glad to talk about it. Actually, this is the most uneasy part of my problem at present. I have not officially informed my present parish that I have been divorced, although some know about it from other sources. I feel that somehow the situation must be made public. Certainly I would not have any one feel I am deliberately hiding the facts."

"Unless I am asked specifically, 'Is your wife dead?' I simply represent myself as having been married and as having already reared a family, which I did. I am not often pressed with such a specific question. When that occurs, I simply admit that my wife is living and that we are divorced. So far that seems to be the wisest policy for me. I cannot see denying the fact; neither can I see making it a topic of general conversation."

"Since my divorce I have been in several local churches. In the first church those who were interested to have me looked over spoke of my divorce to the congregation even before official negotiations began, and they took me. Perhaps they were pretty desperate for a minister! When I moved to another church, the divorce was not mentioned until the Pulpit Committee sat down to talk with me personally. They too assured me this would make no difference; and like the first church, they made good on this assurance. In later years, however, I found that when recommendations on my behalf were made to other churches where I was not personally known, and mentioned divorce, this proved often to be an insuperable barrier."

"My policy has been: the less said the better, although I have discussed it in groups when my experience has seemed to have potential value for others."

"At first I told those with whom I was to be associated. A wise minister counseled against this as it would indicate I felt guilty about the divorce. After that I did not tell about the divorce. It is difficult to know which course is correct. Some people have held it against me for not telling them. Yet others, whom I have told, have assured me it made no difference and then proceeded to demonstrate that it did. In general, I believe those who would not give a man a break after such an experience are the same people who would cause difficulty in other areas as well. In this, I may be biased, but intolerance in one area usually carries over to others. I do believe that general and free discussion of one's divorce is unwise; but at specific points of one's ministry it may prove quite important to say something about it."

"The less said, the better. It is impossible to present a complete picture."

"I have discussed it as little as possible, and only with people who have some right to know because of either personal or professional relationships. I believe that course has been wise. Occasionally embarrassing things happen, but the risk of these seem less than having to discuss the whole thing publicly."

Although we find that these seven men followed a variety of courses, most of them agree eventually that the discussion should be limited in some specific ways but not cut off entirely. One man notes himself as still in dilemma on the point. Another reports his relative openness worked well when he knew the people personally but was a handicap when he did not. As a group, the men lean toward saying as little as possible.

4. The Unexpected?

Our fourth question asked: *Have you found unusual or unexpected acceptance of your situation in some quarters or, conversely, unusual or unexpected rejection or condemnation?*

"Cordial acceptance in some circles but also frigid relationships in others."

"More unexpected acceptance than otherwise. My local com-

munity as well as church was virtually unanimous in its understanding, and my work was not affected. On the other hand, the
man who came closest to being an 'ecclesiastical superior' was
most condemnatory, even to the point of denying the attitude of
the local community. Another minister of my denomination is
considering a divorce at present but believes his community
would not tolerate it even though his wife is the offender on
biblical grounds. Perhaps there is a real difference in communities
and local churches."

"My experience was to find acceptance when the people knew
me personally, but to find rejection and even bitterness when
they did not."

"This is a hard question to answer. I realize that I am rejected
by certain people although they are a minority. After my divorce
I became interested in a girl and did not at first tell her of my
divorce. When she discovered this later on, her reaction was negative, and I found it hard to explain my reasons for withholding
the information."

"I have found some people who resented it when I did not inform them, and others whose actions showed they resented it
when I did. But in contrast, there have been many who have
been more accepting than I expected."

"On the whole, both my relatives and friends have been almost
unbelievably accepting. I have found nothing from any quarter
in the way of unusual condemnation."

"I have found both unusual acceptance and unusual rejection.
The acceptance has come from those who really know me, and
from some who knew my former situation. This is true of fellow
ministers as well as of parishioners. The unusual rejection has
come from those who did not know me personally but to whom
I had been recommended by those who did. Very often I found
them accepting me until they found out my divorce, and then
changing their attitude completely."

These comments speak for themselves. There does appear to be
a real difference in the abstract attitude to a divorced minister
who is personally known.

5. Advice to Others?

Our fifth and last question was: *Sitting on your own private cracker barrel, what would you be inclined to say to the minister who is considering a divorce, from the point of view of your own experience?*

"I refuse to concede to the inevitability of divorce for any reasons other than the refusal to face the issues by one party or both. I believe that no problems are insoluble to two Christians who seek to follow our Master, especially with both psychiatric and pastoral help available to supplement the usual Christian resources."

"A divorce is only a last resort to give a man legal protection against an irreconcilable woman who has made marriage impossible. The divorces I have helped to prevent through my pastoral work were avoided by bringing the man down from his 'almighty throne' and helping him to accept himself as a person not a god."

"This is the easiest question of the five. Divorce may be called a necessary evil in certain cases. However, I am greatly opposed to divorce. I do feel, though, that in many cases people condemn a divorced person too quickly. I strongly advise any minister who is considering divorce to search his heart and make every possible effort of reconciliation before he takes the final action, and then only through long periods of prayer and meditation. If divorce proves to be the sole alternative, I cannot overemphasize that a minister should never be the guilty party in the divorce. I realize that much is involved in the phrase 'guilty party,' and I have no wish to condemn others, but this does seem important in the light of Christian faith."

"To a minister contemplating a divorce, I should not want to say invariably a Yes or a No. But in view of the proper and inevitable function of a minister to 'set an example' (with a capital 'E'), he ought to explore with more than ordinary application every possible way to prevent it. On the other hand, I think a minister is not called upon to continue an intolerable marriage just because he is a minister, although he must be prepared to take the consequences."

"People in most churches will go to any length to sympathize with and help a minister who has a marriage problem, so long as they think it is his wife's fault; but even so, a large number will question his decision to get a divorce. The question of remarriage is also difficult and raises additional questions. I suppose we must admit that, to the public, almost any marriage, however bad, is more acceptable than a divorce, where a minister is involved."

"Definitely, a divorce should be the last resort."

"I would ask the minister to consider the risks involved and how far he is willing to carry his determination to straighten out a mess. A man can secure a divorce and still be a minister, but he may have to change his type of work and his section of the country. Personally, I am convinced that there are more ministers who need to be divorced so far as their creative contribution is concerned. Ministers are not different from other people. As a group they are no better prepared for marriage than others, and do not understand their motivations better than others."

Additional comments are offered by two of our respondents. One writes, "Like every other thoughtful person, the minister ought to be sure before he marries that it will be, so far as it is humanly possible to predict, the right marriage. But he ought to be 50% more sure, if that is possible, of probable compatibility, of his fiancee's interest in his future work and her willingness to share its possible hardships as well as its possible joys, of agreement about children, and all the other factors. For he has to take into consideration that he stands *in loco paternis* to his adult congregation, to his young people and to the children of his parish, in a way which no other professional man does, and in good conscience he ought to exercise the utmost possible care to make a home which shall be Christian."

And the other writes, "Two things are implied. First, we need better preparation for marriage. Second, we need better understanding of our own motivations, and this is always difficult. One may not be responsible for the limitations of neurotic patterns in himself; but unless he does what is needed to get hold of these, they will affect his marriage."

6. Conclusion

We have drawn such conclusions as seem warranted by the data as each point has been discussed. If a minister gets divorced regardless of the reason, he runs more risks than would another person. In every instance the divorce itself was delayed at least in part because the man was a minister. No divorced minister wholly denied his situation in dealing with others, but the best policy seemed to be to say as little as necessary. Most of the men testify both to unusual acceptance and unusual rejection owing to their being divorced, showing in part a difference between knowing the particular minister and considering his divorce in the abstract. All our divorced ministers counsel caution on divorce, which is to be seen as only a last resort.

We present these anonymous comments from seven men to stand on their own feet and present their own conclusions. Our study says nothing about how representative they are. Other things being equal, I would suggest that men willing to make available these comments would be a group considerably above average in sense of social responsibility. Remember also that all these men have remained in the ministry.

An eventual understanding of divorce, or threatened divorce, among ministers will require many things not even mentioned here. Some of them can be helped by better facts. For instance, do ministers tend to marry certain types of women, or vice versa? What types of husband-wife relationships might get along under some conditions but not in those required by the ministry? Other questions demand more than facts. Is the minister's "exemplary" functions to be set above everything else? Or does the doctrine of universal priesthood imply that he can fail and acknowledge failure in this realm as in others, since he is in God's eyes no better than other men? Is the general position of any church about divorce threatened especially by potential divorce among its ministers? And there are many others.

We hope that other ministers will write us after reading this article. We promise the same anonymity as is demonstrated here.

PART FIVE

THE INCIDENCE AND KINDS
OF ILLNESS AMONG MINISTERS

OLDER conceptions of the threat of hell and destruction have lost much of their force, but they are returning in the garb of ministers' discussions of mental illness. Consequently, when a minister decides he was not cut out to be a minister, his fellow ministers are likely to assume that he is "cracking up." However, when other men in other types of work decide to change their work they do not necessarily interpret this as a sign of mental disorder. Nor do they interpret unrest with the status quo in their professions as a sure sign of maladjustment. But ministers are likely to do so.

The imperative necessity of discovering ways and means of strengthening the spiritual fiber of the ministry is apparent even to the casual observer. Nor does this mean that we are seeking to find tensionless, mythically normal, and insipidly average men for the ministry. I agree with Professor Daniel Day Williams when he says that it is not even desirable that we screen out every candidate for the ministry who shows some potential mental disturbance in the offing. On the contrary, some of these men—

given adequate therapy, guidance, and a wholesome education—can become remarkably helpful and discerning ministers. When all the research is added up, we must count in the fact that the biographies of George Fox, John Bunyan, Frederick W. Robertson, H. Wheeler Robinson, George Truett, E. Stanley Jones, Harry Emerson Fosdick, Anton Boisen, and many others, reveal accounts of varyingly serious kinds of emotional disturbances.

But a moving line of distinction needs to be tracked here. The admissions committees of theological seminaries can reveal other biographies of men seeking entrance into the ministry for whom mental illness is not an episode or even a series of episodes, but a chronic way of life. Furthermore we need to cast all that we have to say here against the background of the most positive understandings of the meaning of health itself.

One such conception is set forth by Foote and Cottrell when they say that in the component of health "we include much more than the absence of disease. Rather it signifies the progressive maximization—within organic limits—of all its physiological functions, and to achieve its maximum of sensory acuity, strength, energy coordination, dexterity, endurance, recuperative power and immunity."[1]

---

[1] Nelson N. Foote and Leonard S. Cottrell, Jr., *Identity and Interpersonal Competence*. (Chicago: University of Chicago Press, 1955), p. 52.

The Hazards of High Callings

By John P. Kildahl, Ph.D.,
Clinical Psychologist,
New York City, New York

A deeply perceptive psychotherapist who has had ministerial train-
ing and some parish experience is aware of the subtle but signifi-
cant error that can be made by one who practices a "high calling,"
be he preacher or physician or psychoanalyst or political states-
man. This is when "personal needs become so enmeshed with the
program he espouses that one cannot determine where one stops
and the other starts."

Most ministers are in the predicament of being in a vocation they believe the most important vocation in the world. This is an awesome responsibility; and the responsibility of feeling that one is engaged in the world's most important work carries with it certain unique hazards to one's mental health.

The Ministers Sense of Responsibility

Where could a minister be found who ever believed that his work was done? Or who ever heard a minister say that his work had been done in such a way that it left little or nothing to be desired? One may find ministers who would like to be doing something else rather than being a minister, but rarely could a minister be found who believed that any other profession was more important.

In the eyes of many religious people, there is an aura about the ministry which is not true of any other profession. The medical doctor may have greater status, the attorney may be more feared, but the clergyman is expected to be more "wholly other." His motivations are expected to be more noble, his calling more sacred, his thoughts more pure, his life more dedicated, his sacrifices more generous.

The image of the minister did not develop without reason. It is true that many persons like to invest any father figure with near-divine attributes. But it is also true that clergymen have fostered the idea that "full time Christian service" in the vocation of the ministry is something set apart and different from other callings. Why else do we have Christian service flags which adorn the front of the churches to indicate the number of young men from the congregation who have entered the ministry? There is no other vocation that is similarly honored. And is it not true that there is a special kind of honor accorded by the pastor to those young men whom he steers toward the ministry?

The Feeling of Urgency

It is not our concern here, to interpret what motivations might underlie this unique position accorded the clergy. Rather, the purpose here is to describe some of the consequences of this attitude, particularly in regard to the mental health of the clergyman.

The minister continually feels the urgency of his calling. The task of the church and of its pastors is to call men to faith, to nurture them in the faith, and to help them express their faith in loving service. The grandeur of this task, as well as its immensity, is what complicates making an accurate appraisal of a minister's dedication to his task.

One need not be with a minister very long before one is impressed with his frequent use of phrases like: I must; I ought; I should; I am trying to; I hope to get that done soon; etc. One might well sound positively impious disagreeing with these imperatives which the minister feels to be upon himself. Surely, isn't the minister on the side of the angels? Who could disagree with "doing good"?

But the potential difficulty lies in the fact that the minister says *I* ought, or *I* should, or *I* must.

The capacities people have for self-deception is enormous. That includes ministers, of course. It is generally bad form to criticize a minister—particularly when it is obvious that he is working so hard, and for such a good cause. But in the ministry as elsewhere, one can be doing the right thing for the wrong reason. Our vision may be particularly clouded when evaluating ministers, since their purposes and goals are so "right," at least in the eyes of most of us. But the dangers are particularly subtle precisely since the minister's work is considered so vital. His own personal needs may become so immeshed with the program he espouses; that one cannot determine where one stops and the other starts.

The Dangers of Singleness of Purpose

In the case of the clergy—as indeed in all the helping professions—there is a danger that his vocation may become his whole life—his whole reason for living. Whenever this happens, one becomes so closely identified with his work that he cannot separate himself from it. His vocation then becomes his sole source of emotional security, i.e., the fulfillment of his wishes for prestige, self-respect and the respect of society.

For anyone so entirely wrapped up in his vocation, any failure in his work becomes an intensely personal failure—with attendant emotional distress.

The subtle danger a clergyman faces is that when he says "I must build the church"—his underlying emphasis might be on the *I must* rather than on *the church,* as it should be. Since his own needs for security are basic to his whole sense of equilibrium —and if his whole life is absorbed in the good cause of building the church—he is therefore unwittingly *using* the church to maintain his emotional security and his integrity as a person. The consequence is that the building of the church and the promotion of the church's activities is a *means* to an end—the end being the minister's needs for self-respect, success and personal dignity.

I do not mean here to belittle in any way a person's right to self-respect and the respect of his society. I do believe it is unfortunate to need to *use* the church as a means to this end.

Using the Church to Satisfy Personal Needs

We have all heard the pastor who exclaims "I *have to get* this program across this year." It is as if the Kingdom of God were one and the same as his "program." A person with psychological insight will recognize that his great vehemence indicates that the minister is then motivated by his own personal, emotional needs. Since the program may nevertheless be an excellent one, we may be deceived. But the minister's close personal identification with his pet project is an indication that he is *using* the project to satisfy some need of his own. If a project is not a personally motivated one, then its defeat will not be a major catastrophe, but only a minor disappointment which has nothing to do with the minister's feeling of his own self-worth and self-respect.

The point is this: a minister must have enough avenues of gaining security and satisfaction in his *nonprofessional* life so that he need not use his parish or parishioners as a means for gaining that security and satisfaction. Failure in this regard means that unknowingly he will *need* to add church members, or gain converts, or raise a larger budget, or be a successful pastoral counselor. Again, all this is complicated by the fact that these may be worthy causes. But in the long run, others will sense that the minister is using his parish to satisfy his own emotional needs. Eventually, it will appear that his converts are like so many trophies in his trophy room, or that his counselees have been used to prove what a good counselor he is, or that the size of the budget is primarily evidence that he is a good businessman.

The Need for Nonprofessional Satisfactions

It is in the minister's nonprofessional life that he should gain his security and satisfaction. Else there is a danger that the minister does not help people for *their* sakes, but for his own. An analagous situation is the work of a psychotherapist. (On this same matter, compare Frieda Fromm-Reichmann, *Principles of Intensive Psychotherapy,* University of Chicago Press, 1950.) A psychotherapist must not *need* to see his patients get well. It must not become a matter of emotional life or death to the therapist what the outcome of therapy is. If a certain case becomes very important to the therapist, it is evidence that the therapist is gratifying his own emotional needs through his patient; he is using the patient, rather than being of use to the patient. Most patients will intuitively sense that the therapist is exerting pressure on him to get well. This, in turn, sets up a resistance on the part of the patient, since in some way he senses that he is being used. The psychotherapist must be free enough of his own problems so that he can give to the patient, and not expect or need the patient to give in return. The therapist's unacknowledged and unsatisfied emotional needs not only render him ineffective, but they also create more problems for his patient.

This comparison with the psychotherapist certainly illustrates the need for the pastoral counselor to be free of needs to use his counselee. But in a wider sense, the same situation obtains in all the work of a pastor in his parish. It is altogether too easy to be blind to the way in which a pastor uses his parish, because on the surface his work appears to be so altruistic. When the pastor *needs* to see people converted, or saved from divorce or to be faithful church attenders—he then should be alert to the fact that he is using these parishioners as a means by which he proves his abilities, and from which he derives his elemental emotional gratifications.

Many pastors tend to think that precisely because their work is so important, it is therefore worthy to occupy their every waking moment. The promotion of the faith becomes their whole existence. They eat, sleep, and breathe religion and religious programs. It is then all too easy to make of all of life's activities a means for promoting this religious life—the pastor's own, or that of his parishioners.

Since everyone needs and pursues emotional gratifications, the pastor's religion may tend to become virtually his *sole* source of that gratification. It is absolutely erroneous to think that a minister's pursuit of the faith makes him above or outside the need for these emotional gratifications. It is instead true that any person will use those avenues that are available to gain his gratifications. If the work of the church is his whole life, from it the minister will be forced to gain all those things which make him feel worthwhile—the successful use of his powers, skills, and interpersonal relationships.

Five Elemental Emotional Needs

The minister, naturally enough, has emotional needs that must be met. It is folly to assume that because he is a minister, his needs are less intense, or that they can go unmet. A list of some of these important needs include: 1) a feeling of self-esteem and moral worth; 2) a feeling of being able to cope with one's environment; 3) meaningful interpersonal relationships; 4) the satisfaction of physical functions—oral, excretory, genital and motor; and 5) a unifying view of life that gives coherence and direction to one's existence.

Wittingly or unwittingly, the minister will use every means at his disposal to gain the satisfaction of these needs—or else suffer emotionally when they go unmet, or what is even worse, when they go unacknowledged by himself. The purpose of this paper is to point out the tragedy that occurs when a minister has *only* his church work as his *only* means for him to gain his life satisfactions. It is the common error of putting all the eggs in one basket. The work of the minister then suffers—he presses too hard, he becomes too involved to be objective, he suffers personally with every minor delay in the church's program, and his parishioners begin to resent the fact that they are being used by him.

The Healthy Pursuit of Emotional Gratifications

What then should the minister do? He should make sure that his nonprofessional life is so satisfying that he need not use the church's activities or people as a means for gaining his sense of well-being. He should have nonprofessional activities and relationships which supply the inevitable needs he has for self-respect, success, and personal dignity. The time he spends, and the things that he does away from his job, should be creatively satisfying, rewarding and fulfilling. If at all possible, he should become even an expert at something which has absolutely nothing to do with his professional work as a minister.

He should be able to feel that he is a decent and adequate person—even when he preaches the world's worst sermon, has his official church board ready to lynch him, and sorely offends the president of the Ladies Aid. If he can be this free of the pressures which surround him, it is almost axiomatic that he will do great work in his parish. But he will be a slave, rather than a servant of his parish, if he *needs* his parish to give him life satisfactions. If his own personal self-esteem rises and falls with the climate of the church council meeting, then the minister will lack the freedom necessary to do a creative task.

When the minister takes care to satisfy the five emotional needs noted above, but satisfies them largely outside his strictly professional life—then he will bring to his work a vigor and objectivity which will free the best of his own potentialities. It is therefore essential that the minister work at achieving an emotionally satisfying and independent life for himself and for his family. Despite how important he feels his profession is, and how much work there is to be done—it is essential to his own mental health, and to the effectiveness of his work itself that he pursue and achieve the satisfaction of his important emotional needs. But he must not use the church as a means to this end!

It is not selfish to desire and work toward one's own good mental health, as indeed it is not selfish to work toward good physical health. It is said for example, that the immense cost of a fullscale psychoanalysis will be more than paid for if it adds one productive year to a person's life. This is true in general for the pursuit of all good mental health habits.

Summary

To conclude, it is the concern of this paper that a minister have enough sources of satisfaction and security in his nonprofessional life so that he is not tempted to use his parishioners for the attaining of those needs. The pastor must be free of the need to use his parishioners; otherwise he is not working primarily for the parishioners' well-being, but rather for his own needs for success. He must not *need* to see people converted, nor counseled successfully, nor saved from divorce. This would be only using these parishioners as a means by which the pastor proves his abilities. To guard against this danger, in a work so important as the ministry, is a difficult task. But it can be done when the pastor works at having a successful and satisfying private life. Such a private life pays dividends in the mental health of the pastor, and in parish work well done.

Facts and Fantasy in the Minister's Mental Health*

By JAMES E. DITTES
Instructor, Psychology of Religion,
Yale University Divinity School,
New Haven, Connecticut

We seem to be able all too easily to write articles on "Why ministers break down," but we too readily eschew the difficult and undramatic task of determining whether they really are breaking down . . .

Scientific inquiry has moved only slowly and painfully from the remote to the intimate, from the distant stars to the inner life of man. It is easy to be careful and objective about the movements of stars. But about the still more subtle movements of mental life there are so many nonobjective reasons for seeking one conclusion rather than another that scientific rigor comes hard.

It is difficult to imagine an observer of the stars or rocks protecting his ego or venting his hostilities by asserting an astronomical equation or denying the existence of a geological structure. But it is not even necessary to imagine—too many instances abound—that a person may defend conclusions concerning, let

* Preparation of this article was supported in part by Grant M-648 from the Institute of Mental Health, Public Health Service.

us say, the mental health of ministers, with no more substantial basis than the desire to believe something true or untrue.

On such a subject, so much is at stake personally. Potent threats to one's own self-image and stability seem to be involved. The need to believe or disbelieve certain facts is correspondingly powerful. At the same time, the realm of available facts is so pitifully weak that the motives to believe or disbelieve have clearly controlled most consideration of the problem of the mental health of ministers.

Thus it seems the more necessary to keep prominently in the fore some of the rules of procedure which we all acknowledge as basic to honest inquiry but which become clouded or lost in the heat of conflict, either "inter" or "intra" personal.

Science is concerned with two kinds of questions: What? and Why? (or sometimes How?). So is anyone who is interested in the mental health of ministers. What are the facts? And how are the facts to be interpreted? There is a natural priority in answering these questions. Science has long made it a rule not to try to explain things which aren't so. But this is tormentingly frustrating to the creative, imaginative mind. Facts are such difficult things to acquire, especially the most interesting and important facts, such as those concerning the mental health of ministers. Yet our fertile and creative minds strain to be unleashed with their brilliant theories to explain the facts. We tend, for example, to write articles on *why* juvenile delinquency is increasing, or *why* morality is on the decline, or "why ministers are breaking down." But we too readily eschew the difficult and undramatic task of determining *whether* these things are happening.

The discipline of prior fact-gathering is perhaps the most obvious restriction that needs to be put on our high-soaring ingenuity. But it is by no means the least. Human powers of invention and rationalization are rich enough, and human needs for clear and certain explanations are powerful enough so that theories about everything abound plentifully and in plausible guise. There need to be some rules for screening the more probable from the less probable. Science has gradually evolved such rules, and this paper proposes to list a few of them.

1. "I knew a man once . . ."

"Let me tell you about a minister I knew who had a nagging wife who finally got too much for him, and he had to be hospitalized. I've seen it over and over. A nagging wife makes ministers crack up."

We have deliberately chosen for illustration here an improbable theory. But in the statement above, for "wife" we may substitute "conscience," "schedule," "congregation," "ambition," or some other supposed cause; and for "hospitalized" we may substitute "leave the ministry," "start taking pills," "take a leave of absence," "begin psychoanalysis," or some other alleged sign of mental illness; and we have a sample of the kind of foundation on which rests most of our thinking, public and private, about mental health of ministers. This is the level of evidence and interpretation that appears in the popular press, discussion groups, forum question periods, and even in some of the best research reports.

The basic facts in such a statement could be absolutely sound. The minister may have a nagging wife and he may be hospitalized. But in a dozen ways gross error can intrude between fact and conclusion and render the conclusion utterly invalid and dangerously misleading. Yet the step of transition from sound fact to unsound conclusion may be hardly noticeable. This paper undertakes to make them more noticeable.

2. "This is the cause."

Our usual approach is something like this: We see a man's nagging wife and we hear of his mental breakdown, two "facts" that we know about him, and something compels us to put one and one together; to say "this caused that." We seem unconsciously to assume that out of the intricate pattern of this person's life, the one or few things that we happen to know about him also happen to be those most responsible for the state of his mental health.

Of the complex factors—feelings and conflict, fears and wants, experiences and relationships, aspirations and apprehensions—

which determine a person's mental health or illness, another person can know only a tiny part. Even after weeks of intensive testing, observation, and interview, a staff of sensitive experts may still be baffled. Further, that fractional part we know of another's personality is only that which is accessible to the casual observer. But a person's mental health depends so much more on the inner dynamic forces of wants and fears seeking resolution. About these we know little enough in our own lives, much less in another's.

But unless we speak out and assert our "explanations," our silences seem to confess ignorance, fallibility, and impaired omniscience, which is so often personally intolerable, especially to those of us in the ministry who are accustomed to the role of Explainer and Answerer of questions. So we point out that little which we know: "He had a nagging wife" (or: schedule, ambition, conscience, etc.), and we spin our gossamer theories to show how this caused the illness.

If we are undertaking research complete with questionnaire and statistics, the dilemma may be only worsened. Most research instruments are limited to measurement of relatively external and superficial facts—a minister's denomination, the number of his children, the way he distributes his time, etc. Without painstaking design and administration of more sensitive measuring devices than have been used in any research yet on this problem, the researcher has an accumulation of facts which are even less likely than casual, but personal, observations to be intimately related to conditions of mental health. On the other hand, having launched his project, the researcher is even more committed to producing some conclusions and under even stronger pressures than most of us to assign explanatory power to the facts he has accumulated.

The problem may be still worsened if a writer is using another person's research, especially research which has been well conducted and has been successful in illuminating some particular problem. Even though the questions for which the other research sought answers are almost certain to be somewhat different from those the "borrowing" writer is discussing, the prestige of a carefully accumulated body of data may be so great that these facts may be rushed in to fill the interpretative gap. Their irrelevance can be easily obscured with a sufficiently imaginative theory explaining their pertinence. For example, if the best recent research on ministers (although undertaken for reasons quite other than to study their mental health) happens to relate to the multiplicity of roles a minister fills, then this is what is best known about the ministry as a whole and becomes the candidate for the position of "explanation" or "cause"—just as for an individual minister, his nagging wife may be the best known characteristic and therefore the "explanation" for whatever happened to him.

The factors which we single out as "cause" may be quite unrelated to the actual causative factors. It may be a sheer accident that a particular man had both a nagging wife and some mental instability. Or there may be a relationship, but one different and far more intricate than we suppose. The nagging wife may be related to illness but not as the simple cause. It may be, for example, that the behavior of a man, which justifiably provokes the nagging, expresses certain personality needs—we may summarize them here as Condition X—which have also impaired his general adjustment enough to produce the illness. Condition X, for example, could be frustration-provoked feelings of hostility which the minister finds no way to express except in these types of subtle neglect and domestic discord which provoke nagging retaliation and by eventually breaking abruptly and violently from some of the restraints in a manner characterized as mental illness. The nagging may be empirically correlated with the illness. But it is not the cause. Condition X, rather, is the cause *both* of the nagging and of the illness. It may be perfectly true to say that if the nagging hadn't occurred, neither would the illness; for absence of a nagging wife would have suggested absence of the critical Condition X. But the transition we make so easily from the true statement of correlation to a false assertion of causation bridges a vast difference in facts.

If there happened to be any factual evidence, which there is not, that hectic schedules were correlated with mental illness, this would provide no more basis for concluding that hectic schedules produce mental illness than for the opposite conclusion, that the mental illness produces the hectic schedule. A minister in the early phases of mental illness may already have lost enough perspective and judgment and be unduly sensitive to the demands of others, so that he accepts a far heavier work load than he would under normal conditions. Or, a minister sensing the onset of mental illness may throw himself into a frantic schedule of activity in a desperate effort to affirm his competence and to forget himself in the preoccupations of a hectic calendar.

Still another group of interpretations with equal right to be heard would suppose that the hectic schedule and mental illness were produced by a common cause but have no direct relation with each other. It may be, for example, that the same internal conflicts and frustrations which eventually result in the mental illness also produce frantic work activity as an earlier effort to deal with them.

There is admittedly no available evidence to support any one of these or many other possible alternative interpretations proposed to account for a correlation between heavy work schedules and mental illness, just as there is no evidence that such a correlation exists in the first place. These alternatives do have one merit. They all recognize, as the simple theory of overwork causing breakdown does not, that a heavy working schedule is not exclusively determined by external demands on a minister, but has more psychological roots, too, in the needs and demands of the minister's own psyche.

To summarize abstractly, when phenomena A and B are correlated, the pattern of causation may be that A causes B, as we most easily suppose, or it may just as likely be that B causes A, and it is perhaps most likely that A and B are independently both caused by another factor, C. Psychological phenomena being as complex as they are, notions of simple, direct causation should be highly suspect.

3. "I've seen it over and over."

The central problem discussed above is that any interpretation or explanation of a phenomenon such as mental illness which is based on one set of facts runs the risk of overlooking even more important facts and interpretations. To have any confidence in one interpretation, we need to have grounds for ruling out alternatives. Ruling out alternative explanations is the main business of science, and to this task it brings a large arsenal of procedures, none of them infallible, but each of them decreasing the probability of error.

If a factor is really important in mental illness, it should appear in repeated instances. The value of repeated cases is popularly recognized even in casual statements in which we try to strengthen an argument by claiming repeated identical observations. Actually, the scientific requirement for repeated instances is a necessary, but by no means a sufficient, condition for scientific conclusion-drawing.

Piling up evidence is not a fool-proof procedure. Or better, it is not a *wish*-proof procedure. Confirming cases are too easily sought out and remembered, and disconfirming cases are too easily overlooked and forgotten, even by persons with the best scruples. To overcome this natural tendency, science has learned that one needs to specify in advance just what cases will be examined, then keep a record and report on all of these.

Even in the most sophisticated research, there is a strong tendency, not always resisted, to discard or ignore negative instances on grounds of one rationalization or another: "This man didn't seem to understand the question, or he gave 'incomplete replies.' " "That one has two freckles on his nose, and I didn't really intend to include freckled persons in my sample." Etc. Until the pile of negative cases is whittled down to negligible size, and the original theory triumphs, vindicated by the remaining 50% of the cases, those with confirming results.

Problems of selective attention and memory are troublesome enough in exact sciences with rigorously defined concepts and measures. But the problem is a thousand-fold more serious when dealing with such vaguely defined things as a nagging wife, or repressed hostilities, or mental health. Here, even the most conscientious investigator finds evidence of nagging in the sweetest of wives and signs of maladjustment in the healthiest of men when it fits his theory to do so. And likewise, he is particularly sensitive to the extenuating circumstances, when appropriate to his theory, so that what looks at first like nagging or neurosis can be seen as something else again.

This problem sharpens the other horn of the dilemma faced by a questionnaire-writer. On the one hand, questionnaires tend to deal with externals. To minimize this we are likely to use more open-ended questions, giving respondents more chance to express themselves in their own way. But though this gives us more personal responses, it also gives us less manageable material, into which we are more likely to read the answer that we want to find. In general, as research methods try to probe more deeply and more meaningfully into personality (as with Rorschach or other projective tests, for example), the more they tend to abandon sharp, objective definitions and measures, and the more they become vulnerable to the subjective whims of the researcher.

Three related solutions have been found by science. Research without any two of these three precautions should be suspect. Even when dressed up with tables of statistics based on hundreds of cases, the conclusions may be no more valid than those based on the casual observation of one case.

1. Whatever is to be observed and measured must be thought through thoroughly enough in advance that its defining characteristics can be objectively specified. Presence or absence of nagging or neurosis must be determined by reference to an objective comprehensive definition and not left to the realm of after-the-fact subjective judgment, into which personal preferences so easily intrude. Such advance definition is hard work and is often avoided with the excuse that neurosis (or whatever is being measured) cannot be pinned down, that it can be identified only by some sort of intuitive clinical judgment of a total complex pattern. The fact remains that whatever cues or complex pattern of cues on which such judgment is eventually based can equally well be specified in advance. It just requires hard conceptual labor to do so; in many instances, formidably hard.

2. When more subjective judgments must be relied on, two or more persons should be able to agree reasonably well on the

judgments, or else there is reason to suppose that one or both is subject to whim or bias. If something real is being judged, and it is being judged reliably, there is no reason for disagreement.

3. Bias should be reduced by depriving judges of all possible biasing information. The judge should know only the definition of that characteristic, e.g., neurosis, whose presence and degree he is trying to determine. He should not know how a person has been rated on other characteristics, e.g., nagginess of wife, whose supposed relationship with neurosis is being tested. Otherwise he can too easily let his knowledge of the wife's disposition influence his decision on the degree of neurosis. The research then will not demonstrate a relation between nagging and neurosis in the life of the minister, but only the relation between these two in the mind of the researcher. Ideally, the judge should not even know the hypothesis being tested. This leaves him free to examine the total life of the minister, without fear of having his judgment biased for or against the hypothesis by exposure to contaminating information.

The desire to prove one's own theory correct is such an overwhelming and universal a human trait that the burden of proof is on the researcher to provide evidence that this desire has not been allowed to influence the results. Unless clear safeguards are announced—and they must be more fool-proof than good intentions to be honest—the most likely explanation for any set of results is that cases have been unwittingly selected and definitions and categories variously stretched and twisted so as to make the results what they are. This explanation needs to be ruled out before we can consider as another possible explanation the theory or interpretation which the researcher believes he has proved.

4. Repetition with a Purpose

Since simple multiplication of cases does not, by itself, prove anything, what is needed is a more discriminating kind of repetition, a repetition with a purpose, so that each additional positive instance does make a theory more certain and alternative theories less certain. Three ways of refining such repetition can be listed under the categories of *cross-validation, sampling,* and *controlled comparisons.*

Looking at one case of apparent mental breakdown, we may propose the hypothesis that overwork was the cause. The designation of overwork, it should be recalled, is in competition with the myriad other known and unknown facts of this man's life, or with any pattern of them. If the theory is true, it should be possible to show in repeated instances that overworked ministers are more likely to be mentally ill than other ministers. This should be true even when looking at overworked ministers who are very dissimilar in all respects except this factor of overwork. Overwork needs to be isolated from all other possible causes. If it causes mental illness, it should do so alike for fat and thin, aggressive and meek, successful and unsuccessful, nagged and beloved—in anyone who is overworked, regardless of other characteristics. Failing this kind of general demonstration, or "cross-validation," the most that can be salvaged from the original theory is the supposition that overwork must interact with other factors and that it is the *pattern* of overwork in combination with other characteristics which leads to mental illness. Perhaps more properly, the failure of such a cross-validation should lead to the opinion that overwork was not even the critical factor in the original observed case. Note that in the absence of such a cross-validating procedure, we can assume only that the procedure would *not* support the theory. There are more false theories abroad than true, and an idea can be gradually accepted into the ranks of the latter category only after rigorous screening by such empirical tests.

To mention proper sampling procedures here is only to highlight the importance of cross-validation with persons as varied in all possible characteristics of personality and background as are found in the general population of ministers. For example, suppose we studied middle-class ministers thoroughly and found that overwork did seem to be associated with mental illness, regardless of age, success, or any other characteristic of the ministers that we compared. It still might be the case that overwork as such has no direct relation with mental illness but is only a highly correlated consequence of, let us say, a strong inner need for personal achievement. It may be this need, inevitably frustrated, which is more primarily responsible for the mental illness. Studying only middle-class ministers, we would have no hint suggesting that overwork was an insufficient explanation. But if it happened that among lower-class ministers, overwork did not result from strong need for achievement, but more commonly as a kind of propitiation for guilt feelings; then if we did study lower-class ministers, too, we would find that overwork was not likely to be correlated with mental illness. We might be driven eventually to isolate the need for achievement as the more critical factor. This would prove to be correlated with illness at all class levels—in the unlikely instance that all the illustrative assumptions above are valid.

A procedure related to cross-validation would convincingly cut down still further the probability of alternative interpretations and make the hypothesized factor, overwork—to continue our illustrative but unlikely hypothesis—seem to be the critical determinant. This is the procedure of making *controlled comparisons* of persons who differ only with respect to degree of overwork. For "cross validation" it was proposed that overwork be held constant among persons as unlike as possible in all other respects. Here, the procedure is to find persons who seem to be as similar as possible in all conceivably important characteristics except for overwork. Those who are overworked should end up ill, and their matched "controls" should remain healthy.

The practical problems of making an adequate kind of study, with suitable sampling and controls, staggers the imagination. Yet without it, we must dare to advance or to accept explanations only with utmost caution and humility, in full recognition of the large number of equally likely interpretations.

5. "I knew it all the time"

There is another kind of "repetition" that helps to make a hypothesis seem more probable. So far we have been concerned chiefly with empirical generalization. One observation suggests an interpretation which then needs to be checked by further observations. Yet, this is not the way Einstein worked as a scientist, and even behavioral scientists sometimes can get enough perspective and distance from raw facts to work in theoretical realms.

Theoretical reasoning may lead to a specific hypothesis or prediction—which we proceed to test in ways suggested above—in the same way that an empirical observation may. But the two processes are quite different. The theoretician starts from basic assumptions and principles about mental illness and its dynamics. From these he derives a notion of conditions most likely to produce such illness. Then he proceeds to test empirically whether or not people who live under these conditions or with these characteristics do get sick more often than other people. If so, a theoretical deduction gains probability because it is "repeated" in empirical events, just as one situational inference gains probability when it is cross-validated in other situations.

But this process of empirical confirmation of deductions needs to be sharply distinguished from its counterfeit, after-the-fact theorizing. Our ability, *after* discovering an apparent empirical relationship between, let us still pretend, busy schedules and mental illness, to explain how the busy schedule could cause the illness does not lend appreciable support to busy schedules as the cause. The powers of human rationalization being as imaginative as they are, a similarly intricate and plausible theory could be invented to explain how practically anything could cause mental illness, once the machinery is set in motion by an apparent empirical finding. The finding and the theory are not independent, but the theory is contrived to fit the facts. However, the prior theory and the subsequently confirming facts are independent (assuming the facts are gathered under controlled, unbiased conditions). It is this coincidence of the same conclusion coming from two *independent* lines of investigation —sometimes both empirical, sometimes one theoretical and one empirical—that lends credence to the conclusion.

6. Summary

About such important matters as the mental health of ministers, we all have intense, but frequently conflicting desires. We want to know, but we want to know accurately. We strongly want to have answers and clarity about such vital concerns—so strongly that we sometimes can't tolerate the delay and deliberation necessary to reach more adequate and accurate conclusions. We jump to the first conclusion that presents itself, rather than having no conclusion, while we ponder and search for a better conclusion. We accept those assertions that most closely satisfy what we want to believe.

As controls on these inevitable and universal human impulses, certain procedures and canons have been evolved, and some of these have been suggested in this paper.

The discussion has been focused on those processes by which facts lead to interpretations. However, it is obvious that many of the principles discussed apply equally well to the prior determination of fact, *Are* ministers breaking down? This depends on where you look (selection of cases, sampling) and on how carefully and consistently you define "breaking down," and on whether some base line for evaluation is provided by looking, with careful controls, at similar professions or at the population as a whole. It would be easy, if one wished to, to adopt a definition of mental illness which would show that 95% (or perhaps only 5%) of all clergymen studied were ill. It would also be easy, if one wished to, to shift definitions, either consciously or unconsciously, when lawyers or doctors were studied to show that only 10% (or perhaps 85% of them) suffered illness.

In these matters, science is not a proselytizing cult trying to convert persons to the practice of particular rituals for arbitrary reasons. The canons of science have evolved slowly as necessary means for reducing human fallibility and biases. To some extent these canons can be observed by any individual in his own processes of conclusion-drawing. Certainly any individual can be alert to the fallacies and the absence of necessary safeguards in the opinions of others. Frequently, however, the necessary precautions involve such intricate and extensive procedures that they remove research beyond the possibility of what one individual can accomplish and seem to leave the field open only to comprehensive research projects. This is frustrating. But if there is a reason that most of us cannot discover and decide on the facts of atomic energy even though we are dealing daily with atoms, there is a reason that each of us individually cannot determine the laws of mental life.

Are Ministers Breaking Down?

CO-AUTHORS

Hazen G. Werner
Resident Bishop,
Ohio Area,
The Methodist Church

Reuel L. Howe
Director, Institute for
Advanced Pastoral Studies, Inc.
Bloomfield Hills, Michigan

Carl W. Christensen, M.D.
Psychiatrist, member of the faculty,
Northwestern University, School of Medicine
and consultant to Garrett Biblical Institute,
Methodist Board of Missions,
American Baptist Home Missionary Society

This is an open question. A church official, a teacher of ministers, and a psychiatrist face the question squarely.

A Minister asks:

There appeared in *Life* Magazine in August, 1956, an article by
the Reverend Wesley Shrader, Associate Professor of Pastoral

223

Theology at Yale Divinity School, on "Why Ministers Are Breaking Down." This was a challenging article and if true certainly deserves serious study. What are the facts about this situation, however?

1. What is the statistical evidence with reference to mental illness among ministers?

2. How does this evidence compare or contrast with the extent of mental illness among people of the legal, medical, social work, and other helping professions?

3. What are your hunches as to the emotional factors in personality disturbances among ministers?

4. What mental health measures do you recommend for the parish minister?

I hope that some of your authorities in the fields of religion and mental health can share with us their information about these important points.

A Methodist Bishop replies . . .

When I come to look at the whole range of Methodist ministers (close to twelve hundred of them in Ohio) I have known of extremely few cases of what is commonly called "nervous breakdown." Oddly enough this does not seem to be a malady found in cases of men having the heaviest ministerial load.

I do not believe that the incidence of breakdown is any greater in the ministry than in any other profession. However, it would not be difficult to establish reasons for the likelihood of this experience in the ministry.

(1) Increased number of functions of the modern minister (including the necessity of counseling concerning the breakdown of others). The functions of the modern minister extend far beyond the simple work of the ministry as it obtained a decade or two ago.

(2) The impossibility of putting aside the responsibilities of the minister after a reasonably long day of hard work.

(3) The strain that is upon the minister who works with people engaged in the enterprise of the Church volitionally. Necessarily the modern minister must have some art and some facility

for dealing with all the varying temperaments, fixations and emotional states of persons related to the Church on the basis of good will.

—Hazen G. Werner

A Theologian-Teacher answers . . .

I do not feel equal to answering some of the questions your inquirer asks about the article in *Life* by Mr. Shrader. I do feel free, however, to make this comment: Clergy breakdowns are due partly to a sense of frantic frustration in their work. Many of them do not feel well prepared for what they have to do. As one man put it: "My seminary prepared me to teach theological subject matter, but not to minister to human beings." The experience of irrelevance and inadequacy inevitably takes terrible toll of a clergyman's vitality and morale. A theological education that correlated the Gospel answer to human questions would help to prevent clergy breakdowns.

Breakdowns are also caused *for want of a sense of structure by* which the million helter-skelter demands that overwhelm an active minister may be sorted out, a sense of structure that would help him keep a sense of purpose and direction. "How do I decide what I shall do?" you ask. Replied one parson to my question: "Why that's easy to answer. I do what pushes me the hardest." This approach to the complex and never-ceasing demands of the ministry wears out the minister. Its power is too much dissipated by illness and inefficiency.

But the minister could be saved and the power of the ministry restored if a structure for the work of the ministry could be found. Actually, it is inherent in the work itself. It is to be found in an understanding of the needs of people, of the inter-relation of the various crises in the individual lives, in the correlation of human questions with the divine answer, and in the inter-relation and interdependence of each function of the ministry. The structure might appear if the minister would look for it and if as he looked he would keep asking himself, "What is the purpose of what I am doing?" As a result he might better refuse to do many things he is asked to do and be free to do the things that are his proper work. And he might have the peace that passeth understanding even in this crazy world.

—Reuel L. Howe

A Psychiatrist And Seminary Consultant replies . . .

1. Statistical evidence of the incidence of mental illness amongst ministers is not available since studies have not been done on any large scale. Certain isolated reports have been made; for instance, Jules Masserman in his excellent book *The Practice of Dynamic Psychiatry*[1] reports the results of a certain missionary society in their efforts to screen candidates over a 15 year period. "Of a total of 364 candidates examined, 78 (21%) were rejected for causes distributed as follows: neurotic difficulties, 36; inadequate motivation, 12; temperamental unsuitability of spouse, 10; of self, 8; poor physical health, 3; other reasons (familial objection, financial, etc.), 9."

In my own more limited experience in evaluating missionary candidates for a missionary board, I have found over a two year period that of 73 candidates seen, 17 (23%) were rejected outright because of serious mental illness (psychosis or incapacitating neurosis); 34 (47%) were accepted conditionally, but had some emotional problems which would hamper and limit their work; while 22 (30%) were deemed mentally healthy. It could be said that 70% of these candidates had some sort of mental illness which interfered with their effectiveness, more or less. These evaluations were based on pschiatric interview and psychological testing by an independent observer. Of 70 consecutive people in the profession of religion (ministers, ministerial students, missionary candidates, religious educationalists), 26 (36%) were ill enough to require intensive therapy.

Various seminaries have a psychological screening process in which they attempt to evaluate incoming students for purposes of detecting the presence of incapacitating illness. The Academy of Religion and Mental Health plans to report the results of such a survey in the relatively near future. It must be admitted that statistical information is lacking and a large scale survey

---

[1] W. B. Saunders Company, Philadelphia, 1955, p. 297.

would be of value. The facts which we do have seem to indicate that mental illness is a problem within the ministry.

2. Answering the second question is not difficult, for to my knowledge no comparative studies have been made. Perhaps those in psychology can answer this question.

3. To adequately answer the third question would take a book. Suffice it to say that ministers have the same emotional problems as are generally found. I'm beginning to suspect that individuals who have certain illnesses may be attracted to the ministry as a profession in an unconscious attempt to resolve their problems. What is of concern is the use to which religion may be put in these instances and whether this use is healthy, neurotic, or psychotic as judged by our pragmatic standards. Religion, because of some of its assumptions, beliefs and practices, may seem to offer some individuals substitutive gratifications and is therefore used in an effort to solve emotional problems. Whether such solutions are adequate or not depend upon individual factors, many of which still lack answers. The psychiatrist is often biased in this respect because he sees those in which the solution has not been successful. It seems fairly certain, however, that in these individuals religion can be a part of schizophrenia, obsessive-compulsive neurosis, etc., and is subject to such ego defenses as projection, rationalization, reaction-formation and the like, in an attempt to adapt to life processes. So frequently the question that arises in evaluation religious experience and the usages of religion is whether it is a sublimation, i.e., normal, or a substitute, i.e., neurotic or psychotic. For example, evangelists with problems seem to have to deny their hostile sexual impulses with a reaction-formation as well as needing to compensate for deep-rooted feelings of inferiority and the need for reassurance.

4. The last question is best answered by paraphrasing Dr. Daniel Blain who answers it in his excellent chapter "Fostering the Mental Health of Ministers" in *The Church and Mental Health*.[2] First, Dr. Blain recommends that the minister cultivate

---

[2] Blain, Daniel, *The Church and Mental Health* (New York: Charles Scribner's Sons, 1953).

a capacity to accept limitations and to work within those limitations. Here an objective ability to say "no" is an asset. Second, there is the need to clarify objective in order to maintain a strong sense of direction and purpose and to feel that progress is being made towards goals in order to obtain realistic satisfaction from work. Third, it is necessary to accept emotions without moral judgments and to express them appropriately to circumstances. Emotion and feeling are a part of perceiving and acting, hence, the minister should develop the capacity to love, to fear, to dislike, and to desire. Appropriate expression of these feelings is conducive to mental health. Fourth, the wise minister will seek an adequate program of recreation, refreshment, and replenishment which serves to restore his energies and nourish his mind and spirit. A tired mind has difficulty in being a creative mind. Finally, the minister should avail himself of the values of human fellowship in which he can find realistic satisfactions for dependent needs, assert his independence, and find affection, emotional security, and a sense of personal significance so necessary to that feeling of well-being. If he should need help in achieving these values, he should not hesitate in seeking competent help. While health is a relative concept, one can best minister to illness only out of a fair degree of health. To what Dr. Blain says I can only add—Amen.

—Carl W. Christensen

An Overview of Research on the Mental Illness of the Minister

By Samuel Southard
Associate Professor of Psychology of Religion,
Southern Baptist Theological Seminary,
Louisville, Kentucky

On the basis of current research there is no reason for believing that mental breakdown among ministers is any greater than that among the other professions. There is some indication that it is considerably less.

The mental health of ministers has been the topic of many discussions in the past few years. In 1953, the Reverend George Anderson wrote in "The Christian Century" that emotionally ill clergymen tend to perpetuate the pathology of their congregation. Although he believed that the majority of ministers were mature and intelligent, Mr. Anderson warned that there were enough of the other kind to constitute one important problem of our day. Three years later, the Reverend Wesley Shrader indicted laymen for expecting ministers to fulfill unrealistic expectations. Mr. Shrader hypothesized that this set up a cycle of fear, frustration, and guilt in the clergyman. Then the breakdown happens. Since Mr. Shrader's hypothesis appeared in *Life* and in the *Reader's Digest,* it has reached a wide audience. The personal anecdotes and references to research in related areas has made it so appealing that Chaplain J. A. Davidson offers a facetious warning against "Shrader's Neurasthenia"—"a state of listlessness and apathy, accompanied by mild self-pity, brought on by prolonged meditation on Professor Wesley Shrader's *Life* article on 'Why Ministers are Breaking Down'."[1] In the July, 1957 issue of *Harper's Magazine,* Mr. James Moore concluded that Mr. Shrader's thesis is a partial truth. The minister's sense of failure in the face of impossible demands was the superfical problem. The deeper problem was "the conflict between the role the minister is expected to play as a minister and the kind of life he wants to live as a human being."[2]

All these articles awaken interest in the mental health of ministers. Some persons have assumed from them that many clergymen are going crazy. What actual information do we have? Is there any definitive research on this complex problem.

The Department of the Psychology of Religion, Southern Baptist Theological Seminary, began to look for answers to these questions in 1956. Letters were written to psychologists, psychiatrists, theological professors, bishops, mental hospital chaplains, directors of pastoral counseling programs, and marriage and family counselors. In the past two years, a variety of answers have been received.

Some psychiatrists and theological professors wrote informally that ministers were not "breaking down" more than men in other professions. But ministers were confused about the purpose of what they were doing. The authorities suggested that some of this strain arose from the multiple responsibilities of the pastorate, but that additional tension came out of the minister's lack of self-understanding. If the personal anxiety of the minister could be lowered long enough for him to ask "What is the purpose of what I am doing?" he might find a structure for his ministry. The basic organizing purpose of pastoral work is to mediate God's grace through persons to persons. It is to provide a Divine-personal answer to the needs of individuals.

---

[1] *United Church Observer,* February 1, 1957.
[2] "Why Young Ministers Are Leaving the Church," *Harper's Magazine* (July, 1957), p. 65.

But if the minister is compulsively seeking to win approval through good works, he is tyrannized by conflicting expectations.[3] He is so anxious to *do* right that he neglects the deeper need to *be* a person. How strange that the Christian doctrines of the incarnation and the in-dwelling Christ, which stress the personal aspect of our faith, make so little impression upon some pastors. The rich Reformation doctrine that men are saved by faith is not practiced by them. Instead the medieval Catholic belief in approval through church activity drives them on.

Both theological professors and physicians recommended clinical pastoral education as one useful method of correction for these compulsions. Through a deeper self-understanding, they felt that the candidate for the ministry would recapture the personal emphasis in the pastorate. This does not mean that the authorities believed that all seminary students are unstable and ridden by deep-seated compulsions. Most of the educators were pleading for student knowledge of the basic emotional structure of people and fundamental self-acceptance. They wanted the minister to know how the symbols, words, and roles in the religious community are bound up with emotional patterns. This, they believed, could be best communicated through supervised clinical work. There the student must relate his theological formulations to patients' emotional patterns. In interviews with pastoral supervisors, the student may become aware of his characteristic ways of relating to people. Many opportunities for this type of personal evaluation as a minister are available through the organizations in the National Conference on Clinical Pastoral Education: The National Lutheran Council, the Council for Clinical Training, the Institute of Pastoral Care, the Southern Baptist Association on Clinical Pastoral Education, and the Seminary Professors in the Practical Fields.

Another constructive suggestion was a proposal for better screening procedures. Denominational committees and seminary admission committees are looking for diagnostic techniques which will enable them to screen out candidates who are unfit for

---

[3] See "The Tyranny of Expectations," *Pastoral Psychology*, (September, 1957).

the ministry and discover problems in other candidates which may be relieved through pastoral counseling, psychotherapy, or Christian fellowship. To aid seminaries and denominations in this, the Educational Testing Service, with a grant from the Lilly Foundation, is conducting a three-year study of psychological testing for the ministry. After the psychologists have concluded a survey on "What is a successful minister?" they hope to devise an instrument which will predict the measure of success which may be expected of a candidate for the ministry.

Although the Department may have been unaware of some important research (which we would like to know about), some very interesting reports were received. From these we may form some answers to questions about the mental health of ministers.

(1) Ministers are admitted to state hospitals in increasing numbers, but, at the same time, there are more than twice as many physicians and lawyers admitted. This evidence is reported in the article by Chaplain Leonard Morgan, Jr., who sent a questionnaire on ministers-among-hospital-patients to state mental hospitals throughout the United States, as well as by Dr. E. Gartly Jaco, who conducted a two-year survey of the incidence of psychosis for the state of Texas.

If hospitalization is an index of breakdowns, then the clergy are in a better state of mind than lawyers and doctors, but a word of caution is necessary. An investigation of professions and of hospitalization cannot be undertaken apart from social class factors. Within the ministry there is a tremendous divergence of educational, housing, economic, and professional levels. Dr. Jaco found that fundamentalistic denominations seem to be more frequent among mental patients and that Negro ministers seem to be more psychotic than white preachers. But he points to the possibility that a large portion of these ministers had other jobs in addition to the ministry. Their status was apparently weak and nebulous. Although Dr. Jaco presents this as a speculative judgment in need of more research, it does point to the need to distinguish social class factors in judgments about denominations and their ministers. The research of Redlich, Hollingshead, and associates at Yale University[4] explored this relationship between social level and psychiatric disorders. They found that patients in the lower social levels predominated in state hospitals, while patients in the upper and middle social levels predominated in private hospitals. More than half of the patients of private psychiatrists were in the upper or upper-middle social bracket, while only 2.8% were in the lower-level bracket.[5] When we consider that a majority of persons in Methodist, Baptist, Church of God, Pentecostal Holiness, and various sect churches are in the lower class, it is easy to see why they and their ministers are found often in state mental hospials. Episcopalians, who have more upper-class members than any other denomination except Congregational Christian, were found in Texas state mental hospitals much less frequently than their numbers in society would suggest. Why? Because they more often belong to a social class which obtains private therapy, it seems. The interpretation of mental hospital statistics, therefore, must include a knowledge of the relationship of social class to type of treatment afforded.

(2) Fewer ministers are in hospitals than would be expected from their numbers in our society. Chaplain Morgan reports that only 7 out of every 10,000 mental patients are clergymen, whereas 20 out of every 10,000 persons in a community are clergymen. Again, if hospitalization tells us much about the incidence of illness, the minister is less likely to have a "nervous breakdown" than the people in his congregation.

(3) Ministerial students are sensitive to failure and usually blame themselves rather than others. Dean Harold Massey, Belmont College, administered the Thematic Apperception Test to twenty-five ministerial and twenty non-ministerial college students. One of his conclusions was that "the ministerial group appears to be characterized by rather definite patterns of anxiety reaction, manifested by indecision and negative emotions. There is a sensitivity to failure, especially moral failure. The low oc-

[4] Hollingshead, August B., and Redlich, Fredrick C., *Social Class and Mental Illness* (John Wiley and Sons, Inc., 1958).
[5] F. C. Redlich, *et al.*, "Social Structure and Psychiatric Disorders," *American Journal of Psychiatry* (April, 1953), pp. 729-734.

currence of aggressive scores indicates that the tension is not usually directed against others, but is more apt to be directed toward self."[6] Mr. Fitzhugh Dodson provided a battery of psychological tests for 130 students in three interdenominational Protestant seminaries and for 132 graduate students in three California universities. Seminarians were not found to be significantly more authoritarian nor more emotionally disturbed than the control group, but they were more guilt ridden and uncomfortable about hostile feelings.

(4) A "liberal" or "conservative" theology is not a mark of emotional well-being. Mr. Dodson found that neither group of seminarians were significantly more emotionally disturbed than the other. Dr. James G. Ranck came to a similar conclusion on the basis of tests given to 800 students in 28 theological schools which ranged from extreme conservatism to extreme liberalism.[7]

(5) The way in which a minister uses his time seems to be more of a concern than the amount of time he works. In his analysis of the time schedule of 480 rural and urban ministers, Dr. Samuel Blizzard reported an average work day of about 10 hours: 9 hours and 17 minutes for rural ministers, 10 hours and 32 minutes for urban ministers. These are long hours, but do not account for "breakdowns" in themselves. In fact, Dr. Blizzard says nothing about the mental health of clergymen. But he does highlight the minister's conflicts which derive from the importance, the sense of effectiveness, and the sense of enjoyment which are attached to practitioner, personal and family roles.[8] The minister believes that he must be saint and prophet, practitioner and scholar, general practitioner and specialist. It is this self-image, his inner expectations, which give him the most anxiety.

---

[6] Harold Massey, "Apperception Tests Reveal Ministerial Students' Attitudes," *The Southern Baptist Educator* (April, 1957), p. 2.

[7] James G. Ranck, "Some Personality Correlates of Religious Attitude and Belief," Ph.D. dissertation in clinical psychology, Columbia Univ., 1955.

[8] Samuel Blizzard, "The Minister's Dilemma," *The Christian Century* (April 25, 1956).

(6) The stress of occupation seems to be only an indirect factor in the emotional disorders of ministers who seek marriage counseling. Mr. Edward Thornton, Counseling Director of the Family Relations Center, Louisville, summarized his interviews with twenty persons in church-related vocations. Some of the counselees were passive persons who were afraid of competition and personal relationships. Others were cool, aloof, and emotionally detached. They avoided all personal contacts. All of them shunned any professional role which would require a sense of personal adequacy.

Occupational stress was often presented as the "problem," but long-term counseling revealed deeper problems. These persons had an inadequate picture of self. They described themselves as saints overcome by the flesh, orphans deserving pity and indulgence, or outcasts forsaken by God. Their concept of vocation was distorted. Some believed that a church vocation was morally superior to other occupations. Closely related to this was a belief that good boys and sweet girls would inevitably become ministers or directors of religious education. Others entered the ministry as a bargain with God; He would take away their deviant sexual wishes and they would sacrifice their lives in His service.

The basic difficulties of these persons grew out of unresolved conflicts with children and marital partner, or inadequate relationships with parents. The occupation of minister was a secondary factor in their disturbance.

(7) Although a small percentage of the ministers in one denomination (Baptist) were the sons of ministers, over 90% of them would like their sons to enter the same profession. From a survey of Tennessee Baptist pastors in a variety of churches, Mr. Herbert Miles of Carson-Newman College found that only 10% were sons of Baptist preachers. Yet 93.7% would like their son to be a pastor. Unless a man likes his work and is proud of it, he will probably not wish his son to follow him in it. It may be concluded, therefore, that the overwhelming majority of these ministers were happy in their work.

From these varied studies it may be concluded that many ministers are sensitive to failure, blame themselves more than others, and are in conflict about the inner expectations which they have of themselves, but they are not so harassed by their congregation that they are "breaking down" more than other occupational groups. In fact, their mental stability seems to exceed that of some other professions and of the general population.

The Hospitalized Minister: A Preliminary Study

By Albert L. Meiburg and Richard K. Young
Department of Pastoral Care,
North Carolina Baptist Hospital and
Bowman Gray School of Medicine,
Winston-Salem, North Carolina

There seem to be several factors operating in the mental illness of the ministers studied in this small group: chief among them are the minister's uncertainty about his choice of the ministry as a vocation, the minister's concept of evangelism, and problems relating to overwork.

The Department of Pastoral Care of the North Carolina Baptist Hospital and the Bowman Gray School of Medicine has undertaken a study of the relationship of the minister's vocation to his health. A large number of ministers from a four-state area come to this medical center each year. Several members of the faculty of the medical school have contributed helpful advice and encouragement in planning the project.

The research is proceeding along the following plan. A survey is being made to locate the records of all ministers seen in the hospital over the past fifteen years. The medical records of this group will be consulted and all relevant medical and vocational data recorded on a prepared form for tabulation. The same procedure will be followed with a control group of comparable size selected at random from all males admitted over the same time span. The incidence of various illnesses among ministers can then be compared statistically with the incidence of the same diagnosis among the total control group as well as among its various occupational segments. For example, the data should indicate whether or not stomach disorders appear to be a more frequent complaint of ministers than of other professional workers, white collar workers, or industrial workers, all of whom were admitted to this hospital.

The authors hope to publish in book form the completed study of a thousand hospitalized ministers and discuss any facts that appear significant regarding the minister's health as related to his vocation.

The present article represents a preliminary survey of data collected from the study of the cases of one hundred thirteen ministers selected at random from those seen as out-patients or in-patients in this hospital during the period, 1944-57.

Such a preliminary review has limitations. For example, no comparisons with any other vocational groups have as yet been made. What this article attempts to do is to summarize certain medical and vocational data obtained from a limited number of ministers who came to a medical center.

The communities being served by these 113 ministers at the time of their admission varied from the relatively large city to the open country, with a rather even division between rural (37), urban (33), and village (39) pastorates.

Almost all the ministers were married. Only one of the group was single, and none were divorced. Only in a few cases were there any information relative to the quality of marital adjustment. The number of children most frequently reported was three, followed by two and one in that order.

A rather surprising amount of information relative to the patient's vocation was obtained from the charts. The overwhelming majority of the group was of the Baptist denomination, as was expected. However, a total of five Protestant denominations were represented. Fourteen of the 113 ministers were serving on a part-time basis, four were students in college or seminary, and eleven had retired from the active ministry. The proportion of time given to religious work was not specified in twenty-six of the medical charts.

Although only fourteen ministers reported being engaged in their religious calling on a half-time basis, two individuals reported holding other jobs as well as full-time religious work. One of these, a forty-year-old patient, was pastor of one church, assistant pastor of another, and worked forty hours a week in a retail establishment. He was preaching three to four times a week and conducting revival meetings as he had opportunity. He had a history of recurring headaches since his teens. At the time of admission his chief complaint was headaches, occurring usually on weekends and apparently brought on by shocking experiences and changes in routine. His problem was diagnosed as migraine headache. Following his hospitalization he gave up his work as a clerk and showed some improvement physically. A four-year follow up indicated that a revised work load and medication had helped, but that he still had some headaches.

The age span of the group ran from twenty through eighty years. The age of the patients at the time of first admission to this hospital is shown in Table I, page 240. The peak period for admission in this group occurs during the span 30-34 years, at which ages twenty patients were admitted. The number of patients admitted in each succeeding five-year age period declined steadily from this point until the years 60-64 when there was a small increase. Because of the unfavorable ratio between the size of the sample (113) and the number of possible diagnoses, the distribution of cases among the various diagnoses is inconclusive. The distribution of cases by the major diagnostic categories of the public health code is shown in Table II on page 241.

Multiple diagnoses in some cases resulted in a total number of 144 diagnoses from the 113 cases. Several categories of this table call for a word of explanation: For example, obesity was a definite diagnosis in three cases under III, *Nutritional Diseases*. However, twenty-seven were described as "obese" in some degree.

TABLE I

AGE AT FIRST ADMISSION

Age of Patient	Number of Admissions
20–24	2
25–29	9
30–34	20
35–39	18
40–44	13
45–49	11
50–54	10
55–59	6
60–64	10
65–69	6
70–74	7
75–79	0
80	1
	113

Under another category, VII, *Circulatory Diseases,* the nineteen diagnoses included five cases of hemorrhoids. And under IX, *Diseases of the Digestive System,* the eleven diagnoses included six cases of hernia. Three cases of irritable colon and four of "nervous stomach" were not included here because their psychogenic basis compelled their classification under V, *Mental, Psychoneurotic, and Personality Disorders.* Twenty-six diagnoses fell under category V, but some emotional factor was recorded as bearing on the illness in forty of the 113 cases.

The heart of the problem in this study is the involvement of the minister's vocation in his illness. From the total group studied there was specific information bearing on the vocation-illness relationship in twenty-two cases. The clinical picture of this sub-group is seen in the following discussion in which the elements of age, symptoms, diagnoses, and vocational factors are discussed.

The age span of this sub-group was from twenty-eight to sixty-one years at the time of first admission. This gave a median age of 44.5 years and an average age of 40.0 years.

TABLE II

DISTRIBUTION OF 144 DIAGNOSES IN THE CASES OF 113 MINISTERS
SEEN AT THE NORTH CAROLINA BAPTIST HOSPITAL

Diagnosis (Public Health Code)	No. of Diagnoses	Percentage
I. Infectious and Parasitic Diseases (000-139)	1	.7
II. Neoplasms (140-239)	7	4.8
III. Allergic, Endocrine, Metabolic and Nutritional Diseases (240-289)	9	6.2
IV. Diseases of the Blood and Blood Forming Organs (290-299)	0	0
V. Mental, Psychoneurotic, and Personality Disorders (300-329)	26	18.0
VI. Diseases of the Nervous System and the Sense Organs (330-399)	11	7.6
VII. Diseases of the Circulatory System (400-469)	19	13.2
VIII. Diseases of the Respiratory System (470-529)	14	9.7
IX. Diseases of the Digestive System (530-589)	11	7.6
X. Diseases of the Genito-Urinary System (590-639)	17	12.5
XI. Deliveries and Complications of Pregnancy (640-689)	0	0
XII. Diseases of the Skin and Cellular Tissues (690-719)	3	2.0
XIII. Diseases of the Bone and Organs of Movement (720-749)	8	5.5
XIV. Congenital Malformations (750-759)	0	0
XV. Certain Diseases of Early Infancy (760-779)	0	0
XVI. Symptoms, Senility, and Ill-Defined Conditions (780-799)	6	4.1
XVII. Accidents, Poisoning, and Violence (800-999)	7	4.9
General Medical Examination—No illness	5	3.5
Totals	144	100

Several symptoms tended to appear more frequently than others in this group. The complaints presented in the order of frequency were as follows: headaches—6, chest pains—5, "nervousness"—5, pain in stomach—4, fatigue—4, indigestion—3, feelings of depression—2, pain in side—1, abdominal pains—1, heart skipping beat—1, shoulder and back pains—1.

The thirty-three diagnoses assigned to the twenty-two patients of this sub-group included the following: anxiety state, tension state, functional gastro-intestinal disorder, depression, pyloro-spasm, hypertension, migraine headache, heart disease, bron-chitis, enlarged prostate, duodenal deformity, hemorrhoids, questionable amebiasis, and no disease. Slightly over half of these diagnoses (17), including anxiety and tension states, functional digestive problems and the like come under the general category of emotional or psychogenic disorders.

The chief vocational factors operating in the illnesses of the patients in this small group were seen to be of three sorts: Prob-lems relating to overwork—13; Problems relating to the min-ister's concept of evangelism—5; Problems relating to the minister's certainty of his vocation—4.

The factor seen most often was generally described as over-work. A number of men complained of having multiple respon-sibilities and excessive demands made upon them. Usually they allowed themselves little time for recreation. An extreme ex-ample of a minister with an excessive work load is given earlier in the discussion of part-time religious workers. Assistance in clarifying this problem with the minister's church was given by one doctor who wrote a letter to the appropriate committee. He stated briefly the medical opinion that the pastor's back pain was on a tension basis and recommended that the church help their pastor schedule a half-a-day's recreation a week.

Another example involved a thirty-one-year-old minister who was admitted to the hospital with the chief complaint of severe nervousness. He and his wife were dissatisfied with their field of four churches which were frequently quarreling. In addition to his church work he had other duties and had been unable to complete his educational preparation. Following examination he was given some medication. He planned to move to a former pastorate where he could bring his responsibilities to a more comfortable level.

Overwork related to a building program was seen in four cases where ministers came to the hospital complaining of nervousness, headaches, and depressed feelings. Two of the min-isters had just completed building programs. The other two had encountered problems or had had to make difficult decisions in regard to their building plans.

One patient's doctor, following a complete physical examination which yielded no positive findings, concluded with a diagnosis of "too long application of your nose to the grindstone."

A second vocational factor at work in these cases had to do with the minister's concept of evangelism. Two ministers experienced the onset of their illnesses during or at the conclusion of an evangelistic campaign. Another felt depressed because he could not save more people. One middle-aged minister came to the hospital with the complaint of chronic fatigue shortly after leaving evangelistic work for the pastorate.

The third vocational factor observed was that of vocational uncertainty. The generally held concept that one enters the ministry only in obedience to a Divine call operates to intensify anxiety among ministers who begin to doubt or question their fitness for their profession. One young minister who complained of afternoon headaches was seen five times in the hospital with a diagnosis of anxiety state. He had doubts about his call to the ministry. Another patient, age thirty, presented symptoms of abdominal pains at intervals over the past ten years. However, he reported complete absence of symptoms while away from his parish.

Feelings of inadequacy appeared in some cases in this connection. One pastor of an urban church entered the hospital four times with complaints relating to the digestive tract. He stated that after entering the ministry he had supported his wife and three children while in college and that he felt that his lack of further preparation caused him to spend an exorbitant amount of time on sermon preparation.

Marital conflict is almost as taboo among the ministry as vocational uncertainty. The pastor must be the husband of one wife and must rule well his own household. When a difficulty in his own marriage develops, the minister tends to struggle along as best he can since it is difficult for him to find a discreet source of help. In several of the cases just described an element of marital conflict was also involved. Overwork in a building program is a socially acceptable reason for illness and was given by one minister who also had the problem of a disturbed relationship with his wife.

Summary

The ministers in this sample constitute a selected group in that they came to the hospital. No generalizations can be made in regard to the health patterns of ministers in general because of the small size of the sample and its restriction to the hospitalized patients of one geographical area. The survey of the one hundred thirteen ministers admitted to a general hospital shows that (1) The most frequent age of first admission is during the years 30-34, (2) Approximately 20% of the sample shows some relationship between vocational pressures and the illness. The study is preparatory to research which will greatly enlarge the sample and attempt comparisons with patterns of illness in other occupations.

The Occurrence of Mental Illness in the Ministry: Introduction

BY CARL W. CHRISTENSEN, M.D.

Instructor in the Department of Neurology and Psychiatry, Northwestern University School of Medicine, Chicago, Illinois, Consultant to Garrett Biblical Institute, Evanston, Illinois, Consultant to the Methodist Board of Missions and Church Extension in New York City

The following reflections are from the experience of a psychiatrist in his therapeutic work with over a hundred persons associated with church vocations. This preliminary report appeared in the Winter 1959 issue of the Journal of Pastoral Care, *and was followed in the Spring 1960 issue by another perceptive article dealing with family origins of mental illness.*

The other day a man came into my office, anxious, fearful and guilt-ridden because of a homosexual experience. That afternoon I talked with an individual whom I was to evaluate for a job. It soon became evident that he was a paranoid schizophrenic. A woman was referred for treatment because she was failing her studies. It appeared that her failure was associated with feelings of inferiority and hostility intensified by an inability to date. Another woman sought help because she was afraid of sharp objects, tall buildings, and riding in elevators. These people have two things in common: first, they are suffering from some form of mental illness and, secondly, they are all associated professionally with religion as a life work. The relationship of these two things is the major problem about which we shall be concerned.

Mental illness among those in the profession of religion is not rare. What is of interest and import is the manner in which their mental illness and their work are interrelated. The very nature of this profession is such that it demands the utmost in maturity and mental health. When mental illness occurs in professional people, its consequences may have added seriousness since, by its nature, their work often involves intimate contact with people over whom they may exert considerable influence. Do not misunderstand. Just because we shall be dealing with mental illness among ministers does not imply that all ministers are mentally ill. On the contrary, my experience is that most ministers are mentally healthy, i.e., they have the ability to live a contented creative life with others and withstand the usual vicissitudes of living. However, over a period of years it has been my privilege to study over a hundred professional "religionists" who have had mental illnesses of one sort or another. This report is based on that study.

The material was garnered from ministers, missionaries, missionary candidates, seminary students, and religious educationalists during the course of psychotherapy, rather than as the results of a specific research problem. Thus it has the advantages and faults of this methodology and will present some problems of acceptance to those accustomed to dealing with other types of material. The limitations of such methodology must be recognized, and any conclusions, hypotheses, or inferences must be understood within the limits of the material and not generalized beyond this. The case histories are presented with the kind permission of the individuals concerned. Their anonymity has been preserved and any similarity to others, living or dead, is merely further indication that people are more alike than different. The material was taken from notations made during the course of therapy, at first without consideration of the possibility that it would be used except in therapy with the patients concerned. It was only in retrospect that there seemed to be a certain consistency, a certain pattern or patterns suggesting a relationship between the choice of occupation and emotional conflict and between some religious beliefs and some forms of psychopathology.

A person's behavior is motivated by unconscious factors as well as by conscious ones and the choice of an occupation can be influenced by these factors. In working with these people it became startlingly evident that unconscious factors were often a major determinant in the choice of occupation. This minister sitting across from me was called to his work as the result of an emotional crisis during which he had an acute hallucinatory experience. What were the factors involved in this experience? Why were they expressed in this fashion? How have they affected his life and his beliefs? Was his solution adequate or are there better solutions available?

In an effort to find the answers to these and other questions, I was led to a consideration of the interrelationships of religious belief and mental illness. Do not interpret this to mean that religious belief and mental illness are synonymous. I think that it is necessary to have a healthy religious belief or faith. But religious faith, like other beliefs, can be used defensively to protect against anxiety. Indeed it is often used by the mentally ill for this purpose as we shall demonstrate later. This is not to be understood as meaning that religious conviction per se is abnormal. What is considered normal and what abnormal is in the final analysis a matter of opinion. The fact remains that, regardless of whether a religious faith be judged normal or abnormal by individuals or society, any such belief may be used in a pathological fashion. This aspect of mental illness in ministers is worthy of serious consideration.

Those who have to do with the selection and training of ministers and their associates are well aware of the existence and import of this factor. At times, however, it is difficult to make a value judgment concerning a person's religious faith and how that faith is being used. In psychotherapy, with these individuals, it is necessary at times to examine as objectively as is possible the convictions of the patient in order to understand the manner in which they are used by him in his day-to-day living. For example, the question of belief in God is often of valid import to these people. It would be fruitless to discuss the existence or non-existence of God or the various theological and philosophical concepts of the Deity in therapy. But it may be necessary, at times, to investigate the individual's belief to see how it is being used to satisfy unconscious needs deeply engraved in the character of the individual. Practically, such examination often results in modification of these beliefs from a neurotic defense against the anxiety of a conflict to a more mature application in solving the problems of existence. When a man can realize that his trust in a provident God is, in part, the result of his own passive dependent desires, he may continue with his belief in such a God, but he becomes more active in achieving his goals rather than passively waiting for God to accomplish that which life demands he obtain himself.

This objective attitude poses a real problem for some individuals who may interpret a psychological viewpoint as a hostile attack against religion. It is true that there are those who feel hostile, but this emotion has no place in any scientific investigation. Dispassionate inquiry must be concerned, first, with the compositions and origins of that being studied and, secondly, with its meaning and use. The former involves existential judgment based on knowledge of factual observations, while the latter concerns a value judgment based on interpretation of the observed facts. Neither is determined from the other, nor can they be combined conclusively until they have been separately considered. Unless this is recognized, distorted perception is mistaken for observed fact and value judgments deteriorate into prejudice.

Consider, if you will, the question: When is a religious belief a normal faith and when is it a delusion? An answer cannot be given until facts are known concerning the content and origin of the belief as well as its meaning and use. With this added knowledge relating to a particular set of circumstances it is possible to make an existential judgment of the content and origin and a value judgment of its particular meaning and use. Then and only then can the two be combined to form a conclusion in answer to the question as it applies to a particular circumstance. It is to be noted that any such conclusion is relative. To generalize on the basis of such a conclusion is hazardous, because in any given instance a particular belief is judged to be a neurotic defense, and its effect to inhibit creative potential does not mean that all such beliefs are neurotic or cannot be used constructively.

Moreover, it must be recognized that in the effort to be objective certain errors can occur. Existential judgment, for instance, is based on observation and the unconscious needs of the observer may tend to distort the perceptions unless rectified by repeated observations by the same and different persons. Value judgments present the opportunity for a different type of error, even more difficult to recognize and correct. Usually value judgments are generalizations developed out of past experience; hence they are subjective in nature and tend to vary from individual to individual. Two people may observe a set of facts and agree upon what they see, but their interpretation of these facts may be widely divergent. A flute may be examined by a musician and a mechanical draftsman, both agreeing that the object is a flute. The musician may say that it is worthless since the sound it makes is flat, while the designer, marveling at its construction, will praise it as a beautiful instrument. Both judgments are value judgments based on the past experiences of the individuals. In this case both are valid, but to generalize from this case to all flutes would be fallacious. When we consider, however, the infinitely more complex problems of human behavior such value judgments are not as easy to make. Many individuals who readily make such judgments are either not aware of the unconscious subjective factors determining their conclusions, must deny their existence, or fail to account for the relativity of such judgments. These individuals are frequently disturbed by the existential viewpoint which is necessary when considering religion psychologically, because of their own subjective needs which, in the first place, prevent the making of dispassionate observations and which, in the second place, hinder the recognition of the relativity of value judgments. Hence they react to such objective attitudes as a threat when in actual fact there may be none.

Another problem which is often perplexing to some who are not familiar with scientific methodology has to do with the common medical practice of studying the abnormal in order to gain knowledge concerning normal function. If one is interested in the function of the pancreas, for example, it is a simple matter to extirpate that organ from an experimental animal and compare its function with that of a normal animal. Such observations of extreme conditions where the effects are grossly apparent often lead to knowledge concerning normal function. It is not as simple a matter when studying such subjective phenomena as emotion or motivation. However, we do have ways of overcoming the difficulties and permitting us to make observations of these subjective phenomena in the grossly disturbed individual as well as in the relatively normal.

The use of introspection as a technique, which was developed by psychoanalysis, enables us to understand and investigate not only our own subjective experiences, but also those of others. The methodology of psychoanalysis, the use of modern psychology, and the insights of dynamic psychiatry can be used in working with the abnormal to further our understanding not only of the psychopathological but also of the normal. This is far from being a simple process. The understanding of the subjective reactions of others is limited and understood in terms of our own subjective feelings and experiences. Let no one be so naive as to assume that any description of such phenomena actually conveys the full subjective significance of their meaning to others. Such attempts at communication, honest as they may be, can only describe at second hand, by means of symbols, an experience which can be shared only in this limited way. This is true even when conditions for communicating are optimum, such as during psychoanalysis. In most instances, descriptions of subjective experiences are distorted unconsciously, not only by the person who had the experience, but also by the observer. It takes long and patient training to mitigate these distortions in the observer.

In addition, unless one has had the training to see subjective phenomena as they are, such awareness often engenders anxiety. The anxiety results from the conflict of unacceptable, but similar, feelings in the observer, which are stirred by the observations, with his own thoughts, feelings, and motivations. This is often true when studying religious attitudes or beliefs in a person who uses religion defensively to protect the self from unacceptable feelings or thoughts. Religious phenomena are fundamentally mental, hence are subject to the rules and regulations, the distortions and elaborations, of mental activity. These must be understood and evaluated in any study dealing with religion that purports to investigate the phenomena objectively. Some feel that such study of religious experiences mitigates the significance of religion, thus they perceive such investigation as a threat. In actual fact, it is not a threat. These individuals feel threatened because they forget that a description of such an experience and an understanding of the mental factors involved in no way interfere with any value judgment made concerning the experience. We shall have occasion to elaborate this in detail later when discussing religious experience, but an example will demonstrate what is meant.

A certain minister, when nineteen years old, had a conversion experience while attending a retreat with the fellowship group of his church. Briefly, the experience consisted of seeing the trees glow with an unearthly light and feeling a presence near to him. He heard a voice speaking the words, "Declare for Christ." Feeling a sense of relief, of joy, and the conviction that he had been called by God to preach the gospel, he went into the ministry. From the viewpoint of psychology, this man had had an acute hallucinatory experience. From the viewpoint of some religions, this was a religious conversion experience. Of practical import was the effect it had on his life. When we find that it was used to integrate his personality and resolve some conflicts, thus enabling him to function more realistically in a creative, productive manner as a minister, we can make the value judgment that the experience was of benefit to this individual. Understanding of this man's environmental background, his character structure, his personality conflicts, his motivations and subjective needs enables us to understand the meaning of the experience. Such knowledge in no way detracts from the validity of the experience nor mitigates the significance it had for him. The fact that other solutions were available and that his solution worked merely increases our wonderment at the marvelously complex structure that is a functioning human being. It is only the insecure and the invalid who are threatened by this added understanding.

Now, when attempting to discuss experiences such as the one just described, or religion or psychology in general, we are at once confronted with another realistic problem—one of communication. The process of communication is a complex phenomenon which involves many factors, most of which are beyond the present discussion. A few words must be said, however, concerning communication to avoid misunderstanding by some readers. In the patient-physician relationship, communication takes place on two levels—a conscious one and an unconscious one. The physician must be aware of both and respond appropriately to both. He can do so because of his training and because over a period of time he comes to recognize and understand the meaning of his patient's symbolizations. In working with patients whose religious beliefs are a dynamic factor in their personalities, understanding religious symbolism becomes important to the therapist.

That this is a complex situation, especially if a symbol is associated with a symptom can be illustrated by the following example. The ceiling of my consulting room is covered with square acoustic tile. Patients will often see these tiles as arranged in designs, one of the most common being a cross. To understand the meaning of this symbol it is necessary to recognize that it may have a universal unconscious meaning, a specifically personal subjective meaning, a specific meaning symbolic to a sect within the framework of a church, and a broader symbolic meaning within the general framework of Christianity. It might be necessary to analyze each of these meanings before the symbolization of the cross could be understood and a symptom associated with it clarified. In so doing, the value of the symbol of religion is not destroyed, but is allowed fuller expression once the subjective conflict involved by the patient is removed. I recall a patient to whom the cross subjectively symbolized death and destruction. When he was able to recognize the association to his hostile, threatening father and resolve his childhood fear, the cross became a symbol of hope and love. Further analysis of this meaning was related to his dependent yearnings for mother and eventually he was enabled to accept the cross as a religious symbol free of the constricting influences of his own subjective response. His ministry became realistically more effective as he changed membership from a rigid fundamentalistic Protestant sect to one more liberal. The import of this is that, if the dynamic meaning of the symbol is not understood, its value as a means of communication is lost or mitigated. Practically, a therapist working within the framework of a church may be unable to accept or recognize the subjective meaning of such symbols or their meaning may coincide with his own particular beliefs and his effectiveness will be decreased.

In a broader sense this unwillingness or inability to accept or understand another's symbolizations is a problem that the professions of religion and psychology are just beginning to solve. Consider, for instance, the word symbol "love" and the difference in meaning it connotes to a theologian and a psychiatrist. The theologian may affirm that God is Love while the psychiatrist states that Love is God. When they talk of love they use the same symbol to describe something which may be really quite different. Communication and understanding under such circumstances become difficult or impossible and a situation of confusion, not to say of ill will, may exist. Fortunately, men of good will in both professions are working together toward mutual understanding. They are taking the necessary time to define terms, share knowledge, and clarify symbols.

It is perhaps appropriate at this time to discuss briefly the problems of selection, the material itself, and other related factors, by way of further orientation. During a five-year period, as mentioned earlier, it has been my privilege to see in consultation or therapy over one hundred individuals who were associated in one way or another with the profession of religion. For purposes of discussion, they may be divided into two groups—those who had intensive treatment and those who were seen briefly in consultation. The latter group of forty-four people consisted primarily of missionary candidates and students, with a sprinkling of ministers and religious educators. Most of them had been referred by local seminaries because of specific problems or were self-referred because they felt the need of some help. Generally, the procedure with these people was to take a psychiatric history during the course of a clinical interview. Usually the problems were so apparent that specific recommendations could be made to the individual or to the referring seminary.

Missionary candidates, in addition to the diagnostic psychiatric interview, were given the Rorschach and the Wexler-Bellevue Intelligence Test by a psychologist as a part of the routine evaluation by the board of missions of a large Protestant denomination. Thus there was the advantage of having two independent observers, using different methods of evaluating a person, some to independent conclusions regarding each person. With these missionary candidates the purpose was to recognize disabling mental illness, to search for conditions which might potentially become so, to describe the character structure as an aid in placing the candidates in an optimum environment, and to advise and make recommendations. Most of these individuals did not require therapy since they were functioning in an adequate fashion, but they were advised of any problem areas. Those who needed treatment were urged to obtain it and an effort was made to indicate the treatment of choice and help them accept this. Basically, therefore, with these individuals the material available for study consists of clinical psychiatric data and the data from independent psychological testing.

The remaining fifty-six individuals were referred or came of their own accord for specific problems and were accepted for treatment, more or less intensive, depending upon the usual factors governing the selection of patients. These were consecutive cases, in the profession of religion, seen in my practice and were not specially selected for this study. However, insofar as they were all in the profession of religion and members of a Protestant church, they were in a sense pre-selected. They did not come from the same denomination. The majority were Methodists, but Episcopalians, Lutherans, Baptists, and Unitarians were well represented.

The size of the group precludes any valid statistical evaluation. Further, the type of data obtained does not readily admit to statistical study even if the sampling were sufficient. As an example, a patient has a certain dream and free associates to this dream, producing further material. A psychiatrist, using this material plus his knowledge of the patient, plus his understanding of himself and others, makes an interpretation within the framework of the therapeutic hour. How can the patient's response to the dream interpretation be evaluated statistically? Sometimes the full response is not apparent for a week or longer. In addition, the interpretation given, with its particular emphasis, may be only one of several possible interpretations, each of which may be valid for the dream and the patient, but may not be admissable at the time, therapeutically. In my opinion, any attempt to evaluate such subjective data statistically, at our current level of knowledge, is a waste of time, but the material concerning these people is worthy of presentation. Such empirical data can be compared to similar data from other sources and eventually a body of knowledge may be accumulated. From the practical viewpoint, such data have been of value in the treatment of these patients, but the opinions expressed must await further validation.

Since the material was obtained incidental to therapy, a few words concerning therapy may not be amiss at this time. Therapeutic techniques will vary from patient to patient depending upon the needs of the individual. The orientation for treatment was based on the theory and practice of psychoanalysis, or, perhaps more accurately, of dynamic psychiatry which permits a more eclectic attitude toward patients. It is not necessary to enter into a discussion of the various schools of psychotherapy except to say that each has its advantages and disadvantages. My own basic training is Freudian. Therapeutic goals varied from supporting existing psychic defenses to that of changing or modifying character structure. Patients were seen from two to five hours a week over a period of time ranging from as short a period as six months to as long as five years.

The main sources of data for this study were the psychiatric history, psychological testing, and free association or other verbalizations of the patients during their therapy. Obviously, it is impossible to give a full verbatim account of a case history, because the frank and intimate details of the lives, thoughts, and feelings of people often are unacceptable and are anxiety-producing to some. The selection of material must be such as to protect the privacy of the patient as well as to be consistent with current social convention. No useful purpose is served, in these articles, by detailed accounts of that which was revealed in confidence. It must be recognized that such selection and limitation of the material has a disadvantage in that the step-by-step development to a conclusion cannot always be demonstrated. If the conclusions thus seem less convincing to some, this is to be regretted, but is unavoidable under the circumstances. Part of these data are historical in the sense that they have to do with the past history of the patient in relation to his early environment.

We know that early environmental influences affect the development of personality. To know *what* factors are involved and *how* they influence the character structure is important. A study of such influences is a part of all therapy. Linked with familial environmental influences are cultural attitudes which also affect developmental processes. Of interest to the psychiatrist is the study of how some social mores may be used by individuals to alleviate conflict as well as the study of their effect on intensifying conflict. Blain ably discusses these latter imposed stresses in detail.[1] Our concern will be with the problem of how these imposed cultural strains may be used by the individuals for unconscious purposes. For instance, the sacrifice made by many ministers and their families because of pitifully low income can be a source of real

[1] Daniel Blain, *The Church and Mental Health,* edited by P. B. Maves (New York: Charles Scribner's Sons, 1953), p. 253.

concern. However, to some this sacrifice may be welcomed as a means of punishment to atone for guilt feelings over unacceptable impulses or wishes. Pressures from congregations demanding that the minister restrict personal pleasure may lead to an inhibition of normal emotional expression. A minister who fears to express normal feelings because he is afraid he will lose control may welcome these imposed restrictions as a means of maintaining control. Religious beliefs and practices may be used in an attempt to reduce psychological tensions, but may also be the source of additional conflict.

Finally, a major problem to be considered is the effect mental illness has on religion. Historically, it is known that many religious leaders suffered from various forms of mental illness which influenced their lives and affected their religious beliefs. The effect this had on religious practices and society is important. While this is primarily a sociological problem, psychology may have a few words to say.

These then are some of the problems we hope to consider. To some we shall find answers, to others we shall not.

THE SELECTION OF MINISTERS AND THE PREVENTION OF MENTAL ILLNESS

SINCE the writing of the Pastoral Epistles, the Christian community has been developing both criteria and procedure for selecting ministers. The operational hypothesis of such criteria and procedures seems to have been that a man of "power, love, and self-control," an "apt teacher" of "health-giving doctrine" would be most likely to stay that way as a minister and to impart this same health to the people whom he served. The same spirit prevails today in the effort to understand and maintain the mental health of the minister.

This section is devoted to the kinds of things a person entering the ministry should know about the work he is about to do, and to the observations of professional counselors as to their experience in the selection and continuing care of candidates for the ministry.

THE SELECTION OF MINISTERS AND THE
PREVENTION OF MENTAL ILLNESS

Occupational Information for Church Vocation

By Charles F. Kemp
Professor of Pastoral Care,
Brite College of the Bible,
Texas Christian University,
Fort Worth, Texas

Some problems of adjustment of ministers can be prevented by adequate and carefully presented information about their vocation.

One of the most significant areas of religious guidance and counseling is the guidance given to those who are considering full-time religious work as a vocation. This is true, first of all, because the welfare of the individual concerned is involved (as is true in all cases of vocational choice) and also because the welfare of the church and the Christian cause is involved as well. This is an important field for every pastor but especially so for those who are located in college or university centers, or those serving as university pastors, directors of student foundations, chaplains of universities, secretaries of Student Christian Associations—in any capacity where there are large groups of students who are making such decisions.

This is an area in which other counselors expect the religious counselor to be a specialist. The author made a survey of members of the American Psychological Association who are working on college campuses as to their opinions as to the areas of counseling and guidance in which religious workers ought or ought not to function. Only 5.4% felt the religious worker should give general vocational guidance frequently, but 87.2% felt he should give guidance to those entering religious vocations frequently. It is true that 67.2% did say they felt the religious worker could give vocational guidance occasionally, but 27.2% felt he "never" should attempt such guidance—yet there were none who said he should never give guidance to those entering religious vocations. It is not our purpose here to discuss the reasons for the difference in reply. The fact is very evident that the guidance of those entering the religious vocations is an area in which the general counselors expect the religious worker to be an authority, the one to whom they can make referral and to whom they can turn for information.

This article is concerned about one technique of vocational guidance, that known to the vocational counselors as "occupational information." It is one of the standard tools of the vocational counselor, one in which he and his fellow workers have made considerable study and in which they receive special training. It has an application in this one particular field of vocational guidance as well. Occupational information is defined by Shartle, in his book by that title, as "accurate and usable information about jobs and occupations." It is, he says, "the principle tool in exploring with an individual the jobs, occupations, families of occupations. . . . and relative opportunities that may be ahead for him if he makes certain vocational choices."[1] He further stresses the importance of the use of occupational information, pointing out that many people are making decisions "which affect their future lives" on the basis of the occupational information that they have available.

There are two major considerations in all vocational guidance. The first is concerned with understanding the individual, or

---

[1] Shartle, *Occupational Information: Its Development and Application,* (Englewood Cliffs: Prentice Hall, Inc., 1946), pp. 1-2.

rather, to help the individual understand himself in terms of his own interests, abilities, aptitudes, personality and motivation as he makes his vocational choice. In this particular area of vocational guidance it raises the necessity of facing such questions as conscious and unconscious motivation, and the kind of person that should be encouraged or discouraged from considering religious work as a vocation. Such matters are usually best handled through observation, counseling and interviewing, perhaps testing and securing the opinions and evaluations of others who also know the student. The second matter is concerned with providing the student with an understanding of the occupation itself so that he has some basis on which to make his vocational choice and to make it intelligently and sincerely. This is the need that occupational information attempts to meet. This is the area that is the subject of this article as it relates specifically to those vocations or that family of vocations that are usually considered church vocations. It is not claimed that it is the most important aspect of such guidance, but, it is important, and can almost be claimed to be the most neglected. Francis P. Robinson in his book *Principles and Procedures in Student Counseling* (Harpers, 1950) points out that most of the studies show that high school and college students very commonly do not have an accurate estimate at all as to the nature of the job they have chosen for their life work. All such surveys reveal how surprisingly little is the understanding that people have of the nature of a particular vocation, the training that is required, the income that can be expected, the requirements in the way of conditions or the nature of the work itself. If this is true of other fields of work, it is perhaps more so of the religious vocations. Many young people are urged to enter the ministry without being provided with adequate information as to what that choice involves.

Because of the importance of this matter, the educational and vocational counselors have spent much time and effort in developing occupational information materials that will meet their needs. The most widely used is the Dictionary of Occupational Titles, commonly known as the D.O.T., published by the United States Employment Service. The revised edition includes 22,028 different jobs which are known by an additional 17,995 titles. Along with the definitions, they are all coded and classified by occupational groups with brief descriptions of the work performed and the skill required. There are many other sources such as the *Occupational Outlook Handbook,* "Occupational Guides," filing systems and elaborate methods of classification and reference have been devised for the use of the vocational counselor. There are two points about this, however, that are of importance. First, these general sources of occupational information are very limited in dealing with information on the religious worker; second, the young person interested in the religious field as a life work is more likely to go to his pastor than to an educational or vocational counselor.

The occupational information in these general sources usually mentions the ministry and religious education, with perhaps a reference to the mission field. Actually, the job opportunities in the religious field are very wide and varied. They are divided into at least fifteen different categories (although others have separated them into even more divisions). (1) The minister in a local church is the most common and would include assistant or associate pastors. Within the ministry, there are quite different emphases, such as, city pastors, rural pastors and pastors of suburban churches. (2) The field of religious education includes both opportunities in a local church as a director of religious education and also on a state, area, or national level either within a denomination or an interdenominational agency. (3) The field of administration and promotion utilizes many people, for almost all groups have some state, area, and national organization. There is also the whole field of interdenominational work in city and state councils and the National Council of Churches. (4) The mission field has many specialized areas, such as, educational missions, medical missions, agricultural missions, as well as opportunities for engineers, technicians, administrators and others. (5) American or home missions exist within each denomination with a wide variety of projects—in the cities, among Indians, among Mexicans, mountain people of Kentucky and other states. (6) Social service agencies, settlement houses, homes for the aged, orphanages, hospitals sponsored by church groups, all demand all types of personnel—administrators, dieticians, attendants, nurses, promotion men, social workers, etc. (7) Institutional chaplains are utilized in general hospitals, mental hospitals, prisons and reformatories. (8) The armed services present a constant demand for men for the chaplaincy. (9) A ministry to students is maintained by directors of religious foundations, university pastors, chaplains of universities, directors of religious activities and those with similar titles, as well as by secretaries of Student Christian Associations. (10) Teaching in the field of religion is done through church colleges as well as in some state schools that have a department of religion; some churches maintain their own academies or secondary schools, and on the graduate and professional level through the numerous seminaries and theological schools. (11) Religious journalism and religious publishing, both denominational and interdenominational, employ large groups of people, providing opportunities for writers, editors, photographers and others. (12) Religious radio and television is a new but growing field demanding producers, script writers, program directors and others necessary to produce radio and television programs. Also, the whole field of audio-visual aids in religion has made rapid strides with the promise of more in the future. (13) Sacred music provides some full-time and many part-time opportunities as choir directors, ministers of music, organists, professors of religious music. (14) Church secretaries, receptionists, financial secretaries and business managers are used in many churches and religious agencies. These positions do not usually require theological training but demand an understanding of the church and its function. (15) There are also many related organizations and institutions such as the Y.M.C.A., the Y.W.C.A., the Salvation Army, City Missions and other social agencies which have a strong religious activation, and carry on many religious activities as well as recreational and welfare work and may require religious training. Some young people are fitted for one type of field or institution, some for another.

Occupational information, if it is to meet its fullest usefulness, must be thorough and must present all possibilities. Regular courses of occupational information do not begin to cover all these different areas, specializations and opportunities. Perhaps they should not be expected to. Another problem regarding occupational information in the field of church vocations is a result of the divided nature of religion in America. We not only have what is usually referred to as the three major faiths—Protestantism, Catholicism and Judaism—but Protestantism is further divided and each denomination has its own institutions, its own educational standards and qualifications, its own needs and opportunities. It is no wonder that the general counselors feel that they cannot keep up with all the differences in denominational groups that would be represented by the different students in any one school or university. This is one reason the pastor has to be considered as the resource person to whom the general counselor may turn.

The church has not been idle in this matter. There are resources that are available for the pastor. The Commission on the Ministry of the National Council of Churches has published a series of inexpensive booklets with an interdenominational emphasis, such as, "A Young Man's View of the Ministry" and "We Have This Ministry: Church Vocations for Men and Women," as well as pamphlets on The Rural Pastorate, Opportunities for the Negro Minister, a Statement by the American Association of Theological Schools on Pre-Seminary Studies, and several others. It includes a pamphlet on "Reading About Church Vocations," which contains a bibliography of the books and leaflets that have been prepared to guide young people in the making of their decisions. It also publishes an *Enlistment Manual for Church Vocations,* which was written by John Oliver Nelson for "pastors, teachers, and vocational counselors." It contains instructions for both group programs and counseling and interviewing, and includes samples of occupational information material on church vocations that is available. It would seem advisable for a pastor who is discussing such subjects with his young people to have a supply of such material on hand and to develop his own file of occupational information. Such material, well selected, may go much farther than a mere interview.

In one sense, for reasons mentioned above, each denomination must provide its own occupational information in terms of its own needs and opportunities. Most denominations publish such materials. Some of it is very well done, clear in its interpretation, attractively set up. For example, the Presbyterian Church utilizes the Enlistment Manual provided by the National Council and provides further pamphlets that fit into the packet provided in the cover, such as, "Nine Questions About Entering the Ministry," "Church Vocations for Women," pamphlets describing the opportunities both home and abroad, pamphlets on church social work, office secretary and as a housemother, as well as information regarding schools and training.

The Methodist Church publishes a *Christian Vocation Guide,* and has prepared a Recruitment Packet which includes Volunteer Service Materials, Church Vocation leaflets on a great variety of subjects, such as, "Steps Into the Methodist Ministry," Summer Service Projects and the various Careers in Christian Service that are available.

The Disciples have prepared a booklet "Your Life Work; the Christian Ministry," and "I Would Do It Again," both to give a picture of the nature and extent of the ministry as a vocation. These, like many of the others mentioned, can be used on an interdenominational basis.

The National Lutheran Council publishes a Vocational Guidance Booklet entitled "Who Will Go" with information on Deaconesses, Institutional Chaplains, Institutional Managers, Institutional Nurses, Medical Missionaries, Ministers of Music, Missionary Teachers, Parish Education Field Workers, Parish Workers, Sextans, Student Workers, Teachers in Church Colleges, Welfare Workers, Youth Directors and many others as well.

The Congregational Church publishes a paper or series of pamphlets called "Men for the Ministry" which discusses such items as the choice of a seminary, selective service opportunities that are available and other topics that are of concern to one who is considering this choice.

These are but a few examples of some of the material that is available. There is much more. A letter to any of the major denominational headquarters will secure a packet of such materials, much of it of a very valuable nature that can be placed in the hands of young people who are considering this decision.

Along with such material should be included catalogues of various theological schools. They are especially helpful in giving a student not only a picture of the course of study he will pursue if he makes this choice, but also information as to requirements for entrance, scholarships and loan funds that are available and other factors that would affect his choice.

There are also visual aids that should be mentioned. Film strips are available on the work of the Ministry, the Missionary, and the Director of Religious Education. There are some sound films on vocational choice in general which can be used as the basis of discussion, a few that deal primarily with the choice of the ministry or a church vocation as such, and several missionary films which can be used to present the work of the missionary. These are especially helpful as the basis of group guidance and discussion.

Occupational information as used by religious workers should measure up to the same standards as have been developed in the vocational guidance movement that the religious worker should be aware of. George F. Myers, in his *Principles and Techniques of Vocational Guidance,* includes an outline for the study of any particular occupation. He feels that occupational information should include adequate information in the following eight different areas:

(1) Importance of the occupation
(2) Nature of the work
(3) Working conditions
(4) Personal qualities needed
(5) Preparation needed
(6) Opportunities for advancement
(7) Compensation
(8) Advantages and disadvantages[1]

[1] George F. Myers, *Principles and Techniques of Vocational Guidance,* (New York: McGraw Hill, 1941), p. 111.

Each item has many subdivisions which it is not necessary to include here. There are, of course, other such outlines. They are all very similar and have the common purpose of attempting to make sure that the material is as thorough, effective and useful as it can be to enable the student to make his own decision as wisely as possible.

It is recognized, of course, that good occupational information material does not guarantee good guidance. It is the use and interpretation of the material that is important. It is also recognized that distributing occupational information material does not constitute vocational counseling and guidance. It is only a resource, an aid to supplement the more important aspect of the personal relationship between the religious worker and the student. It is our purpose to make all counseling and guidance as effective as possible. To this end we should utilize all resources that are available. In order that this might be done, religious workers should be aware of the materials that have been prepared; they should study how these materials can be used most advantageously and should seek constantly to improve the materials that we have.

Work and Personality Adjustment

By Leonard Small
Consulting Psychologist, New York City; Instructor, New York University; Consulting Psychologist, AHRO Health and Rehabilitation Services, New York City; formerly, Director of Special Research, Vocational Advisory Service, New York City.

Work is integral to our selfhood. In both its larger context and its specific reference to the ministry, the relevance of work for outstanding emotional health is discussed by Leonard Small.

Increasingly we are coming to understand the implication of an old fact about work: We work not only to earn our bread, but to earn as well our place in the community, and our health of personality. In our country especially the kind of work that we do—not our birth nor even our wealth—establishes our place among our fellows.

The human personality itself can be described according to the work of its several parts. The ego—our primary concern here—has the difficult job of establishing and maintaining contact with the external world of reality. It has the further job of preventing tides of unreasonable impulses from swamping and controlling our behavior. To control impulses, the personality must be able to oppose them with reality. To remain in contact with reality, the personality must be able to move about in it. Therefore, the ego develops skills. The child exploring, touching, smelling, tasting, walking, opening the door, and playing ball, is acquiring skills. At the same time it is developing a sense of selfhood, for as it succeeds in its manipulative exploration, it feels: "I can open the door." The child thus places himself apart from the door as an organization capable of performing something upon the door. From this sense of self and of successful performance flows a feeling of capacity and closely allied to this is the feeling of control or mastery: "I can open the door if I want to,"—all part of the ego's duties.

In addition to being a worker the personality is also an inveterate mirror-gazer. It turns this profile, then the other to its own scrutiny and at all times it is critical of its image. This critical evaluation we call self-esteem—"I am good" or "I am bad"—the job of the conscience or super-ego. Frequent and important among the comments about the self are those that concern performance, the competencies of the whole individual, for the sense of doing something well parallels the sense of being "good." In fact, to be competent so often is equated with being good.

While all the many activities in which we engage involve skills, the skills most important to us are those we use in earning a living. The way in which we work and the kind of work we do are crucial in forming our self-evaluations. It is a question not only of pleasure in skill but of social status, and beyond this the attainment of adult maturity, for work can bring responsibility and independence. Self-esteem, then, is derived from our work as well as from our moral judgments.

We know from our everyday mirror-gazing the importance of seeing just what is reflected in the glass. Sometimes we fool ourselves, distort the first gray hair, perhaps, into a shock of white. So it is with the mirror-gazing our personalities do: it can be accurate or distorted. The self-image of the healthy personality is derived from a reasonably accurate perception of reality. Here again we may link work with the self-image because work for the adult is one of the major reality exercises—work involves continual contact with and perception of reality.

Once we comprehend the importance of the fact that work requires reality perception, we can understand the forces that operate to produce both vocational adjustment and maladjustment.

Let us look at the healthy person at work. He selects a field for which he is equipped by reason of abilities, capacities, interests, aptitudes and training. He develops and progresses in this work. He achieves independence, responsibility, recognition, and self-respect. At every point reality has been perceived and understood with little distortion. The end result is a favorable self-esteem.

Now let us look at a less healthy person: say a mechanically-skilled high school graduate whose grades in math and physical sciences were barely passing. He applies to engineering schools and is heart-broken that he is not accepted. He has not seen himself as he really is and this distortion in perception has brought pain. He has several tests ahead that will all involve reality perception. Will he give up the idea of engineering school and become a mechanic? Will he attempt to bolster his subject weaknesses with further instruction and try again for engineering school, or will he drift into any sort of job and constantly complain that he was never given a chance to show what he could do in college. His decisions and his self-esteem will depend on the accuracy of his perception of himself and of the world around him.

Distortions in reality perception occur with all degrees and with with all possible complexities. Arbitrarily we can set up levels of distortion to illustrate the kinds of vocational maladjustment that occur and their accessibility to assistance.

Easily reached and aided is the person whose vocational problem arises from an accurate but incomplete perception of reality —the young person who needs only some information before he can himself achieve vocational adjustment. Many young people find themselves in this situation, for it is one brought about largely by the complexity of our culture. We have more than

30,000 separately definable jobs. Which job shall a young person prepare for? What is the economic status of this job, that one? Which jobs are in short supply? Which are plentiful? What personal equipment is needed? What training? How long will the training take? Where to get the training? Which fields are expanding? Which are contracting? Vocational information of this kind is the need of most young people. Once they have it, many are able to make realistic decisions and find adjustment in the vocations they select.

Many other young people show the first evidence of vocational maladjustment only after they are well into the initial phases of a work life. These early years can be critical, for during them may emerge the individual patterns of behavior that will characterize the whole life of the person.

The early stage of work life is a time of learning. Sometimes the task is to learn whether or not a certain field of work offers what the youngster is after. Almost always it is the time for establishing work habits and skills that then become the stepping stones to occupational development. As with all learning, a time factor is important; a useful criterion by which to judge vocational adjustment is the length of employment spent in learning jobs by each individual. The healthy young worker remains in the beginning or learning job long enough to derive the maximal training experience from it, and then takes steps to move on, recognizing that movement at the appropriate time is a condition of progress. In such people the self-image is constantly adjusting itself to a changing reality. At first he is a learner; subsequently he becomes a skilled person ready for different things, and so sees himself.

Maladjustment at this stage often is shown in a disregard of the time factor. The person leaves one beginning job for another before he has been able to acquire what the first job has to offer. He plunges into a series of job changes, with the consequence that he is always a beginning worker, but never a skilled one. The driving fantasy distorting the self-image is usually, "Enough of this learning stuff; I'm for bigger and better things." And of course, the fantasy is always at odds with reality.

Another kind of time disturbance at this stage of work life can be called job passivity. A person remains in his first beginning job for years, becoming the epitome of distorted reality—the highly skilled beginning. A typical case is reported in personal literature of a young man who, on the basis of his scores on psychological tests, was promoted from his messenger job held for several years. He promptly developed headaches and stomach symptoms that disappeared when he was returned to his work as a messenger.

Where the self-image is so distorted, the task of making realistic decisions is difficult for the personality and a more serious maladjustment arises. The youngster who over-evaluates himself and fantasies that he has capacities that are not his is on the road to continual frustration and vocational unhappiness. The youngster who under-evaluates himself and plows under his rich assets in low-level jobs is a social and personal waste. In both cases the foe of reality perception is fantasy—or believing we are something other than we are.

Vocational counseling may help young people with such problems. The assessment of aptitudes, intelligence and skills by a competent counselor may be accepted and used by the young worker to alter his self-image to accord with reality. He is then on the way to vocational adjustment. But sometimes reality perception is so weak that the perceptions of the counselor cannot be used to focus more accurately the individual's own self-image. Then the person needs the more prolonged and delicate assistance of psychotherapy.

The seriousness of a vocational maladjustment, therefore, parallels the strength of the individual's contact with reality. Contact with reality is one of the functions of that part of the personality which we call the ego. The stronger ego is more readily accessible to assistance, information and counseling. The weaker ego needs strengthening—psychotherapy—before it can utilize the realistic services of the vocational counselor to combat the pressure of a persistent fantasy and to make realistic choices and decisions.

To assess ego strength and to determine what form of assistance a vocationally maladjusted person needs is not necessarily easy. We may think: we will try information first and then counseling and if they don't work, then there may be a need for psychotherapy. One danger with this empirical approach is that a passive, compliant person will with characteristic passivity and compliance accept information and counseling and make decisions which are not his own, but the ones implied by the counselor. The professional competence of the counselor, of course, is the only guard against this danger.

Pastors today are undoubtedly convinced of the importance of sending people only to professionally competent psychotherapists. Once acquainted with the facts they will accept with equal conviction the necessity to refer only to competent vocational counselors for reliable information and counseling of professional quality because vocational information, if it is to help complete a person's reality picture, must be realistic. It must also be current and reliable. Too often the propaganda of personnel recruitment infiltrates the published information that circulates today. A wise precaution, therefore, is to seek vocational information from a professional person. But if such counselors are not available, material from public sources can be scrutinized by a pastor himself or by the individual with his guidance. Most public libraries have increasing amounts of occupational information and some maintain special files and indexes on job subjects. Several popular magazines publish occupational material as a regular part of their content, though often their releases are directed toward special groups. The accurate and lively job articles of *Mademoiselle* magazine, for example, are written especially for women college students and graduates. The Labor Departments of both State and Federal governments are valuable sources of vocational information.

Since the war, there has been a marked expansion of counseling services and an increasing drive for professional standards among counselors; most counselors now are meeting the membership standards of the American Psychological Association and the National Vocational Guidance Association.

Counseling services will be found in many junior and most

senior high schools. Many colleges and universities have well-staffed counseling centers which are often available to members of the community. The employment services of some states, the Y.M. and Y.W.C.A.'s, the Salvation Army, the Jewish vocational centers, and the Catholic charity organizations are among the groups that maintain counseling services in cities and towns throughout the country.

When in doubt about the existence of a nearby counseling agency or about the professional qualifications of a service, the local council of welfare agencies or a social casework agency can be consulted. An excellent but not necessarily complete source of such information is the list of approved agencies and individuals offering vocational counseling services published by the Ethical Practice Committee of the National Vocational Guidance Association, Box 64, Washington University, St. Louis 5, Missouri.

In stressing professional counseling, I hope I have not created an impression that would lead to hesitancy in making referrals for this service. Rather I want to emphasize the operation of personality factors in work adjustment. It is important for all who work with people to comprehend that work involves accurate reality perception and that work maladjustment reflects an impairment in this function.

Underestimation of the importance of this relationship between work and ego strength has led to the ballooning of the "test myth"—one that no one is more anxious to explode than the counselor himself. The myth is that a counselor gives a person a series of aptitude tests and then *tells him what to do.* A counselor who did that would be as incompetent professionally were he to tell the person what to do without having first examined him in any way. The truth is that a professional counselor seldom tells a person what to do, and that counseling is a far more complicated thing than the mere administration and interpretation of aptitude tests.

Aptitude tests themselves are limited. We are able to measure only a few aptitudes and these few can be evaluated in a general way only—seldom with specificity. Most important, we cannot forecast from an individual's test scores his ability to develop an aptitude into a skill. There is no short-cut substitute for the face-to-face human interchange between the person seeking vocational assistance and the experienced counselor sensitive to nuances of interest, striving and motivation. Aptitude tests are an important tool for the counselor but by no means his only one.

Furthermore, in most instances, telling a person what to do is correctly felt by the person as being authoritarian and provokes either dependence or rebellion, neither of which is the goal of counseling. The counselor's approach to the individuals whom he counsels is founded upon the progressive stepping stones of understanding, integration, growth and independence.

Psychiatric and Psychological Tests for Missionary Personnel

By

JULES HYMAN MASSERMAN, M.D.
Profesor, Neurology and Psychiatry,
Northwestern University,
Evanston, Illinois

RALPH T. PALMER, B.A., B.D., M.S.
United Christian Missionary Service,
Indianapolis, Indiana

The missionary today undergoes much closer scrutiny as to the adequacy of his emotional health for his or her task than does the pastor of a church on the home front. The kinds of insight derived from the psychiatric and psychological examinations of missionary personnel are pertinent to a better understanding of what should be expected of the minister who serves churches at home.

The excellent series of articles in *Pastoral Psychology* constituting a discussion of the general theme, "The Ministry as a Vocation, Part I" which began in the December, 1958 issue, pointed to some of the significant factors relating to the qualifications for entering the several vocations of the church and to the need for understanding more certainly the aptitudes, abilities, and personality traits of any aspirant to one of these ministries. The articles of this series have clearly pointed out the need for an even greater use of psychometric evaluations in helping to determine the qualifications of individuals entering the Christian ministries. Big business has successfully used such tests for several years and it has seemed advisable and even necessary to many of the leaders of the Church to use similar techniques in the administration of the business of the church. To some extent this has been done.

1. Psychiatric and Psychologic Reports to Non-Medical Personnel

It is significant to note that more and more use is being made of certain types of psychologic tests by seminaries and those ecclesiastical organs within the denomination responsible for selecting or at least "approving" ministerial candidates. Historically, Foreign Mission Boards have been forerunners in the use of psychological and psychiatric testing for missionary applicants. These boards have shown the value to missionary personnel selection of those tests that probe deeply into the personality structures of the individual applicant.

Several years ago certain leading foreign mission boards turned to preventive psychology and preventive psychiatry, seeking "predictions of fitness" because of a tragic experience among them. To the sorrow of both missionaries and administrators and to the great detriment of the organization cause they served, many apparently sincere, dedicated and self-sacrificing men and women sent to foreign fields broke down with disabling and sometimes serious emotional difficulties. It was obvious that the mission of the church was being impaired by the sending of personnel abroad who were unable to work effectively within the forceful and often extreme stresses and strains of missionary service in foreign cultures. It was therefore proposed, "that each candidate for missionary, before being accepted, be given a series of psychologic or psychiatric tests . . . to determine his suitability for his final years of special missionary training and future assignment overseas."

This proposal was made to Dr. Jules Masserman in the early

1940's by the representatives of several denominations.[1] The executives of the various denominations agreed on one essential point: that they wanted no more zealots nor fanatics and were, in fact, actually less interested in the detailed theologic doctrines of their missionaries than in their qualities as warm, sympathetic, understanding, dedicated and effective servants of their fellow man as well as of their personal God.

Dr. Masserman and several collaborators trained in psychology and psychiatry accepted the project with these provisions: (1) that all available information be furnished about each candidate; (2) that a detailed description of the various foreign posts and their requirements be sent to the testors, and that they be kept informed of changing conditions; (3) that all reports and recommendations be kept completely confidential; (4) that these reports be considered as only one item among all others known to each missionary board in judging the acceptability of a candidate and finally; (5) that follow-up studies be done at suitable intervals to check on the fairness and validity of the entire procedure. The last was done (described below) and the check proved so satisfactory that the practice of examining missionary candidates has now become the accepted practice by most American missionary societies. Some boards examine missionary volunteers but a few months before final acceptance prior to departure for an overseas post. At least one mission board administers these tests in the junior and senior college years. Results are then used as a guide for stimulating wise vocational choices and proper academic preparation, for directions in counseling the candidates toward an adequate and mature emotional control of their lives as well as for the purposes of screening candidates into or out of

[1] Jules Hyman Masserman, *The Practice of Dynamic Psychiatry*, (W. V. Saunders Co., 1955), see chapters 16 and 17. In chapter 16, "Psychiatric Reports to Non-medical Personnel," Dr. Masserman reports on the use of psychiatric examinations in personnel work. It should be noted that whereas Dr. Masserman limits the contents of this chapter to "psychiatric reports" the use of a combination of both psychologic and psychiatric reports is common to mission boards. Dr. Masserman and Mr. Palmer have discussed both psychologic and psychiatric reports in this article.

missionary service abroad. Occasionally the attainment of emotional stability is accomplished only with the use of professional care and, therefore, early detection is the more advisable.

It must be noted, however, that some organizations have limited their tests to those which merely attempt to ascertain intelligence quotient (I.Q.), certain aptitudes and interests. Used without the support of tests that probe deeper into the personality, these tests results have shown no proven co-relation to success in the missionary vocations of the tested. For this reason one overseas mission board has withdrawn from the use of psychologic testing altogether. Deeper probing into the personality traits and problems of prospective missionaries is necessary to an adequate understanding and use of psychologic and psychiatric examinations. For this reason, several mission boards, such as those of the Disciples of Christ and the Methodists, subject each missionary recruit evidencing other acceptable qualifications to a complete battery of psychologic tests administered by qualified clinical psychologists, to physical examinations and to interviews with psychiatrists. The result is a fairly comprehensive picture of the personality profile of each person's tests. Thus, it is possible to determine to a considerable extent a person's vocational fitness as well as his ability to get along with colleagues and co-workers amidst the known stresses and strains of service abroad.

THE VALUE OF PERSONNEL EVALUATIONS

The validity of personnel surveys such as those here cited can be determined only by the actual performance of the candidates examined under a significant variety of stresses in practical employment over a sufficiently long time.

Fortunately, an objective survey of just this nature was conducted by one of the missionary societies,[2] to which reports were

---

[2] Further to protect the identity of the candidates, this society will not be referred to by name. It must also be made clear that the society's report covered the services of other psychologists in about one-fifth of the cases.

furnished over a period of fifteen years. This society prepared a self-critical ten-year follow-up study of its personnel practices, and a practical ten-year follow-up study of its personnel practices and particularly of the value of psychologic and psychiatric appraisals of the candidates. A transcript of the society's report follows:

Of a total of 364 candidates examined: seventy-eight (21%) were rejected for causes distributed as follows: neurotic difficulties, 36; inadequate motivation, 12; temperamental unsuitability of spouse, 10; of self, 8; poor physical health, 3; other reasons (familial objection, financial, etc.), 9.

Thirty-seven candidates withdrew from their studies at various periods after acceptance. Only 6 of these did so because of the development of neurotic tendencies and 2 were unwilling to conform to certain required church formalities. One hundred forty-four missionaries were accepted by the society, trained and then assigned to field duties under almost every conceivable combination of conditions on every continent of the globe. Of these, 129 served succcessfully, 3 rendered excellent service but had to withdraw out of consideration for their spouses and only 12 were considered to be failures. However, of these 12, 9 had earned only partial and tentative recommendations after their psychiatric appraisals, generally with specific qualifications to the effect that they would require limited duties and especially protective environments and interpersonal relationships if neurotic breakdowns were to be avoided. In effect, then, only 3 of the 135 candidates recommended without such qualifications had failed to perform as predicted— and 2 of these also withdrew because of marital difficulties.

The other 105 candidates not accounted for in the statistics were either still in training or had not served sufficiently long (five years or more) for adequate evaluation. Summarizing these and other more personal data, the society's official report concludes as follows: "All of the 129 who were considered good to excellent risks by the psychologists and psychiatrists (including the 6 who had some psychiatric help before appointment) have done well abroad. Thus these counselors forecast quite accurately the outcome of 141 cases (132 successful, 9 unsuccessful) and missed in only 3 (only one, unless they are expected to know in advance all of Cupid's capers). The men and women who gave the tests and conducted the interviews were in the beginning too lenient in some cases and recommended acceptance of volunteers who, according to their reports, had rather serious personality difficulties. The psychologists and psychiatrists did not then have adequate information about the stresses and strains of life in a mission station.

The secretaries of the foreign division, knowing the difficulties of the life of a missionary, sometimes overlooked rather clear signals in the reports.

When personality clashes caused trouble in the field and secretaries re-examined the reports, they saw these warnings. . . . The secretaries are now very carefully observing students before recommending them for candidacy whose qualifications are no more serious than those of some of the missionaries who were appointed and failed to adjust.

True, such studies, however gratifying, must be taken in their context. One qualification is that there is no practical way of determining how many of the 78 candidates who were rejected might have done well had they been given an opportunity. Again, though the authors have the highest respect for the ability and integrity of those who prepared the report quoted, they recognize that the reporters, too, are human, so that it would be impossible to state with complete certainty that some degree of justification for their own efforts did not creep into their survey.

Nevertheless, the conclusion cannot be gainsaid that diagnostic procedures for personnel evaluation such as those described in the preceding sections have demonstrable value in that most important of all fields of behavior study: the happy and creative adaptation of a human being to his projected life work among his fellows.

2. Reporting Test Results to Non-Medical Personnel

The psychiatrists and psychologists who serve as examiners for prospective missionary personnel are faced with the difficult task of reporting to non-medical administrators. They must report to Mission Society personnel secretaries and other non-medical administrators the results of the tests which have been used and their recommendations, based on these tests as to the advisability or inadvisability of sending the tested missionary recruit abroad. The problem of reporting to laymen is not unique to religious bodies for many secular companies are using psychometric tests for job placements and frequent use is made of psychiatrists and psychologists in courts of law. In every case the reporting doctor must observe the basic rules which provide for intelligible and useful communication.

Therefore, clinical psychologists and psychiatrists making reports to non-medical personnel must not only be proficient in their professions but must have the following:

a. A general knowledge of the motivational, intellectual, and physical attributes required by the various careers and positions (job analysis).

b. Specific acquaintance with probable characteristics of the future employers, supervisors and co-workers in the particular profession, trade or industry the candidate being tested contemplates entering.

It is necessary that all reports include a brief but factual resume of the recommendations and the reasons for the recommendations submitted by the examiner. These reports should be couched in relatively nontechnical language which can be clearly understood by the recipient. At the same time these reports must not be so simple as to import a hazy and less than useful interpretation due to incomplete information. Modern mission boards often require both missionary service abroad plus special academic training in psychology as prerequisites for the job of personnel secretary. For this reason, the reporting doctor must recognize that he is reporting to semi-professionally trained persons and must not allow his reports to become too non-technical nor too general. As will be seen in the examples that follow, the names of tests used, raw scores, the percentile rates and the examiner's recommendation are of the utmost importance to the trained personnel secretary.

3. Psychiatric Reports to Mission Board Personnel Secretaries

We have discussed above the reports of the clinical psychologists and the psychiatrist in general terms. Let us look now at the reporting of the psychiatrists to the personnel secretaries.[3]

[3] For more complete information concerning psychiatric reports to non-medical personnel see Jules Hyman Masserman, *loc. cit.*

It isn't necessary to indicate to the reader that the circumstances of each case will determine the type of report that the psychiatrist makes to the personnel secretaries concerning the missionary candidates. As shown in the example, all reports should give a brief of the important factors in the patient's personal history, followed by a description of the "psychiatric status" of the patient, pointing out the important personality traits of the individual. Recommendations then follow:

FAVORABLE REPORTS

When there is no special question of an applicant's suitability, the report may be made relatively brief.

MISCONCEPTIONS

Unfortunately, even among intelligent and otherwise well informed administrators, a question of "a broken home or adverse heredity" may arise with regard to a candidate and need specific handling. This is a case of educating the administrator. For instance, it is sometimes necessary to state that a history of mental illness in the family does not portend mental illness in the patient. In these reports, the family history is spelled out in more detail than is usually necessary.

ENVIRONMENTAL VICISSITUDES

Not infrequently, unusual environmental stresses may elicit adverse responses in a subject and thus throw his candidacy into serious question with the board. In such circumstances it is the task of the psychiatric consultant to distinguish these reactions clearly from long-term character deficiencies that would truly disqualify the candidate. Discerning and desirable men and women thus can be saved for a constructive career.

QUALIFIED RECOMMENDATIONS

Whenever necessary, the prospective employer should be informed that an accepted candidate has certain vulnerabilities, as in the following report.

The psychiatrist in his report indicates that the patient has superior intelligence yet evidences limitations for originality, imagery and the capacity for verbal communications. The psychiatrist then indicates that the prospective type shows a stereotype of a person suffering from deep feelings of inadequacy and inferiority. The patient is indecisive, anxious and narrow. Such information helps the personnel secretary both in determining whether this person in question can be used abroad, or should be re-directed into service in the United States and also whether he may be aided to mature and overcome some of these problems.

PHYSICAL HANDICAPS

Occasionally, approval must be qualified by appropriate reservations as to physical fitness. For instance, a person showing a progressive rise in blood pressure or an individual found to be diabetic may be given a trial period abroad or deferred for a year or more in the United States while the seriousness and controllability of the handicap is studied by professionally trained persons.

DEFERRAL OF JUDGMENT

While awaiting more favorable developments as to motivation, marital adjustment or other changing factors, it is sometimes wise to defer judgment until these developments crystalize into a clearer picture of the individual involved.

CONTINGENCY OF JUDGMENT

In difficult cases it is not only admissible but highly advisable to maintain an understanding that the employer must make the ultimate decision, and that this is governed by many contingencies other than the psychiatric evaluation and by circumstances largely beyond the examiner's knowledge and control. There are times when the need for personnel abroad makes it necessary to send the persons to "fill in the gaps," even though certain personality difficulties tend to point to the inadvisability of accepting the person. A person is seldom if ever sent abroad when there is a clear-cut negative judgment on the part of the psychiatric and psychologic examiners, but when this is a matter of a difficult case with relative values on both sides of the question, persons are sometimes sent abroad because of special needs.

SODIUM AMYTAL AS AN ANCILLARY DIAGNOSTIC AID

In very rare and particularly difficult cases, sodium amytal interviews may be used as auxiliary diagnostic aids. Sodium amytal tends to relax the subject and causes answers that are more frank and honest than elicited when the subject is under the normal tension confronted day by day.

MODIFICATIONS OF INCOMPLETE OR INACCURATE INITIAL JUDGMENTS

No pretense of infallibility can or need be maintained by the examiner, and occasionally the initial judgments of an examiner may be modified. When more information is needed concerning a candidate and/or when a mission board administrator or the examiner suspects inaccuracies in the initial judgments, candidates are re-examined.

PATIENCE BEFORE RENDERING FINAL JUDGMENT

Occasionally, an even longer wait and interim therapy eventually prove justified, as shown by the interesting young lady herein described:

This young woman was found to have a sober personality. She was inhibited, somber, introspective. She was reserved, formal and distant in all interpersonal relationships resulting in self-isolation and a sense of martyrdom. Although her intelligence was high, she displayed no special capacities. Masochistic tendencies were quite pronounced. Obviously, without help she would never be able to serve as an adequate and inspiring example of tranquility and serenity. It is interesting to note that sometimes a person of this type is considered by ministers and lay Christians as "deeply motivated, consecrated, and mature (sober) person who is willing to suffer and die for the cause of Christ." However these underlying disturbances in her personality made work abroad seem impossible, without improvement. It was recommended that she undertake a program of psychotherapy. The young lady in question was interviewed for a second time at a later date. Again the recommendation was for intensive psychotherapy. It was proposed that this psychotherapy be taken over a period of a year and that at the end of this time, a third interview occur. This interview occurred the following year and the psychiatrist found that the former unpleasant mannerism had almost disappeared. Her efforts to understand and overcome her deficiencies and her remarkable improvement caused a recommendation as a candidate, subject to a continuation of personal guidance.

UNQUALIFIED REJECTIONS

When these seem justified in the best interests of all concerned, the reasons for the decision should be clearly and objectively stated in the report to the personnel secretary. Mission boards are never justified in sending persons abroad who have an unqualified rejection in the examiner's report. Persons who are rejected by the examiner are "redirected" by Mission boards. Mission board policy usually does not consider any person rejected from the Christian vocations. However, personality traits may be such as to indicate that the individual involved should not serve abroad but instead should serve either in a church vocation at home or in a secular occupation which is undertaken as a devout Christian. In each case of a person being re-directed, the policy of some mission boards makes it possible for these persons to be interviewed again by a clinical psychologist or a psychiatrist. At these times the examiners are asked to do what they can to help the person see a way whereby he may overcome his difficulties. Often it is possible for the counselor to advise a program of psychotherapy or of professional counseling which will result in an improvement in emotional health and a more effective and satisfying life in whatever vocation the person chooses. There are some times when the emotional balance is so precarious that an examination of the problems of the individual seems inadvisable. And this is usually because the person has adjusted to his difficulties in such a way that the adjustments which structure his personality would tend to destroy his personality if questioned. In these cases the individuals concerned are helped to find occupations within the United States in which they can work with maximum effectiveness and happiness even though their under-mining difficulties remain.

DELAYED APPROVAL

Sometimes the psychiatrist can take professional pleasure in changing an adverse judgment to a favorable one, even when his recommendations have not been completely followed—as witness this striking case. It should be noted that such cases are rare.

A woman applied for missionary service but when examined was found to be seriously handicapped by severe obsessive-com-pulsive neuroses evidenced in many ways including an inability to tolerate church services, the contemplation of suicide and severe depression. It was recommended that she see two psychi-atrists for therapy. Three years later it was found that she had only partially followed the recommendation. Although she had not undertaken psychotherapy, she did follow the advice of the examiner and regain her position as a field worker. This act plus an intensive desire to improve herself resulted in a marked alert-ness, spontaneousness and integrated personality. She was recom-mended for a further observation and was sent abroad for a trial. She proved to be happy in her duties as a missionary and ren-dered satisfactory service in the field.

The following is a typical report by Dr. Masserman.

REPORT TO: Ralph T. Palmer
The United Christian Missionary Society
222 South Downey Avenue
Indianapolis 7, Indiana

SUBJECT: (the name of the patient and age)

Relevant Personal History

A highly important influence in the patient's life has been her intense, ambivalent and unresolved attachment to her father. She describes this somewhat as follows: When he was sober she idealized him as a devoted and fun-loving companion who was proud of her accomplishments as his only daughter; when he was intoxicated, she spent hours in worrying about his irresponsibility, cruelty to her mother and his "sins." When the patient was 11 years of age her parents were separated although not divorced, creating a schism between them which was not absolutely realized causing the child to hope for the possibility of reunion. She was left with divided loyalties and conflict and conflictual drives: on the one hand toward compensatory self-sufficiency and independence; on the other, a restless yearning for security and belonging. Both were reflected throughout her schooling by a need for status and popularity in various school activities such as concerts, class plays and sports; in her church work she was alternately troubled by doubts or excessive concern with the various service aspects of church life; so also her social and heterosexual development was marked by a series of intensive attachments either to men, like her father, displaying domineering and masculine characteristics or to weakly feminine men which she associated with her mother's characteristics or to the moral, dedicated Christian type which was characterized by her uncle. She manifests inner indecision and turmoil in episodes of tension, anxiety and depression and ruminative obsessions as to whether she has really made the proper choice in entering missionary work. This question is made more serious by her abilities in orchestral music. She has been asked to play the piano for a leading symphonic orchestra with the possibility of future concert tours as a soloist.

Psychological examination:

The patient has superior general intelligence and considerable talent in imagery and both verbal and kinesic communications; in this connection her somewhat exaggerated gestures and mannered speech seem more a part of her training for the role of a musical artist than marks of insincerity. As indicated, she has deep longings for status and companionship, but is at the same time fearful of being unappreciated, disappointed, mistreated and deserted as she had been in her childhood. In the latter regard she is frustrated by conflictful and persistent resentments of persons displaying self-righteousness, religious unctiousness and preachy prejudices against persons in secular occupations. Toward the end of the interview she became more conscious of her inner conflicts about the goals and values and recognized that she needed help to work out a stable decision that would be lastingly satisfactory to herself, the mission board and any person whom she may marry in the future.

Mental Status:

An intelligent, talented young lady deeply conflictful over unconscious fears and yearnings which cannot be resolved by an immediate, arbitrary or impulsive decision. Indeed, if the patient were seriously regretful of her choice of career she would be subject to severe depressive reaction.

Recommendations:

The patient will need a period of personal analysis and expert counseling to help her resolve her conflicts; till then, it would be best to postpone definite plans. If the missionary society so directs, I shall be glad to recommend available resources in whatever city she may be during the next several months.*

Respectfully submitted,
JULES H. MASSERMAN, M.D.

4. Psychologic Reports to Non-Medical Personnel

In reporting to personnel secretaries, clinical psychologists should include in their report the basic facts about the individual such as name, date of interview, age of person and their address. In addition to this, there should be a statement concerning the following:

1. Gross identification of the physical impression the person gives to the examiner, the perception, intellection, emotion, action, relations to self, relation to others, relation to things, items of mild stress, items showing severe stress and aspects of present disequilibration or equilibration should be included in the report along with any other pertinent factors. The following is a very good example of the information desired by personnel secretaries except for the fact that raw scores of each of the tests are not included in this report.

The psychologist should indicate any reservations he or she may feel concerning counsel with the individual. For instance, the examiner may wish to state in the report or in a note attached to the report some such consideration as:

Dear Dr. *(Personnel Secretary)*

On the presumption you might wish to defer any consideration of this patient, I suggest to her that she get a position as a private secretary and allow a year for reflection and maturation.

---

* To protect the confidence of individuals, this report is a sample and is not an actual case in the files of any mission board.

I do not wish to have my report interpreted or reviewed with the patient beyond the points already covered by me with my patient.

Sincerely,

The Examiner

5. *A Letterhead of Examiner Giving Address and Date of Examination*

TO: Dr. (Personnel Secretary)
(Address of Mission Board)
RE: (Name of missionary volunteer being examined)
(Birth date and age)
(Address)

PSYCHOLOGICAL EVALUATION: On (the dates of the examinations,) the following series of psychological examinations were given to this candidate:

1. Wechsler-Bellevue Intelligence Scale
2. Michigan Vocabulary Profile Test
3. Strong Vocational Interest Blank
4. Rotter's Incomplete Sentences
5. Cornell Index
6. Thematic Apperception Test
7. Rorschach Psychodiagnostic
8. Autobiography

A. Intelligence: The following scores were obtained:
Intelligence Quotient, Verbal Scale ....128 (Superior)
Intelligence Quotient, Performance Scale 128
Intelligence Quotient, Full Scale 128

The patient reported that on the Wechsler-Bellevue given by a student at _____ University, he had obtained an I.Q. of 140, a score practically impossible on this test. He is aware that he has excellent learning ability which he has used to good advantage. He does much better in the acquisition of information than in the utilization of facts in practical situations although he is quite acceptable in his performance on any kind of test.

B. Achievement: The following scores indicate that this man ranks in a top third of college students insofar as general verbal ability is concerned.

Biological Sciences   98th Percentile
Physical Sciences   95th Percentile
Mathematics   95th Percentile

Fine Arts	84th Percentile
Human Relationships	77th Percentile
Commerce	23rd Percentile
Sports	23rd Percentile
Government	5th Percentile
Average	71st Percentile

C. Vocational Interest: The heavy weighing of scores for this young man fell in the professional services of psychology, medicine and osteopathy. The two additional vocations for which he seemed to have a strong feeling were chemistry and ministry. There were several occupations for which this young man showed absolutely no interest or inclinations; these included purchasing agent, banking, and sales work. Another important finding on the Strong Test is the abnormal masculinity—femininity scores. On this test the score of 35 is markedly in the direction of excessive femininity as compared with a normal or average score of 50.

D. Personality and Emotional Adjustment: The objective score on Incomplete Sentences Blank indicates an emotional disturbance or lack of emotional peace which merits further investigation. In attitudes toward his family, the patient shows a very close attachment to his mother and a rejection of and coldness for his father. He displays no warmth for anyone except his mother. He regards girls as kind and good but is not strongly drawn to them. He looks upon dancing as permissible when it does not excite sexual emotion. Here we find him demonstrating a puritanical attitude which he himself has labeled as being one of his chief characteristics.

This boy is strongly impelled to find satisfactions in being of service to others. He indicates that life is of value only if he is helping others. Religion has come to serve many of his needs and with it he has withdrawn from the world and contacts with people. He states that his happiest time is when he is sitting quietly and enjoying things, that he feels that God is near sometimes and that he is very thankful for the blessings he has received. What seems to annoy him most is too much Pharisaism on the part of some persons and indifference of others. Most of his sentences are very heavily weighted in the direction of his Christian faith in spite of the fact that the examiner was known to him only as a lay person without any specific connection with the church.

In his original stories the patient's plots did not have to do with mystery and adventure but with real tragedies, such as a mother being killed in an automobile accident or inadvertently drowning her small son. In another case, the mother is told of the death of her son. There is little emotional involvement or dramatization of the personalities in the writing.

In spite of the fact that this boy's behavior and attitude throughout the examination was one of earnest cooperation, the examiners came to feel that there was something awry in his personality before the end of the day. He maintained too close visual contact, was too solicitous and paid too much homage to the women psychologists who were working with him. He was obsequious in his attentions to them; he did not show a free and easy outgoing acceptance of the inter-personal relationship but demonstrated a craven kind of dependence and need for support. In support of this hypothesis it was noted that this boy did not participate a great deal in the selection of the vocation for which he is now being trained but took it on at the advice of an adult whom he could accept as an authoritative figure. His personal and emotional involvement in the choice of the mission field was a great deal more direct and more the product of his own thinking and feeling and is, therefore, probably a more appropriate choice than the choice of medicine.

The Rorschach is alarming in its exhibition of pathological tendencies. First of all the objective score for reality testing is below the limit regarding as a minimum for emotionally, healthy people; actually the score is one which could be expected in the record of a schizophrenic patient. The second point which is alarming is the heavy weighing of scores in the direction of anatomical and sex responses with further screened sex association; this boy's repression of any sexual interest and his condemnation of any of his own natural feelings as "wicked" has actually caused him to develop probably an obsession with this topic of which he is so ashamed. Self-containment, inner-living, satisfying day-dreaming are not possible for this young man. He must find his satisfactions in some other way than in working out his own problems toward happy solutions in fantasy. He has strong prestige drive which he is directing in the mission field with a strong hope that he can gain prestige and acceptance from God as well as from leaders in the religious field.

E. Summary: I regret to say that this very attractive and appealing young man who seems to have a fine physique, excellent health and superb intelligence, actually is so deeply involved in emotional disturbance that he is in immediate need of therapy. While he does not see his need as being serious, he does recognize that there would be value in the association of some fine Christian therapist. I believe that it is imperative that he be given assistance to recover or to gain for the first time an emotional stability which will enable him to utilize the great potentialities which are evidently his. Three years of his education remain during which he could have the benefit of therapy probably from a psychiatrist. I feel that his problem is greatly complicated by his inability to express the normal adolescent rebellion and his feelings of guilt concerning normal adult impulses. Because of this and because of the fact that he is not too rigid in his present personality make-up, there is a good prognosis to be made. I expect that at the end of three years we will find this man adequately prepared academically and ready to render an excellent service for Christ on some mission field.

F. Recommendations: It is the judgment of this examiner that the patient should be deferred for a period of from three to five years during which time he be encouraged to engage in a program of therapeutic counseling. It is recommended that he be re-examined at the end of the deferment period and that acceptance as a missionary candidate be dependent upon the improvement and maturation of the years of this waiting period.*

> Respectfully submitted,
> (Name)
> (Title)

As a personnel secretary examines this report several things jump to his attention with some immediacy and force.

1. The personnel secretary will immediately question the ability of the patient to be involved in the close inter-personal relationships necessary on a mission field both with missionary colleagues and the nationals of the country in which this person might serve.

a. With a statement to the effect that the patient believed himself to have an I.Q. of 140 would come the question of a certain amount of pride readily expressed. Such pride causes dissension among colleagues. This question is made more serious by several other factors. The attainment of only a 77th Percentile score in human relationships would give the secretary concern. The fact that the young man, when asked to submit a picture for his file, submitted a picture of himself in a football attire rather than a normal picture of his head and shoulders strengthens this concern.

---

* To protect the confidence of individuals this report is a sample and is not an actual case in the files of any mission board.

The executive would need to explore this question further to find out not only how the individual would get along with people under normal circumstances but also to determine that his rather rigid religiosity and impelling desire to help people is primarily motivated by a conceit that would cause inter-personal difficulties abroad.

2. The fact that this individual does much better in the acquisition of knowledge than in the utilization of facts and practical situations would call into question concerns related to the practical ministry as a missionary abroad.

His inability to display any warmth for persons other than his mother would lead one to question his ability to adequately display sincere Christian love in missionary service.

3. Concern is sometimes registered over abnormal masculinity-femininity scores for several reasons. One of these is the probability of homosexual tendencies. Other factors in this test report would deny this tendency in this particular patient but it would have to be checked on by the mission board.

4. A happy marital adjustment is necessary to adequate service abroad. The masculinity-femininity factor plus the fact that this person is not drawn to girls due to his relationships to his mother and father and also to puritanical attitudes concerning sex which cause in him deep-seated anxieties would portend a difficult marriage. This would influence the possibility of his serving abroad.

5. In addition to the above are the alarming pathological tendencies indicated by the Rorschach resulting in a score that could be expected in the record of a schizophrenic patient. The possibility of a "nervous breakdown" looms so real in the future of this person that the board would do well not to risk his life and his future by placing him within the multiple tensions of an overseas career.

6. The Future of Personnel Testing

Increase in use and interest in psychologic testing in high schools, colleges, and graduate schools have resulted in a remarkable phenomenon in the United States. In most high schools a number of basic tests are given to the students to determine their intelligence quotient and some of their aptitudes and interests. These examiners seldom and probably never delve into depth psychology. It is right that they refrain from this field. Psychological tests, sometimes duplicating those given in high school are now given in most college structures; sometimes as college entrance examinations and often during the college years as students study psychology, as students need personal counseling and guidance and for other reasons determined by the students and staff of the institution in which they are studying. Prior to entering a graduate school most students are required to take the graduate records examination, which gives a certain bulk of information concerning that student. Prior to entering medical school a prospective medical student must take other examinations similar to the graduate records examinations, providing another bulk of materials. Prior to entering most seminaries of the leading denominations pre-seminarians are asked to take a series of psychological tests to determine their academic ability, their major fields of interest and aptitudes. In some denominations planned programs of recruitment to the ministries have been developed in which basic psychologic tests are given to young people. In one denomination these tests are given in the sophomore year of high school of all students of that denomination. This is later followed by an evaluation by a psychologist who determines whether the student examined has the intellectual ability to continue through college and graduate school in order to prepare for one of the ministries of the church.[4]

This bulk of information available to personnel secretaries of mission boards makes it possible for them to know considerably more about the potential missionary than was known when testing first began by mission boards. This means that a considerable bulk of psychometric information is available to the executive secretary of personnel even prior to sending missionary volunteers to a psychiatrist and a psychologist for the examina-

---

[4] For more information the reader is referred to the Christian Churches, Disciples of Christ. Disciples Guidance and Recruitment Services, 222 South Downey Avenue, Indianapolis 7, Indiana.

tions explained in this article. Thus as we progress into the future it is hoped that the examiners will be able to concentrate more seriously on depth psychology and also on those aspects of one's personality which are not now testable due to limitations of time and material.

Several tests are available for testing special interests, and these are often utilized by the examiners. One very important test as it relates to service abroad is a language aptitude test, now usually given by personnel secretaries or staff members of colleges of missions.

It seems necessary that mission boards begin to move into an even better testing and reporting program which will deal more specifically with certain aspects of the individual personalities being examined such as a candidate's reaction to constant insecurity, to intense rote-memorization programs and other aspects of intensive language training, to work in areas in which one feels unwanted and in work in which one feels called upon to do a variety of jobs in addition to and sometimes instead of the vocation in which he is academically prepared, the missionary candidate's reaction to intense loneliness and to its antithesis, forced gregariousness with constant lack of privacy. Many other aspects of one's personality need to be discovered and related to the tensions of service abroad in this world of revolutionary struggle and inevitable emotional pressures. It is good to know that mission boards are recognizing these needs and in cooperation with the psychologists and psychiatrists that serve as their examiners, are working on a program of increasing the effectiveness of this type of service.

THE RE-EDUCATION AND THERAPY
OF THE MINISTER

THE minister's mental health is really only a part of his total health need. Involved also is his overcoming a fictitious sense of self-sufficiency, and relying realistically upon others—teachers, pastors, psychotherapists, and other medical doctors. In a real way this recognizes his interdependence with his fellow creatures in the helping professions. For, in turn, these persons, especially doctors, need pastoral care just as the minister periodically needs medical care. This part of this volume comes to grips with the religious, educational, and therapeutic dimensions of the processes of counseling of ministers under stress.

Is Psychotherapy a Religious Process?

Contributors:

THE REV. WILLIAM RICKEL,

THE REV. DR. PAUL TILLICH,

THE REV. CARROLL A. WISE,

JOHN A. P. MILLET, M.D.,

THE REV. RUSSELL L. DICKS, and

THE REV. ANTON T. BOISEN

Many ministers procrastinate in getting the professional assistance they need when they are emotionally disturbed. One of their major objections to getting this help concerns the question whether there is a religious character in the process of therapy. The question is frankly confronted here by six men. First, the Rev. William Rickel, Director, Institute for Rankian Psychoanalysis, Inc., and editor of the "Journal of Psychotherapy as a Religious Process," writes; and his statements and questions are then discussed by the other contributors.

As we look at the healing professions today, one of the deepest running cleavages is between those who seek to understand man solely in scientific, rationalistic, or naturalistic terms *and* those who are returning to the more fundamental spiritual insights into the nature of human existence. Often we catch glimpses

301

of this kind of struggle going on in individual thinkers and theologians, a split between the two views. A good illustration of this is revealed in an article by Dr. Paul Tillich in the December, 1952 issue of *Pastoral Psychology* (pp. 11-17): he asserts the valid recognition that the deeper inward forces having to do with ethical values and attitudes toward an ultimate source of power are essential for the complete satisfaction of man, and yet inconsistently he clings to the more limited scientific approach in the practice of psychotherapy.

This attitude reflects the half-way house of some current theological thinking which grasps the issue theoretically but then fails to apply the illumination afforded by the inward experience of truth to the outward practical concerns of living. On one hand we acknowledge his awareness that man, to be saved and freed emotionally, to be healthy (whole or integrated), must reach out beyond all rational understanding, through faith, to find his security in God. On the other hand, Tillich still would have emotionally disturbed, anxiety-ridden people turn to professions whose basic insights are rooted in rational, scientific, and naturalistically determined philosophies that belie their basic spiritual needs.

I believe that the practice of therapy must go all the way rather than pause at this half-way house. The body of scientific knowledge amassed by academic psychology and medicine takes one only to the frontiers of the self. To cross this frontier into the area of spiritual life, involving values, ethics, and a relationship to God, where integrity arises, one must drop off intellectual knowledge and rational evaluation to living and take the leap of faith.

The psychotherapist who has done this and has resolved his conflicts through the *rediscovery* of his own relationship to God, through an intense emotional experience, a rebirth, will be free to help others too. *It will not be the knowledge that modern psychology has made available to him that will enable him to help others; it will be the power and insight which his spiritual experience of rebirth provided him.* I do not think psychiatry acknowledges this. This recognition reveals the practice of psychotherapy to be a religious endeavor, a discipline rooted in the religious life and flowing from it.

Perhaps out of an effort to achieve a rapprochement with psychology and medicine, the clinical theologian and clinically trained clergy are not urging this today. They turn away from the implications of their spiritual beliefs in the actual practice of soul-cure. Tillich, in the article referred to, writes: "Pathological anxiety, once established, is the object of medical healing," and in another place: "but the lack of ontological analysis of anxiety and of a sharp distinction between existential and pathological anxiety has prevented as many ministers and theologians as physicians and psychotherapists from entering this alliance. Since they do not see the difference they are unwilling to look at neurotic anxiety as they look at bodily disease, namely, as an object of medical help."

The relationship of these considerations to psychotherapy is important, because our understanding of human nature determines our therapeutic process. Here in the growth of personality, if we accept Tillich's division of practice between the clergyman and the psychiatrist, we see a split developing. In the normal growth, the person can stand the anxiety incident to change; but in the neurotic this is not so. Growth has stopped and the disturbed person has excluded something from the self. We ask the psychiatrist, who is a scientist and thus a determinist, to free the person from his problem. This, to follow his line of thinking, is a beginning of the renewed growth process. Then at some point not made clear, he asks the psychiatrist to step aside so that the priest may take over with his recognition that basic to a person's ability to take and bear within the total self the contradictory facets of experience is the element of faith, father to security. Hence, according to Tillich, we are to end a process in the religious area which began in the secular area; we are to break the unity of the growth process into two stages, one fully deterministic and rational, and the other existing under grace and faith, irrational from the point of view of science; and the end-product is to be a fully unified person.

This is a typical current view; it asserts the basically spiritual nature of man's neurotic illnesses, and then assigns their cure to those professions whose underlying philosophical orientation is limitedly scientific or else avowedly anti-religious.

In weaving his concept of anxiety into the fabric of Christian theology, Tillich deserves our appreciation for a genuine service to a growing body of therapists who are seeking the more fundamental interpretation of their therapeutic practice in the context of the Christian tradition. They are recoiling not only from the limitations of point of view but also the inevitable falsifications of human nature arising from the scientific disciplines related to human behavior and psychology.

Tillich, in placing anxiety in its true theological relationship to man's existence, gives it a broader understanding than psychologists usually accord it. He deepens our insights into its nature, though I feel the ground for the assertion of a distinction between existential and pathological anxiety is indefensible.

Undeniably the neurotic personality has walled itself off from life. His anxiety is derived from the constant necessity to keep the unexpressed and denied portions of the self in subjection, a denial which indicates the fundamental fact of his separation from God. He can freely express only a small part of the total self, and through this limitation, he tries to circumscribe and control his anxiety—momentarily, to be sure.

The neurotic personality exists in perpetual fear (anxiety) that the repressed parts of the self may erupt into open revolt and reveal the unacceptable portions of the self. The underlying fear is that God will discover what he is like and then punish him.

The universal incidence of anxiety is a tribute, not so much to the unstable and tenuous balance of life in an unpredictable world but to the universal imperfection of the human spirit. It is a recognition of the rarity of the person whose faith is so deeply imbedded in a relationship to God as a source of power and strength beyond the self, so that nothing can shatter the moorings of the self in God. Anxiety need not necessarily accompany all existence, as Tillich would imply; but human weakness and finitude and the limit of faith in God become the conditions of all life, anxiety which can be said to characterize all existence.

To use Tillich's distinction for the moment, one can say that all anxiety is pathological and arises from a sequestering of a part of the self from the rest of the self, and hence of the whole self from God, which is his definition of existential anxiety. Through faith the person rediscovers his original bond of relationship to God and in that return to God, anxiety is scattered like a mist before the warm morning sun. So in his integrity man attains a total immersion of the self in God, so that all the forces and powers of the then-integrated self pull in one direction. *Anxiety is not of existence but of its subversion.*

If the integrated person must remain in a constant state of "existential anxiety" and can go on living only by a certain, shall we say, stoic "courage to be," perhaps such a person has not really discovered his relationship to God. We would then wonder whether the philosophical belief that all existence is accompanied by a state of anxiety is not really a confession, on a high intellectual level, of a failure in experience to find the solace that God's forgiving, divine love can afford man; and may not therefore indicate that there are still parts of the self shut off from God. We do not ask anyone to be perfect—Jesus did not ask that of himself or anyone else—but perhaps we can expect the recognition of what the nature of perfection might be.

The error, I think, arises from a mistaken insight into the inception of anxiety. Tillich describes anxiety as arising from and in the naturalistic order of the world, flowing from simple *cause and effect relationship* between things and selves, physical or mental things, all a part of the natural order. This is indeed to deny and ignore the real source of anxiety in the divine order of things, in the supernatural order, if you will, rather than the natural order. Were Tillich right that anxiety is part of the natural order, then those humanistic disciplines (psychology, psychiatry, etc.) dealing with human conduct, whose philosophical bases lie in a naturalistic interpretation of man, could be called on to cure the emotionally sick person. Perhaps this confusion is what leads Tillich to assign therapy to the medical profession.

I believe that man's anxiety flows from a break between the

self and God and that this break is in the spiritual life of man, and transcends the natural order and has to do with the divine order. Just as God transcends the natural so does man, who is man only insofar as he is related to God. And this area of life lies above and beyond the strictly causal sequences of the natural order of the world and partakes of man's own divine nature. The original separation between the self and God, in the dynamic growth process, took place because of a prior sin, the inadequate love and faith of the parents whose own lack of rootedness in God and consequence emotional instability made them inadequate to minister to the spiritual needs of the child. Hidden areas of parental selves led to distortion and neurotic attenuation of the self. What the parent could not affirm for himself, he had to deny to his child. His own fears sired the fears of his child. The lack of faith of the parent begat the lack of faith of the child. These are the spiritual laws of growth wherein we observe the sins of the parents visited on the child. The result is anxiety, the fear generated by parts of the self which the child could not accept because his parents were not free to accept them for him; and hence the child feared God too would not accept these elements of his self.

Neurosis can be understood only as an illness in the divine part of the self, arising through a break between the self and God as just outlined. Hence any human intervention by parent, foster-parent, parent-surrogate, or psychotherapist, must reach out to the spiritual forces locked in the recesses of the personality, and draw them back into a bond with God. That is the essence of the spiritual experience of rebirth. This is the task of psychotherapy, and was so understood down through the ages. (See *A History of the Cure of Souls* by John T. McNeill.) Hence no discipline or profession which in its rationalistic or naturalistic limitation conceives of neurosis in its own limited terms can provide an adequate cure of the sick person. Only when the therapist, wittingly or unwittingly, can contact this supernatural area of the self, its spiritual-divine essence, can any cure come, and diminution of the anxiety take place. The universal solvent is love, not scientific knowledge, and that love is the love of God. Hence therapy becomes a religious endeavor.

Freedom and the disappearance of anxiety arise precisely because the roots of personality do transcend the natural order of existence. Both the cause and the cure is supernatural, that is, in the spiritual area of the self. Indeed it is even wrong to say "cause" of anxiety, for that is to imply something about anxiety which denies its true nature, for anxiety is the "condition" man finds himself in when he denies his relationship to God.

The Rev. Dr. Paul Tillich,
Professor, Harvard University, replies:

I think the statement of Mr. Rickel is very good and interesting. He, however, somehow misunderstands my division of functions between the medical and the theological faculty and does not see that in reality the physician often is and always should be more than a mere physician. In the same way, the minister often is and always should be more than a mere minister. But this personal union does not mean the identity of functions. I do not believe that the approach of the psychoanalyst is mechanical. But certainly it demands important technical training just as the work of the ordinary M.D. is not mechanical, but has many technical implications.

Only one other remark concerning Mr. Rickel's article: existential anxiety is not always conscious but it is always present and produces the restlessness of the heart which can only, in special moments, be overcome, and is never without the power which Luther called "demonic attacks" (Anfechtungen). Healing does not mean making perfect, but healing means a continually interrupted inner process of reunion with oneself. I disagree with Mr. Rickel in his disregard of psychological fixations which belong in the realm of psychiatry, and his mystical perfectionism. I believe he is unrealistic in both respects. But I agree with him in the belief that a real healing of a person as person is not possible without relationship to the ultimate.

The Rev. Carroll A. Wise, Professor of Pastoral Psychology and Counseling, Garrett Biblical Institute, replies:

This paper is stimulating, and opens up many avenues for comment. Only a few of these will be dealt with.

The first comment should be that it is hard to have a feeling of fairness since the author does not make himself clear as to the meaning of many of his statements and he writes in a way which would seem to force a person to agree with him or run the risk of being labeled as "not spiritual." We could agree with many of his specific insights, but we suspect that he does not mean what his statements seem to mean on the surface. In this he differs from Tillich, who makes clear his meaning. For example, what does he mean by his phrase, "knowledge that has power to transform personality"? He seems to be aware that there is no intellectual knowledge that has this power; later he talks about the relationship of love as having power to cure; does he mean this relationship as a kind of knowledge? Many places he implies that there is a kind of superior religious insight that has the power to cure, but he seems confused as to whether real insight comes before or after growth. We wish Mr. Rickel had been clearer on such terms as rationalism, science, scientism, spiritual, natural, and the like. It is as wrong to confuse science with scientism as it is to confuse genuine spirituality from pseudo-spirituality.

Mr. Rickel attacks Tillich on the grounds that he is trying to find a *raison d'être* for assigning psychotherapy to the medical profession. He does not seem to be aware of his own deep need to defend his position as a non-medical therapist, and that he has laid himself wide open to the charge that he is developing a philosophical point of view to justify his position on religious grounds. While we can understand his feeling of insecurity in being a non-medical therapist in a culture where therapy is dominated by the medical group, this does not lead us to accept his point of view as objective. Furthermore, his understanding and description of medical psychotherapy, it must be said, is neither accurate nor adequate.

The basic problem, however, is the validity of the formulations. Obviously we have here an interpretation, but Mr. Rickel seems to confuse his interpretation with a factual statement. He seems troubled by a misuse and misunderstanding of the nature of religious insights that, in turn, leads to a fear of a sound, scientific approach to life. While we can agree with many specific insights, such as the place of love in therapy, we cannot agree with the need to set the religious and scientific points of view over against each other as he does. It seems to us that he is committing the same error as the scientist who refuses to recognize the religious point of view, only in the other direction, and especially so in view of his dogmatic assertion of his interpretation. He creates a conflict where no real conflict exists; he divides man into two parts, the divine and the natural and sees them in profound antagonism; in denying the validity of cause and effect relationships he certainly gives room for very unhealthy religious rationalizations and projections; these and other objections to his theories could be raised.

What about the issue of religious versus medical psychotherapy? This needs to be faced on both sides, but certainly unqualified claims from the religious side are not the answer to what some consider to be an imperialistic attitude in the medical profession. Rickel makes a contribution to this discussion but he would not seem to me to have the answer to the problem.

John A. P. Millet, M. D., Chief Psychiatrist,
American Rehabilitation Committee, Inc., answers:

William Rickel's comments on the gallant effort to Paul Tillich to define the boundary which separates the role of the physician from that of the priest smack of a claim to certain insights which are apparently all inclusive. Such an assumption is scarcely defensible and savors of a rationalization stemming from a thinly disguised antagonism to the theories of human nature which were originated by Sigmund Freud.

There are, after all, many accredited psychoanalysts—men and women trained as physicians, who are devout Christians, and who, in proclaiming their belief in God and in the revelations of divine truth through the life of Jesus Christ, are conscious of their therapeutic ministry as essentially religious in its significance and aims. The fact that they are physicians, and are thereby better equipped to understand the complicated integrations of mental and physical events mediated through the nervous system, provides them with special tools of knowledge which often make it easier for the troubled person to give confidences, with less fear of such dreaded consequences as rejection, suspicion, or intolerance.

Rickel's contemptuously repeated reference to the "rationalistic" and "naturalistic" approach of the "scientist" to "therapy," would seem to dismiss as unimportant the fact that man has laid claim to his divine essence in part, at least, on the ground that he alone of all God's creatures is possessed of a special quality of intelligence, which includes the capacity for self-appraisal, as well as some ability to forecast the results of actions which he may purpose to take. If this high intelligence, with the assembly of an ever-increasing stockpile of facts about man's total nature which it has facilitated, is to be laid aside as inadequate to meet the problems to which man is exposed, and to assist him in the resolution of the anxieties which result from them, the conclusion is inescapable that God made a great mistake in so endowing him.

No—that is not the real point. The comments of Mr. Rickel, while seeming to propose spiritual re-birth through renewal of faith as the sole means of re-integration of the total personality, are in fact little more than a re-statement of the view that man's nature is basically divided into two parts, the physical being and the spiritual essence, and that his imprisonment in his physical or mortal nature can only be resolved through emotional appeal to the spiritual force within him. Thus he dismisses from consideration as 'therapy' the efforts of medical scientists who are well aware of the need of suffering mortals to find a way to reconciling the claims of the pressures which the demands of their aspirations and the pressures of society make upon them. He becomes the champion of the priest as opposed to the physician.

Experience has shown that neither physician nor priest is necessarily the best therapist for the individual sufferer. The most successful therapist is the one who has come to a sufficient state of inner resolution to offer no threat to the sufferer, and who through his own struggle to attain it is capable of deep understanding of the sufferer's trouble. His is genuinely a religious gift in the true sense. It is the conviction of the best equipped psychoanalysts that a thorough training in the basic medical sciences and in the treatment of the emotionally ill gives them an added advantage in their approach to this ministry of health.

It is perhaps worth commenting that the original work of Rank in emphasizing the significance of the trauma of birth has led his followers to favor the idea of rebirth as the necessary solution for all human ills. Since this can only be conceived in the sense of a spiritual rebirth, a rational basis can be attributed to the emphasis which Rickel lays on this phenomenon. All experienced psychoanalysts are familiar with this deep wish in their patients, through verbal communications as well as the revelations in their dreams.

In conclusion, then, I would like to remind Rickel and the readers of these comments that human beings may experience reintegration of their forces through a variety of therapeutic experiences. Some achieve it through psychoanalysis, some through wise pastoral counseling, some through Christian Science, and many through other sources. The influence of the therapist is often paramount. Above all, it is the interpersonal element in the therapeutic setting which determines the success or failure of the undertaking. Without faith in the therapist no resolution is possible.

The Rev. Russell L. Dicks, Former Professor of Pastoral Care, Duke University Divinity School, with the collaboration of Albert E. Wilkerson, Crozer Theological Seminary, answers:

Spiritual resources and scientific knowledge do not constitute two incompatible entities. Nor is it an inconsistency to draw upon the inner, spiritual forces that God has placed within the personality and at the same time to employ psychotherapeutic techniques. The combined use of religion and psychiatry in the treatment of the emotionally ill constitutes, rather, a total approach to the problem.

In contemporary theology there is much discussion concerning "relatedness to God" and being "at one with God." For the emotionally mature and well-adjusted Christian, such terms no doubt have specific meaning; but to the emotionally disturbed individual these phrases are of small import, since his illness prevents his understanding of what this is and how it is attained. Conflicts and anxieties arise out of the socio-religious expectations of the individual. Whether or not these specific expectations are right or wrong is not an immediate problem for pastoral care, which is an effort within the confines of religion to help the individual to live creatively in a world which it believes God has made creative at its heart. It is no service only to treat an emotionally ill person with religious concepts for it often is a misunderstanding of, or guilt about, these concepts that is at the root of his problem; and religion may or may not be able to treat such guilt. Gandhi once said aptly: "God Himself dare not appear to a hungry man except in the form of bread." The emotionally mature understand deep theology; the emotionally ill need depth therapy.

While it is true that counselors and therapists can give to other personalities only from the overflow of their own inner reserves, we must recognize that they, too, have personal problems and conflicts. Psychotherapy is a highly refined and valid technique. It is to be used only by those who have been trained in its method and who have sound psychiatric orientation. To delegate this role to local ministers at the present time is beyond the realm of possibility. Theological seminaries do not train their candidates to practice depth therapy, and we cannot ignore the emotionally ill until such a feat is accomplished. Similarly, we cannot wait for the psychiatrists and psychoanalysts to be converted. The observation that some psychiatrists are non-religionists does not mean that they are anti-religionists. The professional integrity and insights of these physicians do not permit them to be petty, religious antagonists in the practice of their therapy. Many atheistic psychiatrists demonstrate far more concern for individuals than do some of the most pious of ministers.

Few ministers can practice psychotherapy, but the minister who is intelligent and sensitive can be a helpful counselor. He can help the individual to discover and draw upon the spiritual resources within himself and his world. He can help him to discover and control the healing emotions (such as love) and the destructive emotions (such as fear and guilt) which are inherent within each personality. The minister can listen creatively to the problems and feelings of the troubled person, guiding his thoughts and conversation in such a way as to help him gain insights into his problem. Finally, the minister can use his unique tool, prayer, to help the individual draw upon the spiritual reserve available to him. This process may be called religious therapeutics if you wish; we prefer to call it pastoral care.

The minister must keep in mind the limitations of his training, for that is a mark of true professionalism. The ability to practice psychotherapy cannot be gained by reading a dozen books; however, the minister must read constantly in this field. Emotionally ill persons need psychiatric treatment, and it is a part of the minister's duties to refer these persons to the proper consultants. The minister must realize that for a time in the care of such a person the minutiae of classical theology may have to be set aside and medical and psychiatric treatment employed. The religious counselor must broaden his intellectual knowledge to include whatever disciplines aid him in the understanding of the nature of man. It is the task of psychiatry to describe and treat emotional and mental disorders. It is the task of the minister in his pastoral role to carry on personal counseling up to the point that his training permits, and then to recognize the need for other professional assistance. We admit that psychiatric help is not available to everyone, but it is only a matter of time until consultation services will be.

Religion and psychiatry are not antagonistic disciplines. They are potentially close allies in the total effort to help individuals live to their fullest capacity with their God and their associates.

*The Rev. Anton T. Boisen, Chaplain Emeritus,
Elgin State Hospital, answers:*

Professor Tillich in his interesting article raises two important questions: (1) At what point does anxiety become pathological? and (2) To what extent should pathological anxiety come within the professional domain of the minister of religion?

As a minister of religion who has given himself to the service of those who have not succeeded in "taking their anxiety into their courage-to-be" and who exemplify the pathological in its extreme forms, I am offering certain observations which bear upon these questions.

In the first place it is important to recognize that pathological processes are not all of the same type. Disease, according to Dr. W. A. White,[1] is what happens when the organism comes into conflict with some inimical agent, and the symptoms which arise are signs of what is going on in the organism as a result of that conflict. A splinter gets into the finger, and the inflammation and festering which follow are nature's attempt to get rid of that splinter. Tubercular bacilli get lodged in the lungs. They cannot be removed but are walled off, or encysted, and thus made harmless. And sometimes the defenses fail. We then see deterioration and such phenomena as necrosis.

Now anxiety in its extremer forms is analogous to inflammation or fever in the body. It is the awareness of some threat to the integrity of the personality. It calls for the marshaling of the healing forces to meet the danger. Anxiety in and of itself is therefore not the evil.

In the second place it is necessary to clarify the nature of the threat in "pathological anxiety." I am more and more impressed with the fact that the anxiety manifest in mental illness is due to the operations of conscience and the threat which is feared is that of alienation from the inwardly conceived fellowship of the best. Death, or danger of death, apart from the sense of alienation, or guilt, is not likely to result in mental disorder. It gives rise usually to the hope of a life beyond and of a new start in life. Such hope is found especially in cases of self-sacrifice and even in many cases of suicide or attempted suicide. But hopeless alienation from that fellowship of the best which for the religious man is symbolized by the idea of God means progressive disintegration such as we see on the back wards of any mental hospital.

[1] W. A. White, *The Meaning of Disease.*

Such disintegration is the danger against which the "neurotic" seeks to protect himself and there are many devices to which he has recourse. These devices, most of which involve self-deception and ill-defined anxiety, I need not name. The literature is full of them. What our current writers do not recognize is that acute anxiety, even to the point of severe psychosis, is beneficent rather than malignant. When free from self-deception, it may contribute to a successful reorganization of the personality.

In the third place, it should be recognized that the sense of personal failure and resulting anxiety is a necessary feature of growth. Individuals and civilizations alike have their "time of troubles." Without the blocking of desire and the overcoming of difficulties we would not be men. The personality grows much like the body grows through the constant assimilation of new material. In the case of the personality this new material is the stuff of experience. It is assimilated by being related to organized experience. This involves consciousness. According to John Dewey[2] we are aware of those things which are in process of assimilation. Once a bit of experience is properly related to our system of meanings, it sinks back into the realm of dim awareness, there to function automatically, often with the glow of well-being, or else to lie dormant until it is called forth by some appropriate stimulus or some needed redirection. But all too often it happens that a new experience is not assimilated. This is particularly true in the management of highly charged instinctual drives and other experiences which involve radical alterations in the concept of the self.

Such an experience will then be unable to function smoothly. Instead of being in the "unconscious," it will behave like ill-digested food, clamoring for attention and giving the sufferer no peace until in some way it is taken care of. And many are the neurotic defenses to which he may resort. It is characteristic of those defenses which are known as "neurotic" that they are attempts to obtain peace of mind without correcting the condition which gives rise to the anxiety. Such defenses are

[2] John Dewey, *Experience and Nature.*

therefore unsatisfactory. They result in reduction and malformation of the self. More than that, conscience cannot really be deceived and anxiety is not allayed. When the defenses are ineffective, when hope departs and the disowned and unassimilated tendencies become dominant, anxiety disappears. We have then the adaptation of death.

When now does anxiety become pathological? This question seems of secondary importance. Undoubtedly, when it becomes severe enough to interfere with proper functioning or when serious malformations of character have developed in the effort to secure peace of mind, expert care will be required. The point to be emphasized is that anxiety itself is beneficent, not malignant, and the task of the therapist is to discover and correct the situation to which it is seeking to call attention.

With reference to the respective functions of minister and doctor, I am of the opinion that few psychiatrists have any understanding of the religious factors in mental illness and few ministers are equipped to deal with morbid mental states. And yet it is impossible to understand either mental disorder or religious experience except as we study the one in the light of the other. More than that, no patient is ever truly "cured" until he is adjusted on the level of what for him is abiding and universal, and the message of Jesus and of Paul and of modern psychiatry at its best is that such adjustment is a matter of spirit and attitude, not a matter of freedom from faults. What is needed is not release from conflict but release from the sense of guilt and isolation in order that a man may be set free to strive for the realization of his true potentialities. We have then in pathological anxiety and mental illness a problem which concerns every minister of religion in every parish in the land.

In my own case I draw the dividing line between my province and that of my medical friends not so much with reference to the severity of the disturbance as with reference to the reaction pattern. I am chiefly interested in cases of extreme anxiety in which the better self is seeking to come to birth and is battling desperately against the ills which beset it. In such cases

I find greatest manifestations of religious concerns together with relatively favorable prognosis. I look upon such cases as presenting a special challenge to students and ministers of religion, but I am equally interested in helping my medical friends to see the religious implications of such experiences.

The Significance of an Educative Analaysis for the Parish Ministry

By Harry B. Scholefield
Minister,
First Unitarian Church,
San Francisco, California

An intimately personal and candidly objective report of a parish pastor as to the ways in which he discovered new effectiveness as a pastor through a thorough psychoanalytic exploration of his own adjustment to life.

In the bulletin of the Philadelphia Psychoanalytic Institute the personal analysis of the student in the Educative Analysis Program is described as the "foundation of the curriculum." The significance of the personal analysis for the parish minister is thus a primary consideration in this paper. I confess that it has been difficult for me to see how within its relatively brief span that significance could be adequately delineated.

Manifestly it is impossible to segregate the effects of a personal analysis in any complete sense, saying that one part of the analysis pertains to man's professional life and another to his so-called "private concerns." The analysis treats the whole person and inevitably affects the whole life. The same factors in the unconscious which place a father in competition with his young son may, as he discovers to his surprise, place him in sharp and feverish competition with his ministerial colleagues. The difficulty he has in relating a full and completely satisfying sense to his wife may betoken an overload of guilt and anxiety which colors his relationship to the women in his parish as well as to the women in his home.

Bearing in mind the difficulty of treating the effects of personal analysis in any segregated fashion, I have selected two areas in my field of professional competence upon which the personal analysis focused with illuminating results. The first is the area of preaching and the second the area of pastoral counseling. Here, again, there is no clear dividing line. There is a sense in which a minister's sermons and his pastoral counseling are two sides of the same coin. Frequently it is in the counseling experience that he gains an awareness of the problems of men and women which gives to his sermons a relevance and an insight they might not otherwise possess. Likewise the quality of his preaching, its warmth and sensitivity as well as its thought-content, may determine whether those listening will relate to him as a person with whom they would like to share a personal problem of a perplexing and painful nature.

1. The Relationship of a Personal Analysis to Preaching and Sermon Preparation

I would begin by considering the relationship of the personal analysis to my preaching. To say that sermon-composition has always been difficult for me is an understatement. It has always stirred up in me an array of anxieties which I have long suspected were beyond those which could be placed in the category of normal professional hazards. Insofar as the actual sermon delivery was concerned, I have long been aware, also, that to speak outside of the church, informally, was one thing and to speak from the pulpit, *ex cathedra,* as it were, was another. I found it easier to be myself, to speak with less anxiety and inhibition when speaking outside of the church than when speaking within it. When preparing a sermon which was part of an ordered service of worship, I labored under a sense of pressure and anxiety which while not absent in the preparation of a talk to be given in a classroom or to a non-church group was, in the latter case, much less severe in its intensity and much less inhibiting.

The hours of the analysis often focused on the feelings and blocks experienced in sermon composition. Gradually some of the unconscious meanings which rode upon sermon preparation began to be apparent. As a part of the analytic process, I began to be specifically aware of factors of which I had been aware previously only in the general sense that they occasioned anxiety. I began to be aware of some of the ways in which I was using the sermon for purposes not consciously recognized. I remember well the analytic hour when I meant to say "sermon-composition" but tripped by my unconscious, said "sermon competition." I became aware of the sermon as the critical point on which were centered many of my basic conflicts. Becoming acquainted with my own problems of self-expression, I began to say ironically that a sermon is the means a minister has of concealing his deeper feelings and concerns from his congregation. I became aware of the subtle ways in which in the course of sermons I would use the "solid" quotation, the experience of others, the eminent authority, not as a means of exposition or elucidation but as a means of putting someone between myself and the listening congregation.

I became aware of the meaning of displacement, and began to see how I had displaced upon patterns of sermon preparation fears and anxieties which had their origin in the experiences of early life and the earliest relationships. I had, of course, read of the mechanism of displacement in the literature and had heard it described by instructors. But now I experienced it in the analytic hours and in the relationship which is so slowly and painfully built up between analyst and analysand. It is in terms of this awakening awareness of the student to his own inner difficulties that he perceives that the personal analysis is the heart of the Educative Analysis Program. If he received only the theoretical instruction, the venture, though exciting intellectually, might leave him quite untouched in terms of deep self-knowledge.

I began to see that underlying my difficulties in sermon composition were elements of basic distrust and a sterile kind of skepticism. In my unconscious I questioned my right to seek out the information I needed for sermon-preparation. I questioned the wisdom of using my own life-experience. I labored under what I came to know as "the fear of the empty cupboard," the fear, that is, that when I went to prepare a sermon there would be no food either for my own or the congregation's digestion. This was a very real and painful fear even when my mind was well stocked with ideas and my days well filled with vital and interesting experiences. There was much unconscious resentment against the sermon form, and against the form of the liturgy and the order of worship. There was an exaggerated sensitivity to criticism, an inability to express mildly aggressive feelings without unrealistic fear of retaliation on the congregation's part. There was the need to be right, existing in highly exaggerated dimensions. There was the sense of the sermon as "made work" and a strong and constant tendency to depreciate its worth no matter how hard I had worked at it and no matter how well it was received by the congregation. These were all problems which slowly took shape in the course of the analysis and were examined in terms of their unconscious antecedents.

I would mention now some of the causes of my excessive anxiety over sermon composition. One was my use of the sermon primarily as a means of securing the approval of the congregation. Another was the extent to which I used the sermon as a means of concealing my feelings rather than as a means of sharing them. I used the sermon more as a means of securing the congregation's approval than as a discipline leading to self-satisfaction. Paradoxically, I used it for purposes of self-concealment rather than for purposes of self-expression.

At the age of five under tragic circumstances I lost both my father and my mother. My father disappeared under cruel and humiliating circumstances. My mother committed suicide. My three brothers, two younger and one older than myself, and I were placed in an orphanage. The youngest brother died a short time later of diphtheria. And the next youngest, Ronald, a year younger than myself, drowned when I was ten. This left an older brother and me alone, without any family. Until I was seventeen and a high school graduate, I was raised in institutions marked by the strong discipline experienced in these institutions; though sometimes cruel and erratic, it was on the whole fair and consistent. The values were stern and puritanical, but they were dependable. The rules were rigorous, but they did not change.

It became apparent in the analysis that a good deal of my pulpit work was done for the same reasons that had impelled me to adhere to the strict rules of the institutions in which I had been brought up as a youngster. It also became apparent that the experience of having my world literally shattered at the age of five had made it necessary for me to cling with peculiar intensity to "the rules" of the institution as a means of assuring myself a degree of badly needed security, and as a means, perhaps magical, of warding off some future tragedy. Between my experience of life before the age of five, with a father and mother who were exceptionally warm and affectionate in their natures, and my experience of life after five in an institutional climate characterized by a lack of warmth and intimacy, there was a gap that could be bridged only with great difficulty. I bridged it, but in ways which contained the seeds of later conflicts. I learned that it was easier to try to secure the approval of others than to try to be myself. Trusting "the rules" was safer than trusting my own feelings or the feelings of others. There was built up in my unconscious a heavy store of resentment against the rules to which I clung. It was the price I paid for safety. Later I was to displace onto sermon forms, churches, boards of trustees, etc., a large measure of the ambivalence with which I regarded the authorities who had become my parental substitutes. The institutions of adulthood thus became the objects of unconscious fear, anger, and uncertainty.

One recurrent dream illustrated my plight. In this dream I struggle to put on the academic gown and hood I wear in the pulpit. As I struggle I know that sermon time is close at hand and that this sermon and this church service from which I am being held back are particularly important. This compounds my frustration. Finally, I get to the church service but in a state of great exhaustion and anger. In one dream of this sort a woman is dressing me outlandishly and holding me back. She puts a baby bonnet on my head. It is heavily bordered with lace. When I do get to the pulpit and begin my sermon, my voice seems to lisp and whistle as it sounds through the lace. In annoyance and anger I tear the bonnet from my head and proceed with the sermon feeling much freer and much stronger.

The sermon form which I found so frustrating was not only symbolic of the institutional rules which "saved my life" but which I so much resented, it was also a symbol of the early controls exercised over me by my mother and used by her for various purposes. Conceivably in the months leading up to her death, these controls were accentuated. With the loss of my mother and my father and with their places taken by the orphanage authorities who were the parental surrogates, the controls became impersonal and tighter. They brought added hazards for a young child's development. One of the hazards was the need to feel grateful. I had to be grateful as a sign of appreciation of what they, the authorities, were doing for me. If I was ungrateful, I stood in danger of being cast off again. Of course, mingled with the "gratitude" was anger, largely unexpressed.

Here, again, the same ambivalence was carried over in my attitude toward the "demands" of my profession. In the pulpit I had the feeling that what I "offered" my congregation and, of course, this applied to what I "offered" my analyst—must meet with approval or I was a "bad boy." "Bad boys" get punished, not in any reasonable way, but by having their outward circumstances go to pieces. The sermon was a pivotal responsibility. It was the means by which I could secure good grades, desperately needed approval and security. Sermon preparation thus took on the painful character of studying for an examination upon which life itself depended, an examination to be taken under the eye of the harshest kind of taskmaster or taskmistress. Naturally it was difficult for me to express with comfort even a normal amount of aggression because in my unconscious I confused love with submission and healthy aggression with the kind of hatred that courts destruction.

Material in the analysis which came around the death of my mother, threw light on elements in the unconscious which revealed great anxiety over whether or not I had any right at all to preach. It was indicated that I had guilt around the death of my brother Ronald. The conscious rationale of this guilt was the fact that on the day Ronald drowned, I had expressed to a schoolmate the hope that we would be given the afternoon off from our work. We were given the afternoon off and the tragedy ensued. It was indicated that the guilt experienced here may have screened a deeper source of guilt, stemming from my mother's death. It was indicated in the analytic material that I felt that much of what was happening to me was happening because of my own badness. In some sense I assumed that the loss of my parents was occasioned by that badness. So it was not surprising that one of the questions, most basic in the analysis, was not the question of how to compose sermons—I did this with very satisfactory results; the more disturbing question was the question of whether I had any right to be writing sermons. Granted that I could do them and do them well, did I have the right to *pretend* to be good? Putting it a bit differently, sermon composition was difficult because sermons can lead to self-exposure. To expose a bad self is an unhappy business. The aim of sermon preparation had to be self-concealment rather than self-expression. Self-concealment, however, is a form of dishonesty. Sermon composition leads to self-exposure which is dangerous, or to dishonesty, which is bad. Thus, there can be no pleasure in it.

There were a good many occasions in the analytic hours when my associations to sermonizing were all excremental in character. In my unconscious I constantly downgraded my sermons, regarding them as waste products, taking what comfort I could from the thought that what was excremental might at least have a fertilizing potential. The best thing that could be said of one of my sermons was that a flower might blossom from a dunghill.

It was obvious in the dream material that I displaced much anxiety with regard to sexuality onto the pulpit and preaching. It became apparent early in the analysis that there was a relationship between my difficulty in associating to sexual material and the trouble I had with sermon composition. Silences were a product of a lack of acceptance of my own impulses and feelings. They stemmed in part from my resentment at the analyst for making the same demands on me that were made by my congregation, namely, that I strip myself bare. The discipline of free association was more cruel than preaching. In preaching one at least had a chance to prepare oneself. Nor did the rules of preaching deny the right to that choice between alternative thoughts which is the speaker's prerogative. I found the discipline of free association exercised through hundreds of hours of analysis a curious adjunct to hours spent in sermon preparation. I am not yet sure what the carry-over impact will be. I feel that in my case it has resulted in more self-acceptance, more self-reliance, a more flexible use of the imagination and a capacity to express feelings more directly and less painfully.

I have felt it necessary to refer specifically to ways in which the personal analysis affected my preaching in order to make the point that the personal analysis has affected my professional competency at a deep, feeling level. Another minister with a different family constellation would, of course, be affected in different ways. The effects it had on me can be summed up as follows. In arriving at a higher degree of self-acceptance and self-knowledge, I resolved some of the conflicts which lay back of the excessive difficulty I had in sermon preparation. I became aware that many of the uses I was making of sermons were at variance with my conscious intents. I lived through a good many conflicts which at first I denied had anything to do with sermon composition or preaching. As I lived them through I began to see that I did have a right to preach and I began to put a fresh and higher value on the pulpit and its varied meanings.

2. *Its Relationship to Pastoral Counseling and the Ministry as a Whole*

The area of pastoral counseling is the second area I have chosen to mention in dealing with the significance of the personal analysis. Much of the time of the parish minister is spent in direct person-to-person relationships. The time allotted to what I would call formal pastoral counseling may amount to no more than six to twelve hours a week, depending on the nature of the church, the size of the congregation and the importance the minister attaches to this function. What I would call the more informal counseling relationships, which stem from the occasions when a minister meets people in his role as pastor or administrator or educator, may consume whole days out of each week.

I find that the Educative Analysis as a whole and the personal analysis in particular has had many effects upon my exercise of the formal and informal, ministerial, counseling function. It has made me very much aware of the large distinctions which exist between the role of the psychiatrist or psychoanalyst and the parish minister. Even were the parish minister to undergo the full course of training required for the practice of psychiatry, it would not be possible for him to be a psychiatrist unless he were to occupy a position on a church staff permitting him to devote full time to his specialty. The ministry, except under highly unusual circumstances, makes too many varied demands upon a man to permit him to be at the same time psychiatrist and parish minister.

It is of the utmost importance, however, that the clergyman have access to the findings of psychiatry as a means of making himself a more effective minister. Training in pastoral counseling under competent teachers, an educative analysis, experiences in educative therapy—these can enlarge his frame of orientation and bring him abreast of the tremendous changes which have taken place in recent years in theories of character and personality development. Such a widening of his frame of reference is no small accomplishment if it makes him more sensitive to himself and more intelligently conscious of the various dimensions of all human relationships. My experience indicates that such an orientation makes him more satisfied with his role as a clergyman, and makes him less likely to confuse himself either in phantasy or in reality with the psychiatrist. I find that an educative analysis has made me more aware of the manifold ways in which the parish minister, exercising administrative and educative as well as pastoral and preaching functions, can be sensitive—both to his own needs and to the needs of others.

So far as pastoral counseling in the more formal sense is concerned, there have been specific changes in my work. Earlier in my ministry when a parishioner came to me with a personal problem, I would talk with him once or twice under rather informal circumstances. I now tend to structure the relationship, making appointments to meet regularly at the church, often keeping a brief record of what takes place and limiting the appointment to one hour's duration. I focus more on the creative potential in the relationship itself and I have almost entirely given up the image of myself as a master problem-solver. I am much more interested in the background out of which the problem arose, and the "dynamics" of the person who comes to me. I do more listening and much less talking. I have extended the number of hours I spend counseling a parishioner from one or two to six or eight, scheduled at weekly intervals. I am much more conscious in the parishioner-minister counseling relationship of the importance of my own feelings. I am more sensitive to the kinds of emotional disturbances which lie beyond my own field of competence and more ready, with less anxiety, to refer a parishioner to a psychiatrist or, it may be, to a family agency specializing in case work.

One basic change in this area is not easy to define or describe. My own personal analysis has made me more aware of the reality of the unconscious as a source of health and sickness, and has made me more sympathetic to the long and subtle processes by which character and personality are formed. It is paradoxical that at the same time my method of counseling has become more structured it has become less tense and egocentric. It has become an effort to achieve mutual understanding and insight rather than a means of judging or solving.

3. Concluding Statement on the Significance of an Educative Analysis for the Parish Ministry

More important than the bearing an Educative Analysis has on the preaching function or the counseling function of the minister, is the bearing it has upon the full relationship of the minister to his profession. By virtue of the position he holds in church and community, the minister has countless opportunities to influence people for better or for worse. He visits the sick and the dying as well as the bereaved. The homes of his parishioners are open to him in a special sense as they are open to no other person. He is often called into emergency situations and is given the right to enter troubled waters without being called. On the occasion of marriages and christenings and other celebrations, as well as in times of sickness and trouble, people seek him out. He sits through the interminable committee meetings that are so much a part of the modern church's life and carries a heavy load of administrative responsibility. He is, in the liberal churches, expected to play a part in community leadership and to be concerned with the moral implications of grave social issues. He is expected to exercise a prophetic as well as a priestly function. He has the responsibility for conducting services of worship and, again in the liberal religious communions, of trying to change the forms of these services of worship so as to make them consonant with the needs and thinking of modern men and women. He is given a role in the education of children as well as adults. He falls heir to the freedom and the disciplines of the pulpit.

The parish minister has limitless opportunities to communicate with others from the center of his own life. It is assumed, often over-optimistically, that his life has a center and that he has not only found his way to it, but that he has found it to be reasonably acceptable. I would say that the most significant aspect of an Educative Analysis for the parish minister is that it helps him to accept the center of his life and to speak from it. It helps him to win the freedom to perform—or not to perform—the various offices of his profession. It makes him more aware of himself as a person and more aware of others as persons. It gives him a deeper understanding of the forms and institutions of religion and helps him to use those forms and institutions with more reliance on his own feelings. It helps him to gain more awareness of why and in what sense the forms and institutions are of value to him. It helps him to shape them to ends of self-expression and self-realization.

A Report On An Institute for Advanced Pastoral Studies

By Reuel L. Howe, S.T.D.
Director, Institute for Advanced Pastoral Studies,
Bloomfield Hills, Michigan

The finest features of education, group dynamics in community living, and the mellowed wisdom of mature leadership are combined in the work of the Institute for Advanced Pastoral Studies (non-denominational and ecumenical). The Director gives a detailed report on the work of the Institute in sustaining and guiding responsible pastors.

A new resource in post-ordination theological education has been the establishment of the Institute for Advanced Pastoral Studies in Bloomfield Hills, Michigan, of which the author of this chapter is the director. This experimental project is designed to explore the possibilities of post-ordination training for Protestant ministers. The idea of the Institute grew out of a study conducted by the Pastoral Theology Department of the Protestant Theological Seminary in Alexandria, Virginia, between 1950-57.

Some years ago the faculty of the Department realized that consultation with their graduates after they had some years of experience in the ministry helped them improve the undergraduate curriculum, and that these same graduates were teachable at a greater depth than had been possible for them earlier. Experimental groups of ministers, including alumni and others, were called together to explore the possibilities of follow-up training designed to further their education for the practice of the ministry, and the correlation of their doctrinal understandings, deepened now by their experience and their reflection on it, with their ministerial practice. The results of this study indicated clearly that ministers' training for their work can be greatly advanced by providing them with an opportunity to learn after they have been in their work for at least three years. This insight produced the Institute, which seeks to demonstrate the need for and the possibility of directed theological education for ministers after they have begun their work.

The Institute was founded by a small group of Detroit businessmen who, having heard of the need for a program of continuing education for ministers and recognizing it as comparable to advance training programs for business and professional men, offered to finance an initial two-year experiment. The two years ended with an enthusiastic decision to continue the Institute as a permanent educational resource. The Board of Trustees is composed of lay and clerical men from different denominations, and representing business and professional men as well as clergy and theological educators.

The sessions of the Institute are ten days long and are held about every other ten days from September through June. Attendance is by invitation, but interested ministers may write and ask for an invitation. The attending ministers are expected to pay their own traveling expenses and a fifty dollar tuition, which includes room and board. The Institute is housed in Cranbrook House which is on the grounds of the large and beautiful Cranbrook educational center located twenty miles northwest of Detroit.

1. The Purpose of the Institute

One purpose of the Institute is to provide ministers from different churches an opportunity to reflect on the meaning of their ministry and to learn from it. During the course of the workshop, as much as possible of each man's experience is shared with the others so that through the process of mutual study and discussion all may benefit from the experience of each. Discussions center around the kinds of churches and communities in which the men serve, the relation between the church and community, the kind of ministry being carried on there, the nature of the preaching and the response to it, the kind of pastoral care, the nature and methods of teaching employed, the administrative problems encountered, the whole milieu of their work and with their interpretations of it. The period of ten days in which each group meets makes possible this kind of correlation and reverent study. As a result of these sessions, men leave feeling that they have gained an understanding of their task, of their relationship to it, of its place in the larger work of the church, and of its theological meaning.

The other purpose of the Institute is the ecumenical one. As has already been stated, each group is composed of ministers from different churches. As they meet around the discussion table and worship together, they discover that, in addition to the divisions that separate them, there is much that unites them. They are united by their love and worship of God and their commission to serve His people. They discover that there are no denominational distinctions built into human nature or found in human problems; and they are surprised at how many resources they have in common for their respective ministries to people. Every group thus far has experienced a *koinonia* that has been a source of revelation and strength to them.

2. *Methods of Procedure*

The groups are assembled by invitation. After acceptances are received, questionnaires are sent, designed to draw from ministers their interests and needs. The questionnaires are divided into three parts: First, the clergy are asked to list briefly their irritations, frustrations, and satisfactions in the conduct of their work; second, in the order of their preference, they are asked to check out of a list of sixteen functions of ministry, eight which they would like to study at the Institute. The sixteen functions listed are: the pastoral—parish calling, home visiting; ministry to the sick and shut-ins; ministry to older people; pastoral counseling; ministry to special problems such as alcoholism, homosexuality, etc.; preparation for marriage; preparation for parenthood; preparation for baptism; preparation for confirmation or church membership; Christian education: of children, of adults; training of leaders and teachers; work with groups; administration of sacraments pastorally; preaching in relation to pastoral work; conduct of worship; parish administration and organization.

A third part of the questionnaire asks them to check areas of concern which they would like to have covered at the Institute. These areas include: communication with people today; relation of church to community; tensions between the minister's work and family life; evangelism; the correlation of theology and pastoral work; the minister's role; the ministry of the laity. Then, finally, they are asked to state any aspect of the ministry which they would particularly like to study which has not been mentioned.

When the questionnaires have been returned, the results are compiled and collated and a tentative agenda for each group appears. The group's tentative agenda is given to them when they arrive, as a guide in formulating the actual agenda which grows out of their study and work together.

It is not surprising that the actual agenda which they follow is different from the tentative agenda drawn from their questionnaires. One value of the questionnaire, filled out as it is three months before they come to the Institute, is that it starts them thinking interpretatively about their ministry. By the time they arrive for the session, their evaluations and interpretations are often different from what they were earlier. And, of course, the process of thinking together with their colleagues during the ten days of the conference changes their thoughts about their work still more.

For this reason it has been found wise to require the group to assume responsibility for structuring its own curriculum. The process of coming to decisions about areas of interest and need that they want to study, and the outlining of them for seminar purposes involves them in a dialogue that prepares them for a depth communication that they acknowledge is unusual in their experience.

Because the curriculum is tailored for each group, it more accurately and completely meets the needs of its members. This means that there is always a certain amount of variation in the content of the discussion of the different groups as well as in their manner of approaching their concerns. In spite of this, however, there are characteristics common to the agenda of all the groups.

A typical agenda is as follows:

A TYPICAL AGENDA

I. The Minister as Pastor
   A. Pastoral Counseling
      With limited training and clinical knowledge, what ministry is possible?
      How can we evaluate our capacity, and limitations, in pastoral counseling?
      How is insight gained in problem counseling?
      How is the pastor's functioning as a counsler dependent on his internal correlation of belief and behavior?
   B. What special consideratiions apply to: marital counseling, counseling teen-agers and the emotionally disturbed?
   C. Why do we do parish calling?
   D. What is the relation of pastoral work and preaching, for clergy and for congregations?
   E. What correlations can be made between pastoral work and theology?
II. The Minister as Bearer of the Gospel: Communication
   A. Communication to People Today
      How can the truth of the Gospel be communicated within a secularized church?
      How can we help laymen become more concerned, responsive, and intelligent about Christian faith?
   B. What happens when real preaching occurs?
   C. Christian Education
      With children and adults, how can the tension between concern for subject matter and concern for persons be understood and managed?

Why do we prepare people for confirmation or church membership?

What are the purposes in training teachers and leaders?

In work with groups, what is the function of the leader?

III. The Minister as Leader of the People of God

A. Parish Administration and Organization

What realistic possibilities are there for the organization of time?

Why has this become the frustrating problem it is? How can we handle details, interruptions, pressures, and expectations?

B. Training Lay Leaders

How can we best minister to *and* with laymen?

IV. The Minister as a Person

A. What are the tensions between the minister's work and family life? How can they be managed?

B. What is the minister's role?

C. How can we live and work with personal inadequacies?

V. What is the Mission of the Church in her social context?

During 1959-60 the Institute held four regional sessions for ministers living in distant parts of the country: Seattle, Washington; Halifax, Nova Scotia; Austin, Texas; San Francisco, California. On the basis of this experiment, plans are being made for the development of regional sessions as a regular part of the Institute program. These workshops have been provided not only for parish ministers but for college chaplains, denominational and parish directors of Christian education, clergy and their wives, Bishops and other ecclesiastical authorities, teachers in universities and colleges. In the first three years thirty-nine sessions have been attended by 449 ministers and others from fifteen denominations, from 52 seminaries, and five countries (United States, Japan, Canada, Philippines, England).

The Institute has begun the publication of a quarterly newsletter by which it seeks to keep in touch with its alumni and encourage their continued study.

About the Editor:

WAYNE E. OATES, Professor of Psychology of Religion at the Southern Baptist Theological Seminary, has been associated with that institution since 1948. He was educated at Mars Hill Junior College, Wake Forest College (B.A.), Duke Divinity School (B.D.), and Southern Baptist Theological Seminary (Th.D.). Dr. Oates has held pastorates in rural North Carolina churches and in Kentucky, and served as chaplain for the Kentucky Baptist Hospital. He has also lectured as a visiting professor at Union Theological Seminary.

Dr. Oates is a member of the editorial boards of *Pastoral Psychology* and the *Journal of Pastoral Care,* and has written many distinguished volumes. Among them are *Where to Go for Help, The Revelation of God in Human Suffering, Anxiety in Christian Experience, Religious Factors in Mental Illness,* and—as editor—*An Introduction to Pastoral Counseling.*

About the Author